The Life Of
JAMES BROWN

The Life Of

JAMES
BROWN

A biography by Geoff Brown

OMNIBUS PRESS

London/New York/Paris/Sydney/Copenhagen/Berlin/Madrid/Tokyo

Copyright © 2008 Omnibus Press
First published © 1996 Omnibus Press
(A Division of Music Sales Limited)

ISBN: 978.1.84609.958.8
Order No: OP51986

Exclusive Distributors
Music Sales Limited,
14/15 Berners Street,
London, W1T 3LJ.

Music Sales Corporation,
257 Park Avenue South,
New York, NY 10010, USA.

Macmillan Distribution Services,
53 Park West Drive,
Derrimut, Vic 3030,
Australia.

Every effort has been made to trace the copyright holders of the photographs in this book but one or two were unreachable. We would be grateful if the photographers concerned would contact us.

Typeset by Phoenix Photosetting, Chatham, Kent
Printed in the United States of America by Quebecor World

A catalog record for this book is available from the British Library.

Visit Omnibus Press on the web at www.omnibuspress.com

Contents

Introduction

James Brown had always made much of the importance of Christmas. In the days leading up to the festive holidays it had become a tradition for him to hold annual toy giveaways for children in Augusta, Georgia, and his vast back catalogue of recordings included special Christmas albums and many seasonal singles releases such as 'Let's Make Christmas Mean Something This Year', 'Santa Claus Goes Straight To The Ghetto' and 'Let's Unite The Whole World At Christmas'. So there was something of the inevitable, and appropriate, about the sad and untimely death of the apparently inexhaustible, unstoppable and indestructible James Brown on Christmas Day, 2006. Not that he was fixin' to die. Far from it, for the Hardest Working Man In Showbusiness's date sheet was indeed fully booked up until the following summer, and he had part recorded a new album. But the body that had been driven to its limits on stages the world over in the Fifties, Sixties and Seventies, and was in subsequent decades ravaged by an intake of drugs as he sought to deaden physical pain and escape his demons, had other ideas and finally called time on what had been one of *the* defining music careers of the post-war years.

Indeed, the first sentence of the introduction to the first edition of this book, published in 1996, noted that few artists had had a more profound effect on the course of African-American music since the Second World War than Brown. His influence had, in fact, been much wider, because the funk rhythms he established in the 1960s had been taken and adapted by white rock and pop acts and spread across Europe, Africa and to the Far East. He had become Universal James, as one of his much later, less essential albums was titled.

The pioneering arrangements devised by the singer and his groups in the period 1965-72 had added an entire new genre to African-American music, a genus already rich in history. Having propelled himself to the status of the biggest selling act in black America, and the rootsiest singer to make inroads into the white pop market, all without the assistance of a major record label,

1

he invented the 'funk' style from which Sly Stone and George Clinton evolved influential variants. By the trickle down effect of the boogaloo, his music acted as a signpost pointing large areas of Western popular music to the present day. Forty years on, many of the dance sounds in this new century are direct descendants of his most revolutionary styles.

During his 73 years Mr. Brown, as he preferred to be addressed, set down his autobiography twice. This book was written as an alternative view from a more objective standpoint, but certainly did not aim to do for him what Albert Goldman's texts did for Elvis Presley and John Lennon. In fact, this tome ought to have been written by Mr. Cliff White, unparalleled UK archivist and expert on the Godfather Of Soul. His sleevenotes to the 1991 four-CD box set 'Star Time' had won for him and for each of his co-authors (Harry Weinger, Alan Leeds and Mr. Brown) a Grammy. But waist-deep in unpublished interviews, unheard tapes, unread cuttings and a waning enthusiasm for the book project, Mr. White passed on the mantle to me. Cliff had written for me when I edited a British magazine title, *Black Music*, and here was his chance for revenge.

First, some general impressions of Mr. Brown via Mr. White, who has a reasonably close personal knowledge as opposed to my meetings, which were on the more professional level of journalist/writer to interviewee. You did not need to spend too much time hanging around the James Brown camp or be in the company of the ever-expanding army of his ex-associates to be vouchsafed the information that he was a prickly and sometimes extremely unpleasant piece of work. This revelation was always qualified by a "But...".

Mr. White, shimmying around the fringes of the JB circus since 1973, several times witnessed Mr. Brown in explosive action: irrational, manipulative, divisive, vindictive, extraordinarily egocentric, perverse and forcefully intimidating, with a temper that could be heard, and felt, through a slammed door, along a corridor, around a corner, down a flight of stairs and bouncing off the walls of a far-away sanctuary where the next victim awaited a summons into the gladiatorial arena. If James Brown's volatile temper was all that there was, well, we could close the book right now.

With rare understatement, Mr. Brown himself once said, "I'm not a violent man but I know how to be violent". He might better have admitted to being an ill-tempered, inveterate emotional and physical scrapper. When his needle zapped into the red zone, it was time to put up or shut up. He could be reckless and savage. A list of people physically assaulted by him would not be a short one, nor would it be restricted to the male of the species. He was just as liable to abuse his wives and girlfriends as he was to hurt his male colleagues and enemies, real or imagined.

There are a lot of glib theories that could be expounded about the profoundly underprivileged, dirt-poor, ill-educated, raggedy, short-ass black kid virtually fending for himself without too much love, comfort, parental guidance or proper home in the depths of the segregated South, and what it took him to survive, let alone become one of the most successful and significant black entertainers of the century. Draw your own conclusions from the facts. But, Mr. White adds, in the 29 years he knew Mr. Brown he was never met with anything less than courtesy and friendliness, and he even presumed friendship.

Most musicians who worked for Mr. Brown claim that he ripped off their musical ideas without proper acknowledgement or financial reward. Most everybody who worked for Mr. Brown either came to dislike him or simply got tired of being around him, but overlong familiarity in a working environment can do that to even-tempered souls, let alone what havoc it might wreak among sparky and creative temperaments living in each others' pockets on the road. Some felt bitter, some even came to feel rather sorry for him. But despite everything, they retained an immense respect for what he achieved, even if they felt he only got there by riding on their backs.

So what exactly did James Brown achieve?

Although statistics can be inadequate arbiters, they're a convenient starting point. In terms of American chart hits, James Brown was far and away the most successful African-American recording artist in the history of recorded entertainment. He was also well up there with the Elvis Presleys, Beatles and Bing Crosbys of the white pop world. We're not talking about global sales of individual records here, we're talking persistent and consistent soul power, racking up those hits one after the other.

James Brown dominated the black American music ratings for nigh on 15 years. And 15 years later he was being so extensively sampled that, internationally, his original recordings could be heard more frequently than the music of any other individual pop star. The most reasonable and authoritative estimate of JB samples out there – cut up, at first uncredited and often not paid for, frequently with some jive joker riding a techno-fantasy over the top of his funky riff or simple, visceral "Unh!" – had passed three thousand. They often said the sampling was a tribute. Perhaps it was come-uppance of sorts for a man who had allegedly got many of his best licks from his musicians. At least Mr. Brown employed the people he relied on to back up his bravado, real musicians all, and the music they created together was unique, inspirational and phenomenally powerful.

On top of his chart power and relentless touring schedule, James Brown's single-minded determination drove him on to become an icon for the changing face, fortunes and aspirations of black America. His rise to fame coincided exactly with the American civil rights revolution and he came to represent the extreme of the American dream as he rose from unimagined poverty and brutal segregation to huge entrepreneurial personal success, seemingly totally in command of his own destiny. At the peak of his career, during the second half of the Sixties and early Seventies, James Brown was on an independent roll in the music business that will never be equalled because we live in completely different times. Society has changed, and so has the music business – in the way the music is made, marketed, distributed and sold.

In the few years before James Brown's significant move from the independent King label to the international Polydor corporation in 1971, he was simultaneously overturning the status quo while striving to become part of it. His aims were traditionally all-American, yet his achievements were alarming to the Establishment. Here was a maverick African-American entertainer, literally from the backwoods, suddenly making unprecedented musical moves, wielding national political clout, controlling his own career, heading and feeding an entourage of some fifty people, flitting about the nation in his own private jet, rallying the ghettos, buying up radio stations, announcing the launch of personalised food stamps and soul food restaurants. Here was a very serious contender.

In practice he was politically fairly naïve and many of his business ventures were less than resounding successes. He was never a serious threat to the Establishment, because he believed in it and craved to be part of it. Nevertheless, for a time he seemed to be getting out of control. In the jittery US climate of the late Sixties, it is a matter of wonder that there was no assassination attempt on his life – by one side or the other of the racial divide. Certainly, militant Black Panthers made noises about his allegiances when he wouldn't play ball during those uncertain years, while the white political establishment probably reasoned that James Brown's influence would be finite and that he simply wasn't threatening enough to warrant martyrdom. Or perhaps his very popularity saved him.

At the height of the US civil unrest, an attempt on the life of James Brown would surely have sparked off massive national race riots. Instead he was co-opted to quell precisely the tide of anger, loss and hurt which erupted after the assassination of Dr. Martin Luther King. Nor could black militants take Brown's popularity lightly. Disgusted at his courtship of the Establishment they might have been, but how would they be able to enrol the 'hood when they had just done harm to its musical spokesperson, its most visible national spokesperson? So James Brown survived in a trickily balanced middle ground to face the Seventies.

By the mid-Seventies, his world was falling apart. Even the hits stopped. That's when the heavy paranoia and conspiracy theories first set in and he began using illegal recreational substances. He enjoyed a major, if comparatively brief, revival in the Eighties, which brought the acceptance by the Establishment that he'd always wanted. But his inability to either accept the ageing process or to define a new role for himself as Elder Statesman of Funk – one which by the mid-Nineties he'd happily accepted – meant his musical decline was too far gone for him to make his new music as vital as it had once been.

James Brown's two autobiographies were *The Godfather of Soul*, crafted for him by writer Bruce Tucker and first published in the USA in 1986, and *I Feel Good: A Memoir Of A Life In Soul*, with an introduction by Marc Eliot, biographer of Barry White and Donna Summer, among others, which was published in 2005. Like most autobiographies, or indeed many 'authorised' biographies, the books have their share of half-truths, self-justifications and rewritings of history. For instance, in *Godfather Of Soul*, when talking about his hit recording of The 5 Royales' 'Think', Brown stated, "King Records wanted me to cut it in 1960 at the same session I did 'You've Got The Power', but I didn't want to. I knew that if I did it would hurt The 5 Royales. I held off until they (The 5 Royales) cut 'Please, Please, Please', then I decided it would be all right to cut 'Think'." But the original tape sessions of these recordings are still intact and show that, in reality, James Brown And The Famous Flames recorded 13 takes of 'Think', including the hit release, at the same session as 'You've Got The Power' on 20 February, 1960. Why he chose to ignore this is unclear. At the heart of his own version of events there seems to be an entirely unnecessary attempt to justify why he reinterpreted the other group's song. In this instance, he could rightfully have boasted, "We took it, we changed it, we trashed 'em!"

Despite these flaws *Godfather Of Soul*, the first epistle from Mr. Dynamite, is in parts also a surprisingly forthright and detailed account by a legend of his own lifetime, and thereby gave subsequent biographers a dilemma. Obviously, any full account of his life will cover much the same ground. As we cannot presume to match or question Mr. Brown's recollections about his personal life, especially the early formative days, it is hardly touched upon here. After a very brief summary of those years, this book begins in Toccoa, Georgia, where James Brown was released from prison in June, 1952, a month after his nineteenth birthday.

The next few years are given principally to Mr. Bobby Byrd who founded the group that, with changes, became James Brown And The Famous Flames. At Bobby's instigation, the Byrd family helped to get Brown paroled and offered him some background stability to anchor the waywardness. Bobby and James became close friends and formed a symbiotic relationship that endured on and off – mostly on – into the Seventies. Bobby Byrd is a mirror image of James Brown. An open, uncomplicated man, generally calm of mind, gentle of nature and humorous of spirit, he is universally liked by the cast of characters involved in the James Brown story. He is also, as he has been the first to admit, somewhat shaky of memory when it comes to precise dates, names and chronology. But he is an honest man with a fund of stories and with few interruptions he tells it like it was from his perspective during the early years.

Some of the mid-Fifties to mid-Sixties parts of this book will be familiar to anyone who owns James Brown's Polydor double LP/CD compilation 'Roots Of A Revolution' or Brown's autobiographies. Events of significance crop up in much the same order with much the same emphasis in both the booklet, which Mr. White wrote in 1983 to accompany 'Roots Of A Revolution', and in Brown's later first autobiography of 1986. As Mr. White retains the manuscript copyright of the original booklet, we repeat some of the necessary details here.

One piece of misappropriation, perhaps worthy of the Godfather Of Soul himself, unfortunately did occur during preparation of the first edition of this book and which I am happy and relieved to rectify at this first opportunity. A transcript of an interview with Ralph Bass, the producer and King Records talent scout who in the 1950s heard James Brown's demo and insisted he be signed to the label, appeared in the archive and I assumed it was part of Cliff White's research. Wrong. The interview was conducted by Harry Weinger, keeper of the James Brown flame at Universal Records and reissue producer of a vast number of absolutely essential CDs in soul, R&B and other genres, and remains his copyright. Consequently, the episode described in the interview has been removed from this book... but you can still read it in the 'Star Time' box set sleevenote. Once again, apologies to Mr. Weinger for the misunderstanding.

Finally, the author's personal debt to James Brown started when, as a drummer in what passed for a British 'soul' band in the mid-Sixties, I admit culpability in the crime of mangling numerous and variable on-stage versions of JB classics, 'I'll Go Crazy', 'Think', '(Do The) Mashed Potatoes', 'Night Train', 'Out Of Sight', 'I Got You (I Feel Good)' and 'Mashed Potatoes USA' among them. As I write this, I can feel my wrists seize up, forearm muscles stiffen and shoulders tense into a rockhard hunchback as we funk at speed into another chorus of 'Think' faster than nature, or indeed Mr. Brown, ever intended. Imagine the collision between relief and a sense of betrayal when I saw The James Brown Orchestra on-stage using more than one puny drummer to create those thundering rhythms. Then again, my efforts could have been duplicated ten-fold for all the difference it would have made.

I first wrote at any length about James Brown in February 1973 by which time I had become a journalist and was on the staff of *Melody Maker* in London. I flew to Hamburg to catch his show at the Musikhalle and delivered a piece headlined 'The real Black Moses', a spin on Isaac Hayes's adopted title. Almost 35 years later, it still seems an apt pseudonym for James Brown, a man who gave himself so many alternative monikers. For all his human faults, notably the egotism and ruthless drive without which he would arguably never have reached the top of his chosen profession, James Brown was indeed a Moses-like leader of African-American people, unquestionably so in music and, for a short time, as a role model and high achiever in a hostile society.

And so finally, ladies and gentlemen, it's Showtime! But before gettin' on the good foot to chase down the hardest working man, we would like to name the names without whose help, chat, time, advice and assistance this book could not have been written. First, thanks to James Brown for the music and the career. It's hard to know which has been the more extraordinary, but without them we would not be gathered here today. Second, to Cliff White, keeper of the faith, hoarder of the funk facts and files, whose mighty archive on paper, tape and brain cells keeps the motor running. Third, deep bows to Chris Charlesworth and Omnibus Books for patience and understanding.

For the accumulation of interviews in the aforesaid archive, and some of my own, with Brown's multifarious musicians it's thanks to and please welcome Bobby Byrd, Vicki Anderson and all at the Byrd's nest, the many great horn players, particularly Maceo Parker, Fred Wesley and Alfred "Pee Wee" Ellis, the inimitable William "Bootsy" Collins, Tony Cook, "Sweet" Charles Sherrell, Danny Ray. And to the many other women in the story but notably Martha High, Marva Whitney and the late Yvonne Fair. And to those who have passed on since the first publication, notably Lyn Collins, St. Clair Pinckney and Alphonso "Country" Kellum.

We must also thank the men who served in Brown's organisation in a non-playing capacity: his first manager Barry Trimier, Alan Leeds and Bob Patton, those who've never given up on the funk such as Harry Weinger and Bill Levenson, Bill Millar, Danny Adler, Trevor Swain, Steve Jackson,

Renee Odenhoven, Steve Richards, Tom Payne, Andrew Simons and Neil Slaven.

I must thank two of my current colleagues on *MOJO* magazine, editor-in-chief Phil Alexander and contributor and fellow soul fanatic Lois Wilson, who both kindly made available to me transcripts of interviews they conducted as we frantically put together *MOJO*'s James Brown tribute immediately after Christmas 2006. Finally gratitude and love to Linda White and Catherine, Rebecca and Ella Brown, our own famous flames.

Preface

Macon, Georgia. 1971.

Fifth Street, Macon, Georgia, is a tired, old, quietly decaying thoroughfare two blocks east of the Third and Cherry intersection at the heart of the city. Its focal point is a disused railroad station. Prouder than its neighbours, this ageing heap of Redstone and rusty steel stands by the roadside as a monument to bygone days when freight bays overflowed with the produce of inter-city trade and generations of hopeful migrants passed through in search of the New Deal. Now it is deserted and forgotten. No buses disturb the desolate tranquillity of its old rival, the nearby Greyhound bus depot, an empty, tiled shell with only roaches for customers.

Across town, the big transcontinental buses roll into a modern terminus and way out beyond the city limits, Macon airport grows ever busier as less patient generations jet to their destinations. Multi-lane highways form a cobweb of mobility and diversion through and around the city. Motels, restaurants, bars and ice-cream parlours line these routes for mile after mile, enticing the outward-bound motorist to a last minute stopover or hoping to snare the incoming traffic before it reaches the centre of town.

In adjacent suburbs, families live out their lives amid landscaped estates and weekly visits to shopping malls. Good schools are here, factories and offices, entertainment plazas. It's a familiar pattern. In larger, more famous cities the centres might continue to thrive on tourism but Macon has no national monuments, beautiful parks or spectacular buildings and even if City Hall did briefly house the State Capitol, well that was in the previous century and no-one's interested now. As the city has spread, its heart has grown quieter. And while the faces in the suburbs are nearly all white, on and around Fifth Street they are predominantly black.

Opposite to the disused station, equally decrepit buildings lean forlornly shoulder to shoulder, wearily supported on crutches of billboard hoardings. The block still houses the familiar establishments of such a street – a rat-trap

9

hotel, a barbershop, a small record store, the noise from which is the only sign of life on the whole block, a filling station and an old wooden shack, grandly titled Bryan's Grill. Finally, where the street widens to curve beside the now overgrown freight yard, an off-white single-storey structure sits between two vacant lots like the last yellowing tooth in a bare gum.

Brick archways frame the building's battered doors and shutters which on this Saturday in the summer of 1971 are flung wide open, for although it is only 11am the dusty air is already hot, sluggish and oppressive. Inside, an old man sweeps the worn wooden floor, methodically working his way around scarred tables and rickety chairs, slowly collecting a pile of cigarette butts and empty bottles down at the far end of the room in front of a makeshift bar. Next to the bar, a partition extends from the back wall into the middle of the room. On one side, the tables and chairs crowd the floor space. Before the bar, the other section is clear except for a jukebox and two pinball machines. The front of the room is one large area stretching the width of the building where low pallets are laid to form a stage.

The old man pauses in his work, leaning on the broom to catch his breath. Life has never been particularly easy but recently even his own body seems to have been against him. There was a touch-and-go period a few months ago when he'd been uncertain whether he'd ever sweep this floor again. That time he'd won the fight and now he stands, half lost in memories, surveying the room that has been his second home for the past quarter century. A casual passer-by might mistake him for the janitor but the first of his regulars who are beginning to drift in know him well enough. His name is Clint Brantley and this is his club, The Two Spot.

Clint gathers up his debris and goes behind the bar to break open beers and sodas for the group of young brothers who have strung themselves out around the room. For a couple of minutes, he swaps small-talk, smiling indulgently at their jive and boasts. He's less forthcoming about the show tonight, though. There's a rumour something big, really big, is going to happen. "Stick around. Who knows?" He shrugs and disappears out back into the kitchen to arrange the evening's food.

The fellas take their drinks and disperse to their favourite positions in The Two Spot. One feeds the jukebox: it may be an old club but it gets the latest sounds. Two take up their running battle on the pinball machines. The others just sit around on the low stage or by the open doors where they whistle approvingly at any passing girls. It's midday on a steamy Georgia Saturday and they are tuning up for the best night of the week.

After an hour or so they stretch and saunter out into the brilliant sunshine, off to grab a bite to eat or to seek some shade in the park or to lounge on the sidewalk at the bottom of Mulberry Hill and watch the world go by. They'll meet later, they agree, back at the club.

By 10pm, The Two Spot is livening up. There are about forty people in the club now and more arriving all the time. Up on stage, a local group is well into the first of several long, hard, sweaty sets. Their accent is on rhythm. Up north and across the nation, softer sounds and more complex productions have taken hold of the soul charts but here they still like it sharp and simple. Rhythm heavy but crisp and tight, down-to-earth singing, emotion from the gut. In a word – Funky.

Tonight, the singer is Jimmy Braswell, a local favourite with one or two records to his credit but no hits so far. Like small-time groups everywhere, Jimmy and his band entertain by hammering out competent versions of other people's hits. The crowd wants to dance, drink and have a good time and they want tunes they can recognise. Sometime during the evening, Jimmy will slip in a couple of his own songs. But for the most part, he and the band take the various sounds and styles of the hit parade and turn them into an endless stream of gritty, southern style rhythm'n'blues songs.

Soon the club is as crowded as on any other Saturday night. Up to a hundred noisy patrons dancing, sitting around the tables, laughing and joking, leaning across to shout good-natured jibes at their neighbours. Two or three "waiters", indistinguishable from the customers, pass around the tables dishing out soul food specialities. A steady flow of people jostle between the dancers to the bar or out onto the street for a breath of air.

Just after midnight, the commotion intensifies. Over by the door the crowd seems to have suddenly got thicker. Shouts and squeals waft in from the outside. More and more patrons drift over to catch what's happening or they lean across the tables, straining to peer through the crush. The dancers stop their gyrations, the men at the bar forget their orders, all heads turn towards the door. The band plays on but only half-heartedly now. No one is listening and they too are trying to see what's happening in the corner. The mass breaks away from the door, flowing clumsily back into the club. It parts like the Red Sea, leaving a narrow passageway from the street. Through this human corridor strides a short, determined-looking man dressed in black.

There's not much of him to see, yet he immediately dominates the room. Everyone has on their party best but his suit is sharper, finely tailored to his stocky frame, clean to the bone. Most of the crowd wear jewellery of some sort, many are more expensively clad than the newcomer. But his few pieces are large and genuine, glinting with the fire of a small fortune. More than anything else, it is his face that sets him apart. It is a face of marked contrasts. A forceful wedge of chin offset by high, fleshy

11

cheeks. A broad mouth, now split into an engaging smile full of expensive dentistry, the smile belied by penetrating eyes, alert, probing, seldom soft. A lion's grin. It is not a pretty face beneath that large black bush of skilfully coiffeured Afro but it is, in the truest sense of the word, an attractive face. A face that commands attention and demands respect. A face that in the preceding few years has finally been recognised the world over. Please welcome Mr. Dynamite, Soul Brother Number One, The Hardest Working Man In Show Business … JAAY-YAMES BROWN!

Tonight, he has returned to the first base camp on his route to the summit of soul. Brown's arrival at The Two Spot is truly the return of the conquering hero. While he acknowledges the tumultuous reception, a waiter is dispatched to escort the honoured guest and his small entourage to a hastily vacated table where they are joined by Brantley. The band finds its beat again, the customers struggle back to their tables, the club picks up the rhythm of its party. But it is now on a keener pitch. This is no longer any old Saturday night.

The word goes out. Within minutes the crowd has swelled to twice the normal capacity of the club. The floor space is soon blocked by expectant fans, most of them content just to stand and watch Brown, others eagerly jostling for a position from which they can talk to the star. He's used to this game. Usually, it's nothing more than a ritual greeting, a stylised catch-phrase or two. Occasionally, there'll be a sour grape in the bunch, juiced up and spoiling for a fight. But not here. At The Two Spot in Macon, Georgia, James Brown doesn't have to prove a damn thing to anyone. They all know where he's coming from.

Relaxed in the atmosphere of buoyant but respectful camaraderie, he holds court with his admirers for a while before concentrating on the food placed before him. When the heaped plates of chicken wings have been reduced to a tangle of spindly bones, he allows himself a menthol cigarette and then glances speculatively at the stage. On any visit to any night club, he knows he's going to be asked to sing at least one number with the house band. More often than not, he'll decline, preferring to relax and socialise, understandably chary of performing with unknown, unrehearsed musicians. But not at Clint's.

As if on cue, the leader stops the band and begs him to take the stand. Brown is ceremonially escorted through the crowd, organises a hasty conference to discover which of his hits these local boys know best, then grabs the cheap, fuzzy-sounding microphone. There are no further preliminaries. No flippant introduction. No polite "Hello". Nor does he check again with the band. They have assured him they can cope, now they've got to prove it. He's not about to follow them. They'd better be ready to keep up with him.

He spins quickly to face the audience, hurling out a question that ricochets off the back wall of the club and strikes everyone in the room.

"What We Want?"

The response is immediate and ecstatic.

"SOUL POWER!"

It's his latest record, at its peak on the national soul chart, sales already into the second million.

"Got to have?!"

"SOUL POWER!"

"What we missing?!"

"SOUL POWER!"

Brown and the crowd toss the word back and forth, forming a hypnotic chant that rises in intensity with each call and response. "Soul power … SOUL POWER … soul power … SOUL POWER … power to the people … POWER TO THE PEOPLE … power to the people … POWER TO THE PEOPLE … soul power … SOUL POWER … soul power … SOUL POWER.

"HIT IT!!"

At this final screeched command, the band rips into the riff like a jumbo jet soaring into the sky.

CHAPTER 1

Will the real James Brown please stand up? The subject of this book admits to only two personae: First, there is JAMES BROWN!! the all-singing, all-dancing, internationally renowned entertainer, entrepreneur, peace-maker and consciousnes-raiser, who forged hit after hit after hit from increasingly precious metal between the late Fifties and early Seventies. Although, by the mid-Nineties, this hardest working man in show business had slowed down to a point where his infrequent record releases sold very poorly – and could have said he couldn't get arrested, unhappily that was one thing that was still happening for him – his influence remained powerful: he had become the Hardest Working Sample in Show Business.

Second, we find James Brown, the driven, determined, flawed human being who carries this load, who was apparently born on May 3, 1933, in a country shack outside Barnwell, South Carolina, close across the Savannah River state line from Augusta, Georgia. He claims so and we've found no evidence to doubt it.

However, others do doubt it. A couple of Brown's close associates have suggested that somewhere down the line he clipped a year off his real age. Unless there was a legal snag that called for this slight change during his teenage arrest, imprisonment and parole it seems an improbable ploy. Mutton intent on masquerading as lamb usually makes a bolder cut than one year.

It has also been widely reported that James Brown was really born on June 17, 1928, in Pulaski, Tennessee. This outside runner was first backed in Britain in 1966 by the *Daily Mail Book Of Golden Discs*. Journalists are as ready as the next person to believe everything they read and many have repeated the Pulaski date. Indeed, as recently as 1986, *Penthouse*, naming Brown as one of the Top 25 Most Important Americans, used the Tennessee birthplace and 1928 date. There certainly is, or was, a musical James Brown based in Pulaski, Tennessee and there exists 'James Brown Production' recordings on Pulaski imprinted record labels. But none of them sounds remotely like THE James Brown.

In his ghosted autobiography, THE James Brown says he wasn't originally supposed to be named James or Brown but Joe Gardner Jr. after his father's original name. James Brown it was and, having been so named, he is in crowded company.

Any local telephone directory will be over-blessed with J. Browns, many of them James, Jim and Jas. There are also several known James Browns in the international music industry, including a country singer who recorded for MGM in the Fifties, a Memphis-based keyboard sessioneer, a British classical cellist, a British rock journalist, and the man from Pulaski. It's hard to imagine that anyone could confuse JAMES BROWN with any other James Brown, but here are three defining pieces of evidence. When it was, like, groovy, you know man, to dig the astrological forces, the subject of this book introduced into his act a star-sign routine. Unfortunately, no-one managed to persuade him to drop it when it became redundant. He always called for a drum roll for Taurus. May 3 is Taurus, June 17 would make him Gemini. James Brown will fool with your mind but he will not fool with a star sign. He's Taurus.

Second, if he had been born in 1928 he would have been 21 years old when first imprisoned and 24 when released. In fact, he was still legally a minor, under 21, when paroled in 1952.

Third, when James took Deidre Jenkins as his second bride, in 1970, he invited troupe members Bobby Byrd and Vicki Anderson to make it a double wedding. Byrd and "Mommie-O" had been co-habiting for a while before deciding to do the traditional thing. Vicki's vision of a grand ceremony in Augusta or New York was doused by James's insistence on a quiet and rootsy quickie. He summoned them to a dinky courthouse in Barnwell, South Carolina, his birthplace.

The *Daily Mail Book Of Golden Discs* simply got the wrong James Brown. JAMES BROWN!! is the boy from Barnwell who grew up to call Augusta his home town.

Augusta, Georgia is now world famous as the home of the annual US Masters Golf Championship, and Barnwell, South Carolina has been immortalised in Gil Scott-Heron's song 'South Carolina' as a depository for nuclear waste. In 1933 neither place held such claims to fame or notoriety, although Augusta was not exactly a backwater. Rural, yes, as it still is today. But then it was a thriving and industrious town.

Augusta was founded in 1735, two years after the eventual state of Georgia was first colonised at Savannah by what an aged encyclopaedia is pleased to call "debtors and other unfortunate persons" shipped out from King George II's England. Whether in tribute or revenge, the settlers named the area after the King and Augusta after one of his five daughters. They then set about importing Negro slaves from Africa while slaughtering the indigenous population. The surviving Cherokee and Creek Indians were "removed from the State" between 1832 and 1838.

After the minor setback of being on the losing side of the 1861–65 American Civil War, Augusta gradually prospered to become one of the chief cotton manufacturing centres of the South, and one of many popular southern USA winter resorts for escapees from harsher northern climes. White escapees, that is. By this time, many of Georgia's population, black that is, were escaping in the opposite direction, migrating up the eastern seaboard lured by promises of work in Washington, Philadelphia, New York and the like, with no inkling of future ghettos for the dispossessed.

For a while during his prime time, James Brown made a similar move, establishing a Sixties base in the Queens district of New York City. It was never really home, though. James Brown is first and foremost an American, period. As apple pie as any president's mom could bake. Close on the heels of the patriotic American, he is equally and forcefully a southerner. By the late Fifties, he was aiming at as broad an American audience as then seemed possible. By the mid-Sixties he had become well aware that there was a vast international market out there. Intermittently throughout his career he has recorded other people's songs or employed orchestral arrangers and, latterly, worked with outside producers to try for different targets, some successfully. But catch him in the right light, listen to the bulk of his most important recordings, and you'd need to be blind not to see, deaf not to hear, that the music he makes when left to his own devices is southern. He was not comfortable in New York and by the dawn of the Seventies he relocated back to his home base.

There is a third part of Brown's make-up that confuses the equation and causes him no end of problems. He's an eclectic mix of American Indian – Cherokee and Aztec, he once told Cliff White – and African and, if James's own testimony on this is to be believed, Far East Asian ancestry. His father dealt with the problems of prejudice by being respectful to whites' faces while hating them with a passion. But for all the outwardly confused

17

political thinking and affiliations of the Seventies, James Brown has been determinedly proud at heart since he was first told to know his place.

His upbringing might have been taken from the pages of an early Alice Walker or Toni Morrison novel. He was raised in the sort of rural poverty that has become a cliché for anyone not actually experiencing it. Brown's mother left home for the North when he was four and he never met her again until he was starring at the Apollo and Madison Square Garden in New York. He lived in one-room shacks wherever his father found work – on farms, at gas stations, at a sawmill, in stores, working on roads and highways. Alone for most of the time, Brown taught himself harmonica. "My father bought me a harmonica for 10 cents and I learned to play it in about a day and a half."

After struggling for several years to raise his son alone, the hardworking, hard-pressed father sent for Aunt Minnie to help raise the boy. She it was who had breathed life into his son's frail frame after he had been stillborn. At six, his father left and Aunt Minnie and James moved into a house in the Terry, the black quarter of Augusta, run by another aunt, Handsome Washington, known as Honey. It was a rooming house, a gambling den (do not roll dice with James Brown), a drinking joint and a whorehouse. You could get a good square meal there too.

Brown had a good ear and added the organ to his self-taught repertoire of instruments. "I was eight-years-old," he told Cliff White in a video interview. "My father was working at a furniture store and one of the legs broke off the organ and they were going to throw it out but they gave it to him. He brought it home and we took a cheese crate and made another leg. He brought it home about eleven o'clock that day and when he got back at six o'clock that evening I was playing a tune on it already.

"Then I play bass, I play guitar, I play a little saxophone, I taught myself. I play some trumpet, which I learned from playing the bugle when I was a Boy Scout."

Like his father, he had a very restricted formal education and in his earliest interviews recalled how he wore flour sacks as underwear, went barefoot to school in winter and was sent home from school because his clothes were too raggedy. His real interest was sport – baseball, American football and boxing. "When I did go to school, I adapted to everything real fast because I knew I had to do it. I was the best. Had the chance to play professional baseball, I had three professional fights as a fighter, I was the best horseshoe champion, I was an all-state in football and real super in basketball. I would excel even when I shot marbles. I was just very, very good at everything." Clearly the solitude of his early years never damaged his self-confidence or pride in his abilities. There is no room for self-doubt in his make-up.

He hustled jobs: picked cotton, cut sugar cane, shined shoes. He learned drums, piano and guitar, saxophone and trumpet too. And, of course, there was gospel. At the handclappin', footstompin', tambourine-slappin', testifyin' services, Brown first saw natural showmen grabbing and keeping the attention of an audience. He was learning to do the same, performing at school, where he stayed on only up to 7th grade, but here he met Henry Stallings who would much later travel the world as Brown's personal hairdresser. They tried to earn a few dollars shining shoes and later tried to make some money as boxers but they lost touch when Stallings went into the Army and Brown went into jail. (They would not meet again until Brown, who by that time had a hit with 'Please, Please, Please', went to play a show in New York where Stallings was working at the Golden Gloves, the bar owned by Sugar Ray Robinson, on 123rd Street and Seventh Avenue. Stallings found it hard to believe – James Brown the pool hall attendant and shoeshine boy a star!)

At 11, he won his first talent contest as a singer and at the end of the war he formed The Cremona Trio, named after the group's guitar, and also sang, possibly, with Bill Johnson & The Four Steps of Rhythm. He performed at school. He also got involved in petty crime, shoplifting and, mostly, stealing car batteries and hubcaps to get money for school clothes and for food. This was life as survival pure and simple.

When he was 15-years-old, he was caught stealing from cars for the second time and, he claimed, was held in jail until he turned 16 when he was tried as an adult. He was sentenced to eight to 16 years and locked up for the rest of his teens in the Georgia Juvenile Training Institute in Rome, Georgia, which later moved to the Alto Reform School, a former National Guard armoury and barracks near Toccoa, Georgia. A young man of Brown's race could expect to be subjected to severe treatment and provocation in jail but he showed a positive attitude and there followed a gradual rehabilitation. He formed a gospel quartet, there were other excursions in music, he became a trustee and he earned the sobriquet Music Box, the first of many.

Brown had not long turned 19 when he was granted parole after three years and a day inside, through the good offices of a local family who gave him a home and helped him find employment at a motor dealership. He'd run into Bobby Byrd, literally, during a community baseball match. Byrd was on second base at the time; Brown, a mean pitcher on the Alto team, came through Byrd's base at speed. "After the game," Byrd recalled, "he told me about this letter he was writing to the warden, saying how he was intent on going straight, and he asked me if I could speak up for him. The family put in a good word and they let him out on parole to a job we found for him at Lawson's Motor Company."

Soon after his release, Brown wrecked a customer's jeep. He was saved from a quick return to Alto, just 18 miles away from Toccoa, only by further persuasive pleas from the well-respected Byrd family and others. James Brown re-dedicated himself to singing, for a while.

CHAPTER 2

"Toccoa? Oh, I'd guess you'd call it 'a Thriving Metropolis'," the tall and amiable Bobby Byrd said of his hometown. A deep chuckle rumbled through his whole body. "Naw, it's a small town at the foot of the hills up in north Georgia, close by the Savannah River and right in the heart of the Bible Belt. What built up our thing was the Bible College. And the fishing. They got a dam on the river and there's mighty fine fishing. People would come from all over for that." It was the environment into which Bobby Byrd was born on August 15, 1934, and into which James Brown moved after his release from prison on 14 June, 1952.

"I'll give you an idea of Toccoa when I was growing up," Byrd continued in his rich, husky voice. "When the first streamline train came through, it was due at 12.01 pm and the whole town was at the station to see it. People were selling souvenirs, it was like a carnival. So the train came and didn't even stop, just shot through, whoosh! Then we all went back home again.

"The onliest time we ever saw any act come through was Clyde McPhatter and The Drifters. They stopped in Toccoa to gas up on the way to somewhere else. One person told another person and before you know it half of Toccoa was up there at the service station. Everybody was just staring at them in amazement – The Drifters!"

But Toccoa was predominantly free of racial tension compared to the majority of small towns in the South, Byrd said. It was 'a calm place to be', full of churchgoers. Also, Byrd said, the white elders thought racial incidents would dissuade the folk from coming to fish. "So everything was kept cool.

For the most part, we all got along." Byrd's natural charm and personality has helped him get along with most people.

"Later on, with the group, we had a little local trouble. This white family had moved into Toccoa and they hired us for a birthday party. Now, we'd already gotten to know their kids. We were all friends. It was their parents that had the problem. We played the job and then the kids asked if we could go out there and join the barbecue. The father said, 'No! Feed them niggers, pay 'em and send 'em back to Nigger Town' with a lot of cuss words thrown in. So one of the white girl guests went and told her father what this man was saying in front of all the kids. I don't think the family stayed around Toccoa too long."

On the other hand, Bobby recalled black kids rescuing a white friend of his from an attack by other blacks. "It wasn't a matter of whether you're black or white, in Toccoa you helped the one that needed help. They called it 'Toccoa The Beautiful' – that's what the name means. It's an old Cherokee Indian name. That whole area belonged to the Cherokees before they were pushed up into North Carolina."

Byrd's family was secure and close-knit. Churchgoers. Bobby grew into a relatively stable youth who attended high school regularly. "When we say high school, there was only one school for blacks. An old place at first, then when I reached Ninth Grade a new school was built called Whitman Street. That's where I graduated Valedictorian, the highest honours. That was awarded by the white school board, 'cos there wasn't no black school boards then.

"After that, I went off to college, the A&T [Agricultural & Technical] in Greensboro, North Carolina. Later on, Maceo and Melvin Parker went there and Nat Jones and Levi Rasbury. Jesse Jackson was there too. Not at the same time as me, but we all went to the same place." Bobby had won a basketball scholarship but because he wasn't a giant, like Wilt Chamberlain, "they couldn't get no insurance for me so I didn't get the chance to play." Instead, he majored in music with teaching his minor:

"I'd always been good on piano. I had a real good ear, even at nine-years-old. I don't write formal notation but I learned chords early on. The music teacher could sit up and play something and I'd come right behind her and play it and then add something of my own. She told my mother, 'He ain't learning 'cos he's already got in his head what he wanna do'. When I went to college, that was the first time getting away from home that I was able to listen to a lot of R&B."

Toccoa didn't have a black radio station but there was one just off campus at Greensboro. "I learned a lot. Also, that's when I first started playing with a professional band. This was for a black guy called Williams, I can't recall his first name. He played keyboards too but he wanted to direct so he got me. After Thursday, I didn't have no classes so I'd go off with 'em for the weekend – Goldsboro, Winston Salem, High Point – and come back with all this money. I was making eleven dollars a night which was good money then. I played with him for about a year and a half while I was in college. Funny thing was, the singer with the band recorded for King Records and I didn't even know it. After we got with King I was looking through some old records and saw his name, a tune called 'That I Wanna See'. I thought, 'I can't believe this!' "

There was, inevitably, another side to Byrd's education. Toccoa was in the heart of the Bible Belt and even after Prohibition was as dry as a Mosque when it came to alcohol. "But just across the river, the Carolinas were wet. So you could go across the line and get the liquor. That's when White Lightning flourished. Corn liquor. That stuff be strong, too. But, believe me, we'd drink it like it was water. Later, when we started drinking the government liquor, it was too mild. I mean, 'This ain't nothing here! Let's go back to the White Lightning!' They made it with different flavours, with the taste of apples, the taste of peaches, then they had the taste of cherries. But it was all White Lightning. You'd sit there and sip and sip and sip and then try to get up if you will. You'd fall dead on your face."

From North and South Carolina, even from Louisiana, transportation of the illicit booze was a profitable side line. "We used to haul it, me and a boy named Doyle Oglesby. He and Fred Pulliam were early drop-outs from The Flames. James did it, too. There'd be like 15 or 20 cars on the road. Not in convoy, you'd do what you have to do yourself. My run was from Brebard, North Carolina to Toccoa. Later on, with the group, we played Brebard and I carried 'em right to the spot, 'cos I already knew it so well."

Byrd made the 150 mile run through the Appalachian mountains about twice a week for about 15 months until 'liquor wars' began. He compares it to kids today who earn money from drugs. "You wouldn't get back to town until next day and you'd be late for school so you'd always take a set of clothes with you. At a certain spot on Currhee Mountain there was a cabin where you'd stop off, fix yourself a change of clothes and get yourself together, then go to school. I tell you, once you got up in those mountains, you wouldn't believe it. You'd drive up in the country woods and this great big table would open up and there was like moonshine city up there. If you drove past it, all you'd see was trees. But once through the gate, it was like a city. You could buy clothes, they had bars, women, stores, anything you wanted.

"The police knew. Of course they did. It was like the drugs of today. They knew what was going on. They knew which houses were being supplied and where it was coming from. They were taking pay-offs. But they didn't always know the runs." When the 'wars' and 'takeovers' began rivals informed on each other, but police roadblocks were easy to avoid. "By us knowing the back roads, we'd always lose 'em. But some of those back roads, you gotta watch out. That's how a friend of mine got killed and that's when I decided to quit. He had a souped up '36 Ford with 24 cases of White Lightning in milk jugs. He went off an embankment and that stuff was so powerful it blew up."

But these activities as moonshine-runner were always extra-curricular to music. Byrd's group in school, two girls and four guys, took 'hillbilly' music and interpreted it as rhythm'n'blues. "We used to sing these songs for the little programmes the school would have. Then we'd go over to the white school and do a few tunes. But the real roots of The Famous Flames, the original group that sang gospel as The Gospel Starlighters and R&B as The Avons, that was me, Sylvester Keels, Fred Pulliam, Doyle Oglesby and Nash Knox, with Nafloyd Scott on guitar. This was the group just before James came."

Byrd sang lead and played piano, Keels, Pulliam and Oglesby sang. A little later, bassist Baroy "Baby Roy" Scott joined. Bobby's sister Sarah sang with them too. "What the people have got to understand is that we were brought up in the church from a small age. In our town, like in a lot of other small towns, the church was the most important thing. You had to go to church. During the week, they'd have prayer meetings or Bible study. We all belonged to an organisation called the BYPU – Baptist Young People's Union. Mother would say, 'OK, it's BYPU day'. That means you gotta go. So therefore a lot of the group, me too, didn't like a lot of the things that it took to get over. We always figured that you could do it the right way and get there. Later on, we found out that it's a lot different to that. That's why Doyle and Fred dropped out, because they didn't like what was happening. I kinda hated that because they were the best singers."

But Byrd stuck with the group. "I've got to be a realist and say that if it wasn't for James joining us, me hauling him in, then we probably wouldn't have made it. Not on the same scale, anyway. We were good, even before James turned up. But he was the extra special thing. But with his kind of rootless background, he knows no barriers, he always goes too far. I've known him most of my life now and I truly don't think he knows what it is to love or be loved. He cannot communicate that way. You're either with him or against him. That's the way his mind works. And most of the time he thinks you might be against him, even when you're not."

Before Byrd brought Brown into the group, they'd always played things pretty much straight. "James brought in this competitive thing. Strange things started happening during the time we were trying to make it. The back-biting, so to speak, and the taking people's jobs, the undermining. We didn't do this before. If you were hired to do a job, that's your job. If it was somebody else's job, it's their job. James started this thing where he'd go out for less money than other acts just to get their job. And it hurt, in a sense. Because there were people who'd say 'OK, if you'll do the job for this kind of money, why should I pay that kind of money?' It put a bad taste in other acts' mouths, 'cos they'd been getting used to one level of money and we started going out for less."

Even before the baseball match which brought them together with a clatter, Byrd and James had talked through the wires around the Alto prison. "You know, you can sense it with some people that they got something special about them. When I first saw James my soul said, 'You gotta get him outta there 'cos if somebody else sees him, in gospel or in rhythm'n'blues or whatever, he's gonna be big'. He had something about him, he was just different. He was something exceptional, he really was. That's why I worked so hard to get him over to my group, not really thinking at the time that it would eventually become his group!

"He was really, truly, singing back then. He wasn't hollering and screaming. I guess that all started when he decided to outdo Little Richard in every way he could. Before that, he was truly a fine singer. And dancing … the dancing that y'all seen later on in his years ain't nothing to what he used to do back then. James could stand flat-footed and flip over into a split. He'd just flim-flam then up again. And he could tumble. When you flip, flip, over and over, like on the gymnastics. He was real good at that.

"Man, I thought I was the hottest thing in Toccoa, I was supposed to be THE MAN in Toccoa. And then here he comes, singing like a bird and tumbling and going crazy. They ain't never heard of that in Toccoa! It was fascinating but it made me mad, too, you know. I didn't need him in competition. I needed him with me."

Byrd's family was well respected in Toccoa. They held offices in the church and Bobby's mother worked for one of the richest white doctors in town, a powerful man locally. "Everybody in town knew me. I was working at the theatres, cleaning up at the drive-in and selling tickets at the other two theatres. I got on with everybody, was friends with all the kids, so I had a little bit of clout, too. And then the principal at the school, he helped us out a whole lot. He even went against the system and started James at school in the tenth grade. But James wouldn't go."

When James got out of Alto he lived for a while with Nathaniel and Dora Davis who took him to Trinity CME Church where he sang with the choir, met Byrd's sister Sarah and joined the local Community Choir, The Ever Ready Gospel Singers. "James was a great gospel singer, very good. He could bring the church down. We thought we were good until we saw James. He was something else. He got into this thing with my sister, Sarah, and she was great, too. So now you're talking alchemy. You shoulda heard her and James, it was something. They would come with the community choir, thirty people or so, and most of those people could really sing. Truly, most of them could have been lead singers themselves. But James and Sarah kept the lead parts all the time. They were travelling all over.

"When we first got him out [of Alto] he strictly wanted to do gospel with Sarah and the choir. But I wanted him for my group. It was like pulling teeth, trying to get him out from over there. He didn't want to leave. He did it so well and didn't want to do anything else. But I finally got him with my group and we went into the rhythm'n'blues thing."

There were other matters pressing Byrd. "To tell you the truth, my first girlfriend, who I later married, got pregnant. That's one of the reasons I had to get out of town and go to college. James and I had started our little things, but I had to get outta there. After I came back for good we went into it full force, but in the meantime I could only come back sometimes at weekends or at vacation time. And he was with the community choir. Talk about upset? I was really disturbed then. I was almost instrumental in getting him out of jail, he was supposed to be with me, and they done sent me away. Whenever I get back my sister got him and, oh God, they're going together! Now you know I got a problem.

"Sarah was fighting for James because he was her boyfriend and he was a big asset to the choir. They had this backwards and forwards dual-lead thing going that was the talk of the town. I couldn't get no toe-hold on James because every time we got something going, it was time for me to go back to college. I had to wait 'til the next time off to shoot back there and try to throw a brick in their little thing. But whenever I left and then got back, he'd have always done something crazy. I'm telling you, that boy, he'd always do something crazy!

"There was one time, I came back home one Christmas. Now this is just one incident out of many. James had another girlfriend in Cornelia [Georgia], and he had gone up there with some of the fellas and her other boyfriend was there. So he gets into a fight and almost gets locked up. The other fellas split and come back on to Toccoa. So James and the girl was walking and another friend of James drives by, Horace Brown. He was always a heavy drinker, James hopped a lift back to Toccoa. On the way back they had a terrible wreck. But when the car went over the hill, the door flew open and James was thrown out against a tree, bumped his head up real bad and messed up his shoulder. But at least he was still on top of the hill. The other guy was dead in the wreck at the bottom.

"The rest of us are all back down in Toccoa, having drinks and a good time, when this white fella came by the house. His name was Taylor, never will forget. His father owned the local Buick outlet. He said, 'I thought I saw James Brown walking down the mountain but I'm not sure 'cos I don't pick up hitchhikers'. Maybe he meant he didn't pick up niggers but at least he had the courtesy to come by and say something. Now all the other fellas are back, right, but James is still missing. So we knew it had to be him. And he was, like, in shock. He couldn't say anything but he kept pointing back up the hill. We went there and found the wreck.

"Now you'd think he shoulda changed his ways right there, just missing death and one of his best friends killed. But you wouldn't believe, he gets back into Toccoa and immediately there's another fight. He gets back and finds Velda, I think it was, who became his first wife, she was with this other guy, Nelson. So he jumps on Nelson, and James and Velda have a knock-down, drag-out. So what I'm saying is, I come home for Christmas and already there's two fights, a car crash, a death and James is up to his neck in trouble again."

This lively ability to seek out experience in its infinite variety was not the only facet of Brown's character that those who knew him much later in life would recognise in the youth rebuilding a life after jail. "He was kinda paranoid even back then. He always thought that people were trying to do something to him. It was hard to get it in his head that most of the people you'd talk to in Toccoa were some kind of kinfolk. Being from Augusta, James didn't know the town or the people too well. Everybody in Toccoa knows everybody. You're either some kind of kin to 'em or you've known 'em so long you know their business. You can be talking to a girl, then you go to another girl and she'd be her first cousin. Or you might mess with some girl and brag to the fellas about it and they'd turn out to be her cousins and whop your head! Every time I came home there was always something crazy happening around James."

Byrd and the group decided to switch to rhythm'n'blues at roughly the same time as Brown joined. "When we first saw Hank Ballard and The Midnighters and The Clovers and those groups, all of our eyes went like that, wide open. We said 'Oh, this is what we wanna do!' The girls were hot and screaming and carrying on." At first they worked local gigs in social clubs and recreation centres. "Although James became the main lead singer we still didn't have a new name, people just knew us as 'that Bobby Byrd group' ... we didn't do any original songs for quite some while, we'd just sing our favourite R&B hits: The Five Royales' 'Baby Don't Do It', The Midnighters' 'Annie Had A Baby', The Spaniels' 'Goodnight Sweetheart', The Clovers' 'One Mint Julep'. As a matter of fact, 'Julep' was the highlight of our act, we were pretty good at that."

Shortly after switching from gospel, 'that Bobby Byrd group' became The Avons. "Now as long as we'd been doing gospel everything was fine with everybody at home and in the church. But when they found out we'd turned over to R&B, that's when they hauled us up. They didn't find out at first because all the jobs we were doing as The Avons was outside of Toccoa and we'd always make it back home just in time to get to church. Gradually, people got to hear about us and we'd be playing a place like Athens, Georgia, and when we look up half the congregation from Toccoa was out there dancing and having a ball." Eventually asked to explain himself to the church conference, Byrd apologised for his heinous sins. He'd be sure not to play R&B in Toccoa.

Nonetheless, the city's only professional black music entrepreneur in the Fifties, Barry Trimier, became The Avons' first booking agent cum manager. He's now a funeral director in Decatur, a suburb of south Atlanta. "This man did a lot for us," Bobby asserted, in Trimier's funeral parlour. A tall, slightly stooped, quietly spoken old gentleman with the disarming, conciliatory manner his current trade demands, he was not willingly forthcoming on the subject of The Avons and James Brown. "One day I will publish my own story." As he had been on the critical list in the emergency ward of the local hospital a few months earlier, time was clearly of the essence.

But the erstwhile group manager gradually vouchsafed his story. He'd been born in Toccoa on 18 October, 1912, to "the most wonderful woman in the world. My mother, Savannah, was a nurse and midwife. She raised some of the big white folks in town. The old 'uns would say proudly, 'My baby was spanked by that nigger woman down there'. Everybody liked her and that helped me." But not enough to assist him at the age of 28 when he was drafted during World War II. "I was too old but some of the white people wanted me out of town. I was operating cabs and making more money than they thought I ought to be making."

Stationed near Liverpool, England, with the 372 Quartermaster Battalion, Trimier and his comrades were given advance invasion training and sent to France. "One night some of us bivouacked in the middle of a field while the others slept by the road. They were all shot by the German planes that strafed the roads at night. They called it 'Bedcheck Charlie'. Later, in Cherbourg, we were going to spend the first night in a German submarine headquarters but the infantry ran us out. Next morning, they were dead. The headquarters was booby-trapped. The good Lord didn't intend for me to get killed."

In Europe, the army companies were integrated for repatriation. "From New York we were all sent by train to Augusta, Georgia, to be discharged. As we got down into Virginia, MPs came through the cars splitting us up again. The white soldiers who were with us in France, they'd felt safer sleeping beside a black soldier while the Germans were still around. There weren't no black German soldiers. But we get back home and we're second-class niggers again."

He stayed in Toccoa to look after his mother. He went back into the cab business and had some trouble from white drivers who'd taken his business while he'd been away defending freedom. Despite getting no help from the local law enforcement agencies, stubborn Trimier prevailed.

He bought a corner lot, built a café, club and poolroom called Barry's Recreation Centre. "This was half a block from the school. It became the hang-out for the kids. That's when Bobby and his friends started coming round. They first started playing in the Recreation Centre, then we branched out to other little towns, into high schools, colleges and the University of Georgia. Bobby was the main organiser of the band, just a natural born musician. If it hadn't been for these boys, we wouldn't have had anything to eat.

"Then James Brown turned up. I have to say with all his trouble and stuff, the boy was unusual. He was always in trouble but he had something different about him. James came out on nine months' probation. Unknown to me, he went and bought an automobile, kept it for two or three weeks and then traded it for another one. Being on probation, he wasn't supposed to do this. He had lost citizenship. The sheriff came to pick him up, was going to send him back for nine years. The only thing that saved him, he was still a minor. Also, the monied people in Toccoa who booked these boys for gigs, we went to them. They had the clout. Always we had to get somebody with clout."

With Brown still available, Trimier booked Byrd's group into schools on Fridays and Saturdays and clubs on Sundays and Mondays. "We would send out two or three bands at the weekends," Trimier continued. "James sang with different bands at different fraternities. One band was fronted by Bobby, one by James, one by Sylvester. James Crawford was in there too. The student council recommended us around to other schools. We'd make a deal on the phone, there were no signed contracts. It wasn't a matter of a whole lot of money for a band. Maybe $125, maybe $150.

"When James hit the big time with 'Please, Please, Please', he was already well known in our area. He'd get a bigger turn-out than Little Richard. It wasn't the song that made him, he didn't even like it at first. He was never sure what the people wanted. Originally, he had to be told. The song didn't make him. It was the folks who helped him that made him. He was somebody unusual but he had to have people like Clint Brantley and Ben Bart to take him further. There was no way in the world that I could go out there and socialise. He took our name and our song but I told him, 'just leave me out'."

Trimier worked the group steadily during 1954–55 on the north Georgia and South Carolina semi-pro circuit. The instrumentation, Byrd recalled, was fairly primitive. "Benny Jones had a station wagon, Barry Trimier had a car. We had a cymbal made out of steel or real heavy duty tin. You'd hit it and it'd go CRASH! not swish. We got a bass drum from school, a big ol' marching band drum. Then we messed around and got us a foot pedal. James was working at the plastics factory by then, and they welded up all this stuff together so it'd never come apart. So now you got 'Boom-bang-CRASH! Boom-bang-CRASH!'

"Nafloyd had a regular guitar with a pick-up on it. We had no bass. I was doing the bass vocally. We had one mike and one little amp about the size of a modern TV. We'd all sing through it. When Nafloyd's brother, we called him Baby Roy, came in with the other guitar, that was a regular guitar too. It wasn't a bass but we put bass strings on it. He didn't know too much about making it sound bassy so a lot of times he'd sound like Nafloyd only playing a different part. Eventually, we got us another amp."

Rudimentary though the equipment was, it was theirs and they could make gigs regularly, their reliability and consistency making them popular locally. "We were different because we had a lot of variety. We'd ring the changes. Although I was the principal piano player and bass singer, I'd also drum and sing lead. Before Baby Roy really started playing what passed for the bass guitar, he'd take over on keyboards. In Toccoa, there was a lot more piano players, the kids were into that. Baby Roy was real good, almost like me."

Byrd, Brown and Sylvester Keels were the principal singers. "So when James got ready to sing I would drum and when I got ready to sing Sylvester would drum. 'Cos James and I would be back and forth on the lead part. Our voices always did go well together. What we were doing then was like the foundation of all those later things like 'Licking Stick' and 'Soul

Power'. James would drum too and Sylvester could also play piano. So we'd switch it around, rotate around. That was part of the act and that would fascinate people."

Instruments were not the only things they switched. Around this time, while still working as The Avons, they also played their first gigs as The Flames. They were also using other names – like The Trenells and The Rhythm Masters – and were possibly still doing the occasional gospel date under the Gospel Starlighters banner, whatever it took to get over.

Johnny Terry had been in the same prison as James and, before Brown was released, had brought a group from Atlanta to Toccoa. "It was about the first time we looked seriously at the R&B thing." Byrd can't recall the band's name "but the boys could sing, all except Johnny. He never could sing but we didn't find that out till later on. So Johnny decided to make Toccoa his home and he tried to get in school. But then James got out of jail and they started to run together. So that was that, they both didn't go back to school.

"Johnny was always the one left not doing anything because he couldn't sing with my group and he couldn't sing with the community choir. He wasn't singing with nobody, I'm sure he was glad when James finally got him in my group. He first came around as a writer, not singing. He was a good writer. Then he finally joined us full time after we'd gone over to R&B. James wanted Johnny to be in the group and that's when we found out he couldn't sing. But he was a good dancer. So we handled the harmonies and he joined in the routines.

"As far as I can recall, we didn't do any original songs for quite some while. We'd just sing our favourite R&B hits, The Five Royales' 'Baby Don't Do It', The Midnighters' 'Annie Had A Baby', The Spaniels' 'Goodnight Sweetheart', The Clovers' 'One Mint Julep'. But we didn't just do group hits. Somebody would do like B. B. King, somebody else would do Big Joe Turner. That was me, I sang 'Shake Rattle And Roll' and that kinda stuff. Fred Pulliam did Lowell Fulson's 'Reconsider Baby' and some others. Sylvester Keels would do Clyde McPhatter, James would do Wynonie Harris and Roy Brown. As far as the horn parts, if there was supposed to be a saxophone solo either James or I would whistle it or we'd scat-sing it together. Turned out to be all right too. We did have one sax player for a while, this boy Neil who was a friend of James's from Augusta. He was with us briefly in Toccoa and then again in Macon but he didn't think anything was going to happen. He sure missed the boat."

As well as their clubs, schools and colleges act, the group would also play afternoon tea parties singing pop ballads. "That's what we'd been doing as

The Avons before James joined us and he could do that stuff good too. He'd do some of those ballads that were later recorded, 'So Long', 'Prisoner Of Love', 'Blue Moon' was another one, and 'White Cliffs Of Dover'. As a matter of fact we did record all this stuff before we ever got with King Records. I can't remember when, but we definitely cut some stuff in Atlanta and over in Florida. [Brown says South Carolina.] I wish we had re-recorded 'White Cliffs Of Dover' for King 'cos James could really sing it beautifully and the arrangement we had on it was fantastic."

It would be some while before the rotation of roles stopped to reveal James Brown permanently out front. But during 1954–55 the changes gradually came to move at James's speed, fuelled by the manic energy that had impressed Byrd when he first saw "Music Box" do his thing inside the prison fences. One night at Bill's Rendezvous Club, the hottest spot in Toccoa, the Byrd-Brown group contrived its début there by jumping up on stage during the intermission between sets by one of the southern chitlin' circuit's most popular acts, Little Richard. They tore up the place. After the invasion and the rest of the main attraction's show, Lucas "Fats" Gonder, Richard's tour manager/MC/pianist, introduced himself to the group and suggested they get in touch with Clint Brantley, Richard's manager across state in Macon. Brantley put them up at his club, The Two Spot, and got them a few other local dates. But he was too busy working on the booming career of Little Richard to be able to spend much time and energy on the younger act. However, two things soon forced Brantley's hand: Brown's propensity for getting himself into trouble and Richard's departure to Specialty Records.

"Another time," Byrd continued, "James was over in South Carolina at four o'clock in the morning. At that time, being black in the south, you can't be caught travelling those kind of times in the morning especially 'cross a state line, especially when you're on parole! But we got word he was over there in a fight and he had took the fenders off somebody's car. Now lemme tell you, James could strip a car in no time flat. He had a thing about cars. You could come in here and me'n'you sit and talk for twenty minutes. When you go back out there, the body of your car is sitting on blocks. He'd have the wheels, the fenders, the motor and be gone. We told him 'James, you don't have to do this no more. This you gotta do no more. I mean, you got my mother on your front, she done went through all these people to get you out of jail …'

"So we drive all the way over there to get him out of this mess. He was driving like a '37 Ford with a rumble seat in it. The other guy's fenders, hub caps and parts of the motor, all this stuff was in the rumble seat. The rest of the motor was hoisted up on chains ready to be taken out. I guess James was fixing to put that on top of the car. So we get James away from this other boy and got him out of there. We came with two cars, so we put James in one and sent him right on. Then we got all the stuff out of his car, threw it anywhere we could, put a chain on his car and hauled it back to Toccoa. Now, here we gotta come back from South Carolina in the middle of the night, all the way across the line, towing a car – all black folk. And James ain't got no tyres on his car! But anyway, we made it back to Georgia. I had a talk with him but, you know, he just could not stay out of trouble."

Not even marriage to Velma Warren and the responsibility of his two sons, Teddy and Terry, seemed to slow Brown down. "While he was in Toccoa I kept thinking, 'Lord, they're gonna put my mother in jail for speaking up for this boy'," Byrd said. "When we got to Macon they transferred his bail [to Brantley], so my mother and them was off the hook. I was so glad of that. So now Clint was on the hook."

CHAPTER 3

Compared to Toccoa, Macon was Big Time Georgia. Major R&B acts regularly played the Macon Auditorium, booked by Clint Brantley, and on the rise they all played at his Two Spot. With the club-owner's more professional set-up, Brown, Byrd and band made an increasingly strong impact on the Macon scene but, bearing in mind his continuing parole, James's activities away from the stage often caused just as much excitement.

"Clint bought James a car," Byrd recalled. "A brand new Buick '55, I think it was. We didn't have no record yet but we were gigging regularly and James was working. He had a job in the bus station, so he could sign for the car. James decided he wanted to drive to Toccoa to let everybody see his new car. Now, there weren't no super highways back then, just two lanes. We told him, 'Don't go', but he just headed off one night. Next thing we heard, six o'clock in the morning, he was in jail again. In Madison, Georgia. Being black, this was no place to be at any time. A very peculiar town.

"James had run into a man on a tractor. Had it been a young white guy it might have been different, but this was an old white man who knew everyone in Madison. Now, James ran into the man, right? But instead of saying, 'I'm sorry for messing up your tractor', he beat the man up 'cos his new car was all tore up. In Madison, Georgia in 1955! Bam! That's it. James was in big trouble. I don't know to this day how Clint got him out of there. But after four or five days he got him back to Macon. A little while later we played Madison two or three times and never got paid. Obviously, Clint must have owed someone a big favour."

35

Back on stage, Brown and the group were developing a wild act, tear-down-the-walls singing and powerpack playing but, like local hero Little Richard and dozens before and thousands after, James knew by instinct that in front of an audience, an artist had to look clean. Not scrubbed behind the ears and pared down fingernails clean, but slick, smart, cool. All the best groups were, like the hip Orioles or Flamingos, and so were the most magnetic front men, such as Louis Jordan, whose ability to catch and keep an audience's attention with snappily arranged music, witty lyrics and an eye-popping show mightily impressed Brown. Trying to emulate them was not without its problems for a hard-up act.

"James is very particular about his hair," Bobby said. "I don't know where that came from, although it might have had something to do with when we were starting out. There were these groups like The Flamingos and others who were smooth, good looking, with nice hairdos. So although we had a different kind of act, we wanted to look like that. We couldn't afford the suits and stuff at that time, but at least we could try to look sharp with our hair. Just like all so-called 'black' people are all different colours on the skin, so we all have different coloured hair. Just like Caucasians, right? You're not all naturally blond, we're not all naturally jet black. So we used to dye our hair. And at that time we used shoe polish. That was our thing. Put that stuff on your hair and try to dry it out, it take forever.

"Now, Johnny Terry was real auburn so he had to use a lot of that stuff. But Johnny was always a sweater. When I was younger, I was like always the cool one. I'd do my routine, click, click, click, but I never would sweat. I didn't start sweating 'til later on. We all get older. But Johnny, he was a sweater. So sometimes, when we got real energetic or it got really hot, man, that stuff would be running down his face … oh boy, the things that we went through just to get over.

"We were playing a place in the Atlanta area one time and we came in on the rim. The tyre burst just outside of town and we didn't have no spare. We made the gig and jumped out of the station wagon trying to be sharp, you know, 'We are here!' The people got to looking and said, 'Oh no, I don't see how y'all made it with this heap here'. But we went in there and did a good show, talk about tore up the place. Rattled 'em to death. Then came time to leave. We come out there and the car wouldn't start. So we're frantically trying to push this thing down the highway before the folks come out the place and see us. Man, that was both tragic and funny."

One night in Macon, between sundown and showtime, James made a startling revelation to the rest of The Flames. He was about to "sell his soul to the devil". "This was at The Two Spot," Byrd recalled. "He was talking to me and Johnny Terry. He said, 'Do you want to go with me? They're taking me back tomorrow night'. I never did know who 'they' were. I said, 'Oh no, I'm not going out there on no dark country road to meet no devil'. And Johnny Terry wasn't going. He said, 'You're crazy. What are you talking about?' But James was very serious that night."

The legend of selling one's soul to the devil in exchange for the power of innovation in music – or for the possession of great wealth or the love of another human being – is scarcely a new twist in any mythology. It pursued the innovative blues singer Robert Johnson to his early grave and remains a potent symbol for the emergence of genius from a wild, torn soul. The tug of war between spiritual salvation and venal sin among African-American singers raised in the church on gospel music is now so obvious as to verge on cliché. A catalogue of singers – Little Richard, Sam Cooke, Al Green, Marvin Gaye and many others – have experienced it. In their church community's eyes, it is an equivalent of actually striking a deal with the devil.

"Nobody saw him for a day or so. We were wondering what he was doing. Then he turned up again and suddenly he was sweating a lot. And he had a shortness of breath. I don't know whether he'd walked from wherever he went off to, but he was tired and sweating. And that very same day, Clint got into a huge argument about Little Richard because James said Clint was pushing Little Richard too much and not giving us a proper chance.

"I'll say one thing for James. He told us, 'I'm not going to tell you to be like me or to go with me. I'm going to take you all with me anyway. Don't you even worry about it. We're going to be the biggest thing out there'. He said that often around that time. And let me tell you something strange, we started to get very popular after James said he'd sold his soul to the devil. Now we weren't going anything much different 'cept James started to push himself harder than ever. But all of a sudden the phone started ringing for The Flames."

Some of their precipitate popularity could be explained simply by the process of elimination. Little Richard had a national hit with 'Tutti Frutti' and disappeared from the local scene. "So suddenly we're the number one local act in Macon. See, Richard had the city sewn up. It was his home town. And as flamboyant as he was, people are going to come to see him whether he had a record or not. You wouldn't believe the houses he would draw before he had 'Tutti Frutti'. You could not believe it. He'd fill the auditorium. I'm talking about the auditorium now, not some small club or theatre. And he hadn't had no hit or nothing. People would be coming to see him change clothes, and to see how his hair is going to be looking. This big pompadour he had. He was real flashy.

37

"Richard was always trying to be nice to us but James had this thing about Richard because he was a good looking fella and was successful. And we were like a struggling act. Richard was sharp but all of us looked like we were straight from the sticks, you know what I'm saying? Richard and his band were well groomed, suits and ties and things. Girls were always hanging around them. James couldn't stand that at all. He had a powerful hate for Richard there for a while.

"Also, the money situation. None of us was getting much back then. But whereas we were making, say, twelve dollars a night each, sometimes eight or ten, Richard's band was making like fifteen or twenty dollars a man. And Richard was getting thirty-five or forty. So James was mad because Richard was getting all this extra money for being the front man but James couldn't get any more than us because we were a group together. There wasn't no James Brown And The Famous Flames at that time. We found out later on that Clint would slip him a few extra dollars. Actually, I was the first one to find out so then he slipped me a few dollars extra too!

"The meanest person in our group was Nafloyd. He didn't take nothing from nobody. Even James was frightened of him – I was, too. 'Cos he didn't want to ever say nothing. He'd just walk up to you and bash the hell out of you. Very talented guitar player, but didn't take nothing from James or nobody. Leave him alone and he'll do the job. Pay him, though. Don't talk about no fines to him, no sir. That's why he got lost along the way, James couldn't handle him.

"So anyway, naturally there was some mess started when everybody found out that James was getting a little extra money when everybody was doing the same work. Because at that time, we were still switching it around somewhat. James wasn't leading all the songs, Sylvester was a very good leader, too. We had a few problems but that time they eventually got ironed out and, with Richard outta the way, we started to make our move."

When Little Richard's "Tutti Frutti" hit the Top 20 late in 1955, the Georgia Peach wasted no time in heading west to California. He rang Macon with the useful information that he wasn't about to come home and play dates that had been booked weeks in advance. "So all these dates, I'm talkin' 'bout forty or fifty dates that Richard had, we did all his dates. Which was good for us because we finally saw some real money." Although they played a few of the dates as The Famous Flames, for the vast majority of the gigs the billing stayed as "Little Richard and The Upsetters". "James had long hair and we fix him up and he'd go out there." Occasionally, they'd admit to their true identity afterwards. "Some of the places didn't want to hear that. I mean, you better stay Little Richard. You might not be Richard but you better be him tonight!"

The subterfuge was helped by the lack of promotional photographs of the acts in those days "and the pictures on the placard didn't look like nobody no way. During that time, you throw somebody's picture on the fire and you go do the job. So we got away with a lot of that in most of the places. Some of the places we had some problems, but we really had to get out and do a show."

Of course, impersonating Little Richard and The Upsetters had the effect of making Brown the prominent, sole front man. "I've never seen a man work so hard in my whole life," Byrd said. "He would do extra. He would go from what we rehearsed and leap from that pattern off into something else. He just drove himself, you know, driving, driving, driving. We'd say 'What's wrong with you? By the time it's time for us to try to make a record, you'll be done killed yourself'. He just had to outdo Richard, that's what it was. He wanted the people to forget about Richard and talk about him.

"He did it too. I remember one gig in particular, in Alabama. The people found out that we weren't no Little Richard and started to chant 'We want Richard. We want Richard'. James started climbing on the piano, jumping off the piano into splits, flips, tumbling. He threw in everything. And he got the people's minds off Richard and on to him. When we left they was all cheering for us. So who's Little Richard? You know, that kind of thing."

Thus far, their recording experience had been limited to unreleased tapes made at local Georgia radio stations. One demo cut at station WIBB in Macon in November, 1955, suddenly upped the stakes. According to Byrd, 'Please, Please, Please', a fervent supplication which had evolved into a blisteringly emotional, hypnotic chant that had become a vehicle for James's gripping showmanship, had developed from their version of 'Baby Please Don't Go', as rendered by Bill Johnson's group based in Augusta. Because it was a group version, The Orioles' reading of 'Baby Please Don't Go' influenced their arrangement of 'Please, Please, Please', though they had probably also heard the 1951 version of 'Turn Your Lamp Down' by the Atlanta-based and locally very popular Billy Wright.

WIBB dee-jay Hamp Swain played the tape of 'Please, Please, Please' and Brantley sent demos to local labels and bigger, more ambitious independents. Don Robey, the boss of Duke Records, was keen but couldn't agree terms with Brantley. In Chicago, Leonard Chess was interested and sent Brantley a contract but the deal faltered when Chess's flight to Georgia was grounded. Meanwhile, producer and talent scout Ralph Bass heard the demo. He worked for King and Federal Records, two labels owned by Syd Nathan and based in Cincinnati. Bass's rhythm & blues signings were released on Federal. He eventually signed The Famous Flames on January 23, 1956.

Bass told the story in detail to Harry Weinger, and it was entertainingly recounted in the aforementioned Grammy-winning booklet to the 'Star Time' box set. In brief, visiting the Atlanta, Georgia branch of King Records, Bass found a demo that had been left there for him. It was marked, 'The Flames'. He asked where he could find the group and was pointed in the direction of Macon, Georgia. There, Bass headed straight to the local black radio station where he was redirected to Clint Brantley, who owned several entertainment franchises and businesses "across the tracks". A clandestine meeting between Bass and Brantley was arranged at a local barber shop to avoid local whites discovering that the latter was doing business with an outsider.

Bass told Weinger that he offered Brantley $200 for the group's signatures and the deal was struck then and there. He took The Famous Flames to Cincinnati and recorded 'Please, Please, Please'. Three months later, still on the road but now in St. Louis, Bass received a message to the effect that King owner Syd Nathan was on the warpath and wanted Bass fired. "That's the worst piece of shit I've ever heard!" Nathan famously ranted down the phone, "You're fired!". But because of the reaction he'd been getting to the single while out on the road, Bass knew better and urged Nathan to test market 'Please, Please, Please' in Atlanta. "Fuck it," Nathan replied, "I'm putting it out cross-country just to prove what a piece of shit it is."

CHAPTER 4

The Platters' 'The Great Pretender' (a No. 1 pop hit) and Frankie Lymon & The Teenagers' cheerier 'Why Do Fools Fall in Love' (No. 7 pop) were the No. 1 records on *Billboard*'s rhythm & blues charts for the first 15 weeks of 1956. Roots sunk deep in doo-wop but arranged to top pop charts, these comparatively gentle strains were blasted aside by the unrestrained energy of rock'n'roll.

Little Richard consolidated his position as the big noise in the South with two double-sided hits for the Specialty label – 'Long Tall Sally'/ 'Slippin' & Slidin'' and 'Rip It Up'/'Ready Teddy' – while Imperial's big wheel, Fats Domino, topped with 'I'm In Love Again'/'My Blue Heaven' and 'Blueberry Hill'. Elvis Presley, who had lately moved from Sam Phillips' Sun label to RCA Victor, was repaying the major label's investment with a gold disc rush. 'Don't Be Cruel'/'Hound Dog' even topped the rhythm & blues lists in 1956. Chuck Berry had had his first hit, 'Maybellene', the year before. All of these records moved massively into the white pop charts. Little Willie John, one of Brown's idols if he owned to any, and Bill Doggett, King's biggest-selling act at the time, had No. 1 rhythm & blues hits with 'Fever' and 'Honky Tonk' respectively.

Doo-wop was fading and the appeal of rhythm & blues was wavering in the shockwaves of the rock'n'roll explosion when Syd Nathan called Ralph Bass's bluff and released 'Please, Please, Please' on Federal on March 3, 1956. The first pressings named the performers as James Brown with The Famous Flames which did not amuse the other members of the group. They were also less than thrilled by what they thought was the single's lack of immediate success.

"We had all quit," Byrd said. "As far as we're concerned, ain't nothing happened. So we went home, even James. He started back at the plastics factory, I went back to the shop and the theatres, Sylvester went back to the nursing home. All the original group returned to Toccoa. That's how green we were."

Brown, in fact, had a wife in Toccoa and a girlfriend back in Macon "so he was running back and forth down there. A lot of us were. I'd married this girl, Gail Harvin. But we'd met these women when we were playing in Macon and they thought we were the biggest thing. You know how that goes. Anyway we carried on doing our little thing locally. But we had no idea the record was selling. See, we didn't hear it on the radio."

'Please, Please, Please' was being played in Mississippi, Alabama and Florida but not much in Georgia and the Carolinas. "And we certainly didn't know nothing about no *Billboard* nowhere. Charts? What's that? We were so down. We didn't realise that – what we had to do was get out behind it and work the record."

In fact the record was already selling well. Listed as a "territorial tip" by Atlanta in *Billboard* at the end of March, it was named Buy O' The Week in the first week of April. "Emerging from left field ... a sleeper to watch. Atlanta and Cincinnati for two weeks have reported very strong activity." Those areas, of course, had strong Brown or King connections but the Bay Area and Virginia also reported good sales. Although 'Please, Please, Please' was breaking on both coasts, it was some while before it passed the million sales. The song had legs. It stayed on the catalogue and was to be the crazed climax to Brown's exhausting live show for decades. It entered the *Billboard* rhythm & blues chart on April 21, 1956, reached No. 6 and sold well enough in various territories at different times to jive around the Top 20 for 19 weeks.

Byrd said that the record was in the charts at No. 60 before they knew it was in the shops. And the record kept selling. In November 1956, two months after it had dropped out of the national lists, 'Please, Please, Please' was the No. 3 rhythm & blues record in St. Louis, according to *Billboard*, which ranked it as the 16th most played rhythm & blues record of 1956. Despite his initial dislike of the record, Nathan was enough of a business man to still feature it in his company's trade ads in the early part of 1957. Four more James Brown & The Famous Flames singles – 'I Don't Know'/'I Feel That Old Feeling Coming On', 'No, No, No, No'/'Hold My Baby's Hand', 'Just Won't Do Right'/'Let's Make It' and 'Chonnie-On-Chon'/'I Won't Plead No More' – had come and gone on Federal in that time with barely a flicker of interest. Record buyers would pass on another five, making nine flops in a two-and-a-half-year span, before Brown & The Famous Flames made the charts again.

Why? Why had the follow-ups been so poorly received? Since setting King up in 1943, Nathan had established one of the very few self-contained independent labels. Built on the site of an old chemical plant, King had its own recording, cutting, pressing, printing and, to an extent, distribution facilities. And although it was best-known for its rhythm & blues acts, King had a wider church. The set-up was ideal for channelling records into specific ethnic markets but rock'n'roll changed the rules of the game. Ethnic markets slowly began to break down and King was ill-equipped to promote and market its acts even though many of them would have appealed to the rock'n'roll audience.

As Nathan will reappear not infrequently to do battle with Brown over releases, a quick sketch of this not untypical independent record company boss is useful. Born in Cincinnati in 1904, he was an asthma sufferer with profoundly poor eyesight and, from the age of five, a drum kit. He left school at the age of 13, worked in a pawn shop, worked an elevator, bucked rivets, was a dining room busboy and played those drums. He went into his father's real estate business, the jewellery trade, was a wrestling promoter, managed a radio store, sold refrigerators and ran a chain of shooting galleries. A one-man enterprise economy gone berserk. He tried to start businesses in Phoenix, Arizona and Miami, Florida, but always returned to Cincinnati.

With, legend has it, capital of three dollars, he took a lease on a shop in the black section of the city, got records from distributors on credit, bought old juke box stock and opened for business. Just before the USA entered World War II, Nathan played a hunch and bought up 12,000 records. Soon they were like gold dust. One batch, bought from a record store owner soon to retire to fish, turned out to be 85 per cent hillbilly stuff he'd never heard of. Don't worry, said the vendor, the customers will follow the records. He was right. Nathan had broken into another market. He also started to record hillbilly musicians who were drawn to Cincinnati by the plentiful work offered in factories experiencing a boom during the war years. But he thought that the pressing plants were ripping him off so he set up King Records in August, 1945.

Nathan built much of the plant's infrastructure with his own hands, tearing down walls and putting up new ones until it could produce everything it needed except the cardboard boxes in which to ship the records. It was while the building's fitting out work was going on that his eyesight was at its worst and he was often led from place to place by a colleague or friends.

It took four operations for cataracts and triple-lensed glasses to help him see normally again. His energy and input in the early years made him proprietorial in the extreme about his label and affiliated publishing companies. At dinners and meetings he would hold forth to the assembled employees, often into a tape recorder, in cadences similar to W. C. Fields with a somewhat blunter wit.

At one such meeting he recounted the story of a trip to Europe in the Sixties as a series of collisions with inadequate hotels, indifferent cuisine and insanitary streetwalkers. In France, they "go for hot jazz and there's a lot of coloured musicians over there. White men can't get a chance over there with the gals because of the coloured men. There is absolutely no colour line over there. None whatsoever. In fact if there is, the white people are thought a little less of than the coloured people. Just the reverse. Because of that, why, when those fellas go over there, they stay if they can because it's Shangri-La, it's something that they'll never find in America and I'll tell ya, I guess the reason for it is because most of the coloured people who came over there were of the arts, musically inclined, they could do things that were out of the ordinary and that is why [the French] have probably formed the opinion that they are a super-race.

"If the quality of the coloured people was equivalent to the ones I met over there," Nathan concluded, "this would be a better world over here if we'd accept them more on an even plane like they do over there. You don't see any bigotry going on over there. They're just people." Oddly, he told his audience that because he suffered from asthma he could detect a person's race by smell.

He recorded other tapes and discs for circulation to his salesmen and employees in affiliated companies. "Unfortunately," he prefaced his remarks on King's business strategy, "you or other people may disagree with me one hundred per cent but somebody has to be the chief and I am elected as the chief. I'm spending my money, not yours, therefore unless I change my ideas it has to be as you will hear on this record." His theories are simple. "I go on the assumption that nothing is any good … Let me see the sales after 90 days, then I'll tell you how good it is. That's how much of a goddam genius I am. There are no geniuses." He referred to staff writer/producer Gene Redd. He had "written some songs. Some good ones, some bad ones. Gene Redd's trouble has been that he was a jazz musician. Thank God he is losing this. And I think he's saying 'Amen' himself."

Songwriting kept King in business. "King Records in 25 years has not made a dime," Nathan said. "The money that has been made has been made by the publishing companies, leasing our stuff foreignwise, doing custom pressing, et cetera, et cetera. Having your own plant, getting things when we want them and that is where we've put the whole ball of wax together and made a good living and we're happy. Now, we don't want to become millionaires because you have to work too goddam hard. We're all satisfied to wear good clothes, eat good food and be content to be a normal human being. That's the only kind that can last with this Dutch organisation. I say Dutch because Cincinnati is a Dutch town. I'm Jewish but the town is Dutch. I'm more Dutch than I am Jewish. Don't forget, we are in the mid-West and we're not contaminated by New York, Los Angeles or Chicago."

After the war, the major labels did not understand nor see much profit in the ethnic and specialist markets. Their disinterest opened the door to regional independent labels which expanded quickly to cater for the untapped market. Soon, *Billboard* estimated, there was in the region of 500 labels operating and Nathan, with typical modesty that produced a figure probably not too far from the truth, reckoned King was fifth or sixth in terms of record volume. At its peak, the King plant employed 400 staff.

In common with many independent labels in their early years, King's offices doubled as recording studios at night with the furniture stacked away in a corner. The label's first record was a hillbilly opus by Cowboy Copas, 'Filipino Baby' with 'I Don't Blame You' on the flip. An early big-seller came courtesy of Benjamin "Bull Moose" Jackson's 'I Love You, Yes I Do', named best race record of 1948 by *Cashbox*. It sold well over half a million copies. 'Race' music, as African-American music was known in 1945 when Nathan set up King, accounted for 60 per cent of King's output and the balance had not altered greatly some years later as Brown and The Famous Flames struggled to find a follow-up to 'Please, Please, Please'.

Years later, when very dependent on his output, Nathan said of Brown that "from one minute to another you can't tell how this guy James Brown is going to act but we all love him and we consider and respect the fact that he has made it. Now we are hoping that he has not only made it but he stays there for many years, the same as Bing Crosby, Sinatra and others, [Perry] Como." But the stubborn Nathan's initial opinion of the Brown & The Famous Flames' ability and appeal looked as though it had been vindicated by the flat sales figures of releases after 'Please, Please, Please'. Besides, Nathan had even more dramatic failures to concern him, like Hank Ballard & The Midnighters. The label's hottest rhythm & blues act from 1953–55, they should have been a natural cross-over act into rock'n'roll but despite immense popularity as a live act they never made the leap into the newer market and even slipped out of the rhythm & blues charts for three-and-a-half years. Perhaps Nathan was unwilling to pay the right people the right amount of money to get his acts accepted in the new scene. In fact, Brantley had wised them to a few worldly truths about the business and began booking them further afield. That, Byrd said, was "when we found out about payola".

They were still hicks, largely unknown as a live act outside the south eastern states. One of the few shows they played outside the area at this time was a date at Laurel's Garden Ballroom, Newark in New Jersey. "This was the first time we'd seen Little Richard since he'd left Macon with 'Tutti Frutti'," Byrd said. "We were on the New Jersey Turnpike. It was the first time we'd been that far north and it was a huge show. Richard, Ray Charles, Fats Domino, Solomon Burke ... course, he was as unknown as we were back then although he had his little thing going in the North like we had in the South.

"We broke down on the highway and Richard came by. He asked 'What's wrong?' We told him and asked where he was headed. He said, 'Y'all on the same show that I'm on, let me help you make it'. He went back and opened up the trunk of his car and I've never seen so much money in all of my life. I'm trying to figure it out to this day why he didn't have a briefcase or suitcase or something. He had loose bills all over the trunk of his car, thousands of dollars, just laying out. He just reached in the trunk and grabbed a handful of money, didn't count it or nothing. He gave it to us and said, 'Get this thing fixed and get on into town'."

They also continued to play the kind of tricks that first brought them to the attention of Little Richard's entourage at Bill's Rendezvous Club. Byrd recalled a date at Little John's Grill in Climpson, South Carolina. "We were booked there just after we had 'Please, Please' out. It hadn't done nothing yet. There was another act on close by that same night. We run up to where this other act is at and they're on stage. James asks the man 'Can we watch 'em?' and then he gets up there and kills the people. I'm talking about salivate 'em. Then he gets on the mike and says 'We're right up the street at Little John's Grill, ladies and gentlemen, come on!' We get out and here comes a wild crowd behind us. He would do things like that. I said to myself, 'This is a man who's on the way up'. It was amazing to the rest of us that he had this much nerve to do things like that."

Brown never lost it. Much later ... "Otis [Redding] was playing the Howard Theatre, Washington. We had been up to Waxie Maxie's record shop, signing autographs and I said to James, 'Let's go see the show'. When we got there, there was a lot of people hanging around the stage door. So we went through the front instead, straight into the auditorium. The rest of us was trying to stay inconspicuous and find some seats but James walks all the way up to the stage so everybody could see him. The people are in uproar. And he doesn't stay for Otis, he just turned around and walked back out again. Everybody gets up and comes out, a big mob of people outside the theatre by the time Otis is in there singing. They had to call the police and the fire department. I couldn't believe it. He did it to Ben E. King, too, at the Apollo. Went in there, started his one-leg [dance] down the aisle, did a little Mashed Potato and then came back out again followed by a huge crowd of people."

But for now, the group played all over the south and, yea, even unto the West Coast where the hit had picked up respectable plays and sales. In a few years, California was to become a regular pitch for The Flames but at this stage the team was falling apart, the players disenchanted with the ever-increasing ego of the captain. Things were no less fraught in the studio. As noted, 'Please, Please, Please' was followed by nine straight commercial failures. By no means unlistenable, and better than their consistent failure suggests, the flops lacked a genuine spark of originality or the jolt of a thousand volts of electric excitement given by Brown's live performances of 'Please, Please, Please'. The raw grip of his lead vocal against the much mellower group harmonies sounds unorthodox, even in the varied rhythm & blues market, but the records make nothing special out of this promising juxtaposition. The unusual and potentially unique sound is used in fairly unadventurous styles and on standard, unexceptional material.

One side of the first follow-up, 'I Feel That Old Feeling Coming On', was the only uptempo side cut at the 'Please, Please' session. 'Just Won't Do Right', Brown's favourite flop, was the fourth single and allegedly the biggest-seller among the failures (he would go on to re-record it five times with slight amendments) and the seeds of 'I Don't Mind', a later hit, can be heard in 'Hold My Baby's Hand'. There were obvious influences being worked through in his recording at this time. 'No, No, No, No' pays dues to The Drifters, 'Let's Make It' is a Midnighters-styled vocal version of 'Honky Tonk' cut before Bill Doggett's instrumental became a smash and he imitated Hank Ballard's ballad style on 'Begging, Begging'. Even James admitted that 'Chonnie-On-Chon' was an attempt to baldly copy Little Richard's wild rock'n'roll. Most of these sides sound like James Brown trying to sound like someone else, the sounds of an act searching for its own voice and style.

Using a changing cast of local musicians at King's Cincinnati studio, Brown and The Famous Flames had recorded 22 titles in five sessions during 1956-7. Drummers Edison Gore and Reginald Hall and bassists Clarence Mack and Edwyn Conley laid the rhythm, guitarists Eddie Freeman and John Faire replaced Nafloyd Scott and the saxophonists were

Ray Felder and Cleveland Lowe. Bobby Byrd and Fats Gonder played piano. From now until 1968, the records were almost always credited to Brown and The Famous Flames. Not that they actually appeared on every side from the second recording session – March 27, 1956 – onwards. By April, 1957, The Famous Flames had retired, mostly hurt by their lack of success but also partly by the way in which Brown's strength of purpose and personality had begun to dominate proceedings.

Royalty payments also became an issue. "We was on three per cent artist royalty as a group," Byrd recalled. "At the beginning we were splitting it equally. On 'Please, Please, Please' the five of us were supposed to be credited as writers but this is where James made his devil's dash. He and Johnny Terry got 'Please, Please' whereas me, Keels and Nafloyd got the B-side. For a while we all got a fifth of 'Please, Please' but then it got cut off. After the advance I think I got maybe two cheques and that's it. They said, 'Don't worry about it, you got the other side, so as long as 'Please, Please' sells, your side will sell too'. But of course we weren't thinking about all the reissues down the years.

"One thing about King Records. When they had all those publishing companies, Lois, Armo and so on, they would pay you. They wouldn't owe you nothing. Syd Nathan would say 'I don't want nobody to ever come down here complaining or going out bad-mouthing the company'. So you got paid on the dot. Later on, we found out that the advances and percentages we were getting was pitiful but at least we always got what we signed for. Many other acts with other companies didn't even get that courtesy."

With the record company's waning interest and his group disbanded, Brown spent the summer of 1957 playing small dates in Florida with Fats Gonder and pickup musicians. Here, he met Henry Stone, the Miami-based producer and distributor with whom he struck up a long-term friendship. Stone's Tone Distributors were a significant outlet in the area and had had business connections with King for many years.

On October 9, 1957, Little Richard suddenly announced that he had received the first of several calls from the Lord, forsook rock'n'roll and enrolled in Bible school, leaving his manager Bumps Blackwell, his band, The Upsetters, and his singers, The Dominions, with 40-odd dates to fulfil. Once more into the breach stepped James Brown to become Little Richard, at least for the southern swing of the tour. Dates completed, he enlisted The Dominions as a new set of Famous Flames and also used some of The Upsetters. The Flames were now Big Bill Hollings (or Holland), Louis Madison, who also played piano, and J. W. Archer. Their first recording with Brown, on October 21, 1957, was his fifth and final flop session.

Two songs co-written by Rudolph Toombs, distinctive composer of The Clovers' 'One Mint Julep', among many other hits, were taped at the session. The aforementioned 'Begging, Begging' was one and the other, 'That Dood It', co-penned with Rosie Marie McCoy, was a cautionary tale out of Ray Charles' 'It Should've Been Me' and 'Greenbacks' bag. Fine though they were, neither sold and, for the time being, Nathan washed his hands of Brown and his only marginally famous Flames.

Bobby Byrd sums up the period. "After 'Please, Please' came out, the original Flames stayed on the road about nine months to a year. Then we all left James. He hadn't hurt me too much at that point. There wasn't too much he could do to me 'cept maybe cheat my money, 'cause he needed me as a writer. He'd say 'Fix this so it makes sense'. And then he'd go about his business. But I didn't like the way he did the other cats. It was supposed to be a group thing.

"So I went back to Toccoa for a while, working at the theatres again. And I formed me a group called Bobby Byrd & The Drops Of Joy. I was lead vocalist and pianist, James Styles and Roy Mayfield were on saxes, Billy "P. V." Key played guitar and we had Ben Payne on drums. It was a very good group. We went back 'round the colleges and the same circuit I had done before with The Flames and we started to make some noise. Then Clint called me in Toccoa, said, 'Would you like to gig with James again?' "

CHAPTER 5

Over the next three years, from 1958–61, the apprenticeship Brown had served in the King studio paid big dividends. His career as a recording artist blossomed. His punishing road work, driven by that determined and competitive nature, ensured that the records he made received maximum and very positive exposure. He built his reputation as The Hardest Working Man In Show Business on sweat. Syd Nathan was not a man blessed with the patience of Job and his deep misgivings about Brown's ability to cut it on record had increased. But the dynamic live performer's second success as a Little Richard Mark II, persuaded the label boss to give him one more chance in the studio. It was payback time for the nine consecutive flops. Hindsight is a treacherous friend full of easy answers. However, in the case of Brown's recording career it is more than fanciful retrospection to suggest that nobody, least of all the singer, quite knew how the runaway success of 'Please, Please, Please' had occurred. What followed it was the recording equivalent of a man in a clothing store trying on shirts, jackets, slacks, ties, hats and shoes of various types to see which style best suited him. He found the answer in the United States of America's beach wear department: Florida. Bearing in mind Nathan's views, 'Try Me (I Need You)' could not have been more appropriately titled.

"The lyrics James had, he got from this boy down at The Palms in Hollandale, Florida," Bobby Byrd said. "It was something like the way we got 'Please, Please', an adaptation from something else. This boy was singing the song around and he gave James the lyric. But it was originally more complicated. We went back and did it again in New York, simplified it

51

structurally but made it smoother and more sophisticated sounding musically. I wasn't on the original demo but I was a part of the issued recording, singing and helping with the lyrical adaptation."

Although they'd remained in contact, Byrd had moved out of Brown's immediate orbit. In Florida, the singer had been using Little Richard's secular singers The Dominions – or Dominues depending on which poster or handbill you believed – and Fats Gonder-led musicians. "Apparently James was having trouble with this other group he had. They were good singers. As a matter of fact they were probably better singers as a group than the original Flames. But they weren't working out."

Ralph Bass, James's main ally at King, was having the same sort of luck as Brown with his other Federal releases – nothing but bad – and was on the verge of leaving the company for Chess. And Nathan was on the verge of tearing up Brown's contract. He was so down on Brown that the singer and Brantley paid for the demo of 'Try Me'. Good investment. "James and the other group had cut a demo acetate of 'Try Me', which wasn't like the final recording. Clint had paid for the session and James had taken it to certain dee-jays and it was getting good reaction. King were persuaded to go with it but they wanted it different." One more session was scheduled at the Beltone Studios in New York for September 18, 1958.

"Clint wanted me to pick up Sylvester and the other original guys and bring 'em on. I actually tried it, too, but they said they wouldn't work with James no more. But he caught me at a time when I remembered all the good times we'd had so I went on up there. The original was good, but I think the issued one was much better for what King wanted. James had started a few little screams in the other one. And that's what [producer] Andy Gibson was trying to tell James, they had a huge argument about that. James thought it should have been put out the way it was, he didn't want to change it. But they were trying to get him to go for gold and try to get some pop play. Anyway, at that time it was a lost cause for James because Syd Nathan and Andy Gibson [who was also known as Albert Schubert] were tight and James was going to be dropped from the roster. So we changed it."

'Try Me' is a heartfelt plea for love and if Brown did rein in his vocal then the restraint has worked to the benefit of the lyric because the understatement gives his singing a vulnerable quality that is at the centre of the record's success. Self-pity is kept at bay by the edgy yearning in his voice. The song's potential for excess sweetness is evident in the solo which consists of a conversation between the saxes and the honey-toned guitar of jazz player Kenny Burrell.

Other, more mundane but financially significant factors changed too.

Nathan usually set up publishing companies for his producers. The singer's publishing moved from Ralph Bass's Armo company to Nathan's subsidiary Wisto until 1961 when it moved again to the King boss's main publishing company Lois. So in addition to recording sales, Nathan could anticipate a larger share of the publisher's profit if James's music sold. The web of publishing companies at King was a not uncommon tactic. When Nathan sanctioned Brown as a producer by setting up the Try Me label, a publishing company, Jim Jam Music, was also set up. The label lasted for three singles. When Brown started recording singles for Smash, he set up another Try Me company as publishing outlet for the 45s. Try Me was a talisman title. The song itself was the first one to be published by Wisto and the record, released in October, 1958, met with immediate favourable response in a wide spread of regions. King possibly put more muscle behind it and certainly persuaded Dick Clark to preview it as a contender for exposure on his influential *Bandstand*. But "he turned it down flat" according to Byrd. The record didn't need Clark. By the early weeks of 1959 it was the No. I rhythm & blues record and nudged into the pop Top 50, Brown & The Famous Flames' first appearance there.

As things came together in the studio, so they did on stage. Shortly after the 'Try Me' session, Brown made two equally important connections. He was signed to the Universal Attractions booking agency and, late in 1958, met and hired a permanent road band. After the 'Try Me' session in New York, Brown was booked in to the Apollo Theatre in Harlem. Nathan asked Ben Bart, the owner of Universal, to run his practised eye over Brown.

Bart knew the business every which way. He'd run his own label, Hub, and produced records as well as being a powerful booking agent. While at the Gale Agency he'd handled the careers of Dinah Washington and Billy Eckstine, among others, before setting up Universal. Brown made an immediate impression on him. The raw talent, its unfettered energy, the electrifying performer on stage and what he perceived to be a willing and determined learner off stage. He had little hesitation in signing Brown and his group, soon devoting increased time and energy to developing their career and to all intents and purposes replacing Brantley as manager, though the latter would continue to take the weight in the South where he had strong contacts. Byrd actually has an interesting and slightly different slant on the group's signing to the agency. "Ben and Syd Nathan and King's lawyer, Jack Pearl, were all inter related in some way either though blood or marriage, so it was like if you recorded for King you were automatically booked by Universal Attractions. When we first went up to Cincinnati to record 'Please, Please' I'm sure we signed all three contracts at the same time, for recording, publishing and booking. Of course, we didn't know nothing about contracts back then. We all just signed on the dotted line."

Brown, of course, states that the contract with Bart and Universal was signed later in New York, after the success of 'Try Me' in 1958. The confusion was perhaps understandable because there seems to have been quite a few contracts flying around at the time. In addition to the Universal deal, the recording contract with King was renegotiated to give an improved five per cent royalty and Brown's publishing deal with Lois was improved to give, among other items, five cents on sheet music sales and 50 per cent of all net mechanical rights. A more important change at King was the appointment in June, 1958, four months before the release of 'Try Me', of Hal Neely, formerly a vice president of Allied Records in Hollywood, as general manager at King. He would act as a sort of buffer between Nathan and Brown during their the worst disagreements.

Bart's enthusiasm and the success of 'Try Me' made it imperative for Brown to do something about the transient band personnel and get out on the road to cash in on the record's popularity in the untested northern cities as well as earn money on the southern circuit where he was already popular. Few singers or vocal groups had their own band at this time. Most had to be satisfied with the band provided at the club or theatre and rely on the competence of their own musical director, usually a guitarist or pianist, to lead the pick-up band through the performances. But as well as being wild and enthusiastic, Brown & The Famous Flames' shows cried out for a disciplined, skilled band of sympathetic musicians who could keep the music rooted and give a dramatic coherence to his energy and ceaseless outpouring of emotion.

Throughout 1957–8, Brown's volatile nature had kept the band line-up in a state of flux. Guitarist Bobby Roach had been recruited from California as a belated replacement for Nafloyd Scott, and The Upsetters' tenor saxophonist Lee Diamond and drummer Charles Connor began playing gigs with Brown on an irregular basis. By the start of 1959 they, and sax player John White, a transient band-member, had drifted away. By then, however, Brown had met another sax man, J. C. Davis of Burlington, North Carolina.

Davis was hired as nominal bandleader and brought with him a bonus not to be underestimated – his own station wagon and equipment truck. "There were a couple of other fellas that came with James, too," Byrd recalled. "The bass player, Bernard Odum, had been with the original group, quit, then came on back. Apart from the singing group, Baby Lloyd Stallworth was valeting for James and Bobby Bennett was J. C.'s valet. I do know that my first time meeting with Bobby Bennett was when we got to the Apollo. I think I must have gone home for a while and then went back up to New York." New York drummer Nat Kendrick also joined at this time.

"We were staying at The Cecil Hotel. They had a basement down there where we rehearsed, got the voices together and worked out the routines. Now, I had two new people to coach who didn't know anything about entertainment at all, Baby Lloyd and Bobby Bennett. Between us all, we pulled it together. Eventually, me and Bennett and Baby Lloyd wound up being the permanent Famous Flames, but not right away.

"I did the week at the Apollo and a few more dates on the tour – Hartford, Connecticut and others – then here comes the confusion between me and James again. I don't know what game he was trying to play but he said 'I can't afford all of you. So y'all got to decide between yourselves which one is gonna leave'. I had my own group, The Drops of Joy were still doing pretty well, I could go back and get right into it, so I said, 'Me, I'll go'. I think that's when Johnny Terry went back into The Flames again.

"What you gotta understand about being around James, you get periods when everything's pretty cool, everybody together, and other times of change and confusion. People getting fired and rehired, quitting then coming back. Then sometimes somebody don't make a gig or a recording session, so somebody else fills in. This was one of those times."

One of the bigger bust-ups occurred in the spring of 1959. Big Bill Hollings, Louis Madison and J. W. Archer, who had sung on 'Try Me', "had a big confusion" out in Oakland, California "and James left 'em all out there". It led to one of the many confusing backwaters of Famous Flame discography. Of the marooned ex-Flames, Madison was the busier, forming (or joining) a group called The Fabulous Flames. They recorded a single in 1959 for the Baytone, a San Franciscan outlet started by Bradley Taylor. In 1960, the Time label of New York (prop: Bob Shad) had a single by The Fabulous 5 Flames. Back on Taylor's Baytone, a group called Claude & The Hightones had a single out coupling 'Buckethead' and 'Doodle Bug', which, though they share the same titles as two unsuccessful JB instrumentals, are actually different songs. Other musicians augmenting the basic team to varying degrees of permanence in the late Fifties were bassist Hubert Perry, who alternated with and then replaced Odum, guitarist Les Buie, alto saxophonist Alfred Corley and trumpeter Roscoe Patrick. Keyboards were played by Fats Gonder, Byrd or Brown. The core band was Davis, Roach, Odum and Kendrick.

The live work boomed because Brown's shows gave top dollar value and through Bart's unstinting efforts at Universal. But the end product of the Universal pact was a very full date-sheet. "It wasn't too long before we got uniforms and two brand new station wagons, one for us and one for Fats and the band he'd put together. I don't think Clint paid for all that, that was an advance from Universal. They took a little money back each time we played. 'Please, Please, Please' was a splattered hit, so to speak, so we started to travel to where people wanted to hear it. Apart from our own area the people all over California took to the record, so we spent a lot of time out there.

"At first, Ben was concerned with all of us. He always told us it took more than one person to make it to the top. But from time to time, him and Clint and James started having private conversations. I felt there was a division. There may have been schisms off-stage, but whenever they hit show-time, they got better, tighter."

Byrd remembered the Apollo gig after 'Try Me' had hit the charts. "We were down on the bill but it was still a big deal for us. The star of the show was Little Willie John and there was another group on the show called The Vibrations. Man, they ate us alive. That was the first time we'd been beaten at our own game, they really had their act together. After the shows in the South that taught us a lesson."

Brown told the story slightly differently. The Vibrations shook The Famous Flames at the Uptown in Philadelphia. After he'd seen them do the splits, spins, dips and dances that the southern group thought were pretty much their dynamic own, James claimed that, as an improvised response that night, he developed the imaginary exhaustion and fainting fits at the end of 'Please, Please, Please'. Then the headlining Isley Brothers came on and blew out The Flames. They were those kind of stand-up, knockdown nights. Soon after, he saw the American wrestler Gorgeous George on television. At the end of his bouts, an aide would cover his sweat soaked shoulders with a robe which, after a few moments, the wrestler would fling aside to bask a while longer in the glow of victory, repeating the action several times. Brown sent out for a robe the next day and added the piece of theatrical business to the end of his show.

The emotional distress and fainting fit, the cape of comfort and its swift restorative powers, have been there in his show ever since, for three-and-a-half decades and became as much of a James Brown signature as hurling the mike stand away followed by a spin, a dip and an elastic spring back up to meet the mike on its return to the perpendicular. Or the splits or the one-legged 'walk', an uncanny sight as he appeared to slowly water-ski across stage without water, ski or boat, the moves which the child Michael Jackson watched in the wings and, years later, renovated as the Moonwalk. Every time a group like The Vibrations (who had no hits behind them and would not have one until 'The Watusi', a Top 20 rhythm & blues record in 1961) gave The Famous Flames a hard time, James would come back stronger, leading from the front with the determination and drive that Ben Bart saw and admired so much.

The peripatetic nature of Byrd's association with Brown again absented him from the group for a short while: he didn't tour or record with James again until 'Think', which in fact was scarcely any time at all. "I went back to my group and stayed home for a while. But soon after I got into that, James needed someone to go to King in Cincinnati to make sure that his records was done right, no faults. At that time, the machines they had would manufacture batches of records with skips in 'em, that kinda stuff. So now I'm up there, looking after that. It was kinda exciting. I had me a little office and along with looking after James's stuff, my other job was to change or rewrite songs. People would send in demos and if they thought it was good for Hank Ballard, I'd fix it for Hank – or The Five Royales or Little Willie John, him too. I did a song for Little Willie John that Sam & Dave sent in from Florida. They'd called it 'This Is The Sweetest Love'. If Willie couldn't do it, King was considering signing Sam & Dave. So I fixed it from a duet to a solo, added a bridge and we changed the title, can't remember what to. I was there when Little Willie John recorded it and I got mad at myself 'cause what I should have done was put in my own lyrics and got some of the writers' share, you know what I mean? I was just on salary to do all this.

"A lot of the songs was changed that way, even some of the things James did. 'This Old Heart' and 'There Must Be A Reason' [both credited solely to Brown] were originally country tunes. When I got back with James, I got back with 'Think' and we turned that around too. Because James came unprepared to record for that session. He had a few little things but they were in the same ol' bag. He didn't have a really hot new tune."

Fundamental to the longer-term evolution of James's music was his own observation about this period: "I began to hit somewhat of a different feel. The thing that made that was my eyes started opening. As long as I lived down South I would have cut the other kind of songs but the minute I started seeing different things and my brain started to intercept new ideas and new thoughts I became a big city thinker."

There is no bigger city than New York. Although Brown would be a hit at almost every club and theatre he played, no-one among the many, many great performers who have triumphed at New York's Apollo Theater is so readily associated with that Mecca of African-American entertainment. He would record three outsanding "live" albums there which define, like no other recordings, the excitement of live soul shows in the Sixties and early Seventies.

In the Fifties, the famed marquee entrance dominated the Harlem sidewalk on 125th Street between 7th and 8th Avenues. The grey, three-storeyed building was modest to the point of drabness but you didn't notice that because of the bright purple-on-white lights that picked out the theatre's name, flashing an invitation to the biggest rent party in town.

Hustle through the sidewalk throng and turn into the alleyway at the side of the building. A short step down is the stage door. Push on into the backstage area. There are thirteen dressing rooms on four floors with unadorned, cement-painted walls. The tactful would describe the rooms as functional but they were better facilities than The Famous Flames were accustomed to. Even after 1958 and the success of 'Try Me', Brown's appearances at the biggest theatres his market offered in the northern eastern cities – the Uptown in Philadelphia, the Royal in Baltimore, the Howard in Washington – all packed with the latest generation of migrants from the South, were exceptions to the rule. Up there, he was a comer, a name to watch. But there were many other bigger attractions. In the South, he was a big and getting bigger draw and it was in the dance halls out in the sticks and the large, sparse arenas where an evening's show meant hours, not minutes, on stage that the James Brown Revue of legend took shape.

On those barnstorming swings through the South, Bart would co-promote dates with local dee-jays. Giving the jocks a piece of the action not only meant that each show received plentiful and good local publicity but in time built up a nationwide network of positively inclined dee-jays who could be relied on to spin any new James Brown release. If the singer and the show were third-rate, of course, the tactic would not have worked at all. But the breathtaking, soul shaking, ball-breaking act was so hot and wild, and toured so extensively and intensively, that the ploy paid off long into the Seventies. And Brown's photographic memory for names and faces enabled him to keep a log of essential contacts, venues and their capacities intact in his head.

Just as Brown, and Nathan's company, had been unable to capitalise on the success of 'Please, Please, Please', so 'Try Me' proved a singularly difficult hit to follow. But this time there were identifiable reasons. The first follow-up, 'I Want You So Bad' (which actually reached No. 20 on *Billboard*'s rhythm & blues charts) was released while 'Try Me' was still a selling item. The next single, 'I've Got To Change', again came out far too

James Brown, the young man making his way in the early 1960s. (HARRY GOODWIN)

Mr Dynamite! James Brown in the late 1950s.
(MICHAEL OCHS ARCHIVES/REDFERNS)

Friend and Famous Flame, Bobby Byrd.
(MICHAEL OCHS ARCHIVES/REDFERNS)

Rehearsing the band in the mid-1960s. (FRANK DRIGGS COLLECTION/CONTRIBUTOR/GETTY IMAGES)

Soul Brother Number One takes rehearsals to the stage in the mid–1960s. (MICHAEL OCHS ARCHIVES/REDFERNS)

A publicity still from the sixties.

(MICHAEL OCHS ARCHIVES/REDFERNS)

Brand New Bag! James on the Ed Sullivan Show, New York City, May 1, 1966.

(CBS PHOTO ARCHIVE/CONTRIBUTOR/GETTY IMAGES)

Gimme some horns! James and the sax section find the groove. (CHUCK STEWART/REDFERNS)

Are you ready for Showtime! Backstage at Harlem's Apollo Theatre in 1964 with long-time emcee Danny Ray. (DON PAULSON/REDFERNS)

The rehearsals went well. (GAB ARCHIVES/REDFERNS)

Knitwear! Publicity still from the 1960s. (LFI)

On the set of the *Ready Steady Go!*
TV show, 1966. (DEZO HOFFMANN/REX FEATURES)

Martin Luther King shows the way forward on the Freedom March Day
in Michigan through Detroit. (BETTMANN/CORBIS)

Forces favourite: James Brown meets American troops in South-east Asia, 1968. (SIMON PIETRI/REX FEATURES)

With (from left) Gertrude Saunders, Ann Morman and Marva Whitney on the USO Pacific Tour to Korea and Vietnam, June 1968. (FRANK DRIGGS COLLECTION/CONTRIBUTOR/GETTY IMAGES)

Arriving in London in the early 1970s with second wife Deedee. (EVENING STANDARD/STRINGER/GETTY IMAGES)

Down on the double bump, emcee
Danny Ray still in attendance. (LFI)

Black and proud as the afro replaces the process.
(MICHAEL OCHS ARCHIVES/REDFERNS)

Amen!: As the Reverend Cleophus James in John Landis's 1980 Blues Brothers movie. (LFI)

soon after the preceding single. King was also preoccupied with the success of Hank Ballard & The Midnighters. After three-and-a-half years in the doldrums, they were suddenly hot again with a double-sided hit – 'Teardrops On Your Letter'/'The Twist'.

A third Federal single, 'Good, Good Lovin'', was the unluckiest, least deserved flop of them all. Arguably his most exciting performance on record up to January, 1959, it's clear that Brown was in the process of creating a new sound on record to match the dazzle of his live shows. By now, he was touring so exhaustively that he would record in whatever city was convenient if he had time and could find a studio free. 'I Want You So Bad' had been cut out in California with his newly assembled band. But much of the material he was recording now would not be used until his third King album a year later.

By the end of 1959, the band was slick as grease and tight as a vice. As well as accompanying Brown and The Famous Flames, they were featured as an opening act and he campaigned to get them on record. Nathan was not inclined to fritter away his cash on studio time for such a venture. Nonetheless, in mid-1959, Federal released 'Doodle Bug' and 'Bucket Head' by James Davis, Brown featuring on organ and intermittent hollering.

Later that year, with the band really smoking and the leader creating wild scenes with a new dance routine he was developing on stage, James pleaded with Nathan to record the band again. The owner, still stubbornly miffed by the earlier failures, didn't play, even though by now his artist was manifestly the hottest new black act in the southern States. So Brown took his band to his friend in Florida, Henry Stone, who cut a session in Miami using the leader on piano and local dee-jay/comedian Carlton "King" Coleman as vocalist/shouter. (Brown's contract with King meant he could play sessions for another label as long as he didn't utter a sound; and besides, Stone did business with Nathan and had to show some business sense and decorum.) The melody and lyrics to '(Do The) Mashed Potato Pts 1 & 2', credited to 'Rozier', presumably a pseudonym for Brown and, possibly, Stone, were fortunately not demanding. But the drive generated by the band, named on the Dade label single as Nat Kendrick & The Swans (Kendrick was the band's drummer), was compelling, and the single rose through the rhythm & blues charts to the Top 10 in February, 1960.

While in Jacksonville, possibly on one of the earlier swings through Florida, Brown had been visited in his dressing room before a show by Jack Bart, Ben's son, who at the time was a deputy in the Sheriff's department. There was a crowd of about 8,000 waiting to see the Hardest Working Man and there were some legal papers in the Sheriff's possession waiting to be served on Brown. Jack's superiors leaned on him, ever so gently, to serve the papers, which he later recalled were pertaining to a legal suit brought by a woman demanding money.

So Jack changed into civvies, made the visit, made the small talk and, in passing, mentioned Brown might have a legal problem in Florida and his own employment status as The Man. "He looked at me for a moment and he said: 'Well, I know you gotta do your job. It's just like I have to go on stage tonight no matter what happens, and get up there and entertain the audience, because they've paid to see me here'." So Bart slipped the papers to Brown and they talked about show business again. "Deep down, I felt bad that I was the one that had to do it because I'm sure that he sort of felt that maybe it was a dirty trick on my part or on the part of the department."

Fortunately for Brown, he was approaching a phase in his life when paying bills would not be a problem for, in tandem with 'Mashed Potatoes', he hit pay dirt under his own name that same month. He would be on a roll for a very long time. The variety of styles on his records from 'Please, Please, Please' up to 'Try Me' at last gelled into a definable James Brown sound. This was evident on three sides in particular: 'Good Good Lovin'', recorded at Beltone in New York in June, 1959 and released in the following month; 'I'll Go Crazy', cut at King in Cincinnati in November, 1959, and released in January, 1960; and 'Think', taped at the United Studios in Hollywood in February, 1960, and released in May.

'Good Good Lovin'' is ostensibly a straight, rockin' 12-bar but the rhythm and the horn sections lock in a much more cohesive band arrangement. But this was small beer next to 'I'll Go Crazy', whose pleading vocals were carried along on a far more imaginative and audacious arrangement. They recorded eight takes of 'I'll Go Crazy' before deciding, as quite often happened, that the first was the best. Over the years, Brown's singing of it on stage became immeasurably more impassioned.

Compared to those two tracks, however, 'Think' came from a different planet and was a potent example of the way Brown could alter material quickly by using his own band in the studio. His third million-seller, it had been written by Lowman Pauling of The 5 Royales and recorded by them in February, 1957. " 'Think' got me back with James," said Byrd, who had rejoined for the tour after 'Try Me' but quit again. He was working at King's plant in Cincinnati doing quality control on Brown's pressings and rewriting songs for Nathan's publishing companies. "James came in for a session with a few old-type things run down but nothing special. We reworked 'Think' right there at the session."

There are no passengers on the arrangement. Every instrument plays its full part from the horn section's repeated, baying riff in the introduction, repeated at the end of each verse, to the plucked Bobby Roach guitar line which drives the verses, while Nat Kendrick's drumming holds the whole thing together, albeit somewhat unsteadily at times. This is new stuff, a fresh sound and style. That it seemed to come together so quickly at this time had much to do with the road work Brown's stable and practised band had put in over the preceding weeks. Like a prize-fighter after months of serious training and sparring, Brown had a succession of knock-outs.

"We got the show really tight with signals," Byrd recalls. "That meant we could change it around at will. I mean, no two shows are ever going to be exactly the same. But we still all know what we were supposed to be doing. James didn't want anybody else to know what we was doing, so he had numbers and certain screams and spins. There was a certain spin he'd do and if he didn't do the complete spin you'd know it was time to go over here. Certain screams would instigate chord changes, but mostly it was numbers. James would call out [American] football numbers, that's where we got that from. Thirty-nine – Sixteen – Fourteen – Two – Five – Three – Ninety-eight, that kind of thing.

"Number thirty-nine was always the change into 'Please, Please, Please'. Sixteen is into a scream and an immediate change, not bam-bam but straight into something else. If he spins around and calls thirty-six, that means we're going back to the top again. And the forty-two, OK, we're going to do this verse and then bow out, we're leaving now. It was amazing. Then there was the fine system, that kept everyone on their toes."

A system of fines for mistakes on stage – usually a cue missed or a very serious bum note – was a method of penalising errors that was by no means exclusive to the James Brown Band, although legend has occasionally made it seem so. Most leaders of the big bands of the swing era, of jump bands of the Forties and Fifties, and of the larger rhythm & blues bands of the Fifties had instituted the fines to ensure that their musicians maintained a reasonable standard of performance. Many also extended these required standards to appearance and sobriety. The difference was in the rigour with which they applied the rules. In the case of The James Brown Band, however, the idea of fines did not come from the leader. According to Bobby Byrd, it was Johnny Terry, Brown's former jail mate from Alto, who first had the thought.

"Many band leaders do it but it was Johnny's idea to start it with us and we were all for it 'cos we didn't want to miss nothing. We wanted to be immaculate, clothes-wise, routine-wise and everything. Originally, the fines was only between James and us, The Famous Flames, but then James carried it over into the whole troupe. It was still a good idea because anybody joining The James Brown Revue had to know that they couldn't be messing up, and anyway, all the fines went into a pot for the parties we had.

"Ben Bart would always say that with these many people on the road, you gotta have some rules, some discipline. You got to know where everybody is at all times, and you got to be sober on the bus, you can't be rowdy. That was a big fine! You couldn't be up in the aisle of the bus, raising hell, you had to be in your seat."

Unfortunately, Brown began to use this authority with the sort of dictatorial touch usually associated with totalitarian regimes. "The onliest thing that I think started people to grumbling was that James ... well," Byrd continued after a ruminative pause, "for one thing he sometimes seemed to fine people for no apparent reason. Like he'd make up a reason just to get at somebody. But also he started this thing on the bus where you always had to travel in a suit and tie. In hot weather maybe you could loosen your tie and take off your jacket during the journey. But when the bus pull up at the hotel, your tie better be tight and your coat better be on or you were in trouble. I'm telling you the truth. There's no kinda way we could have dressed like they dress now. So you see, it started out as a good system but like everything else with James, he took it too far. Push a man too far and he's eventually gonna walk out on you." (In *The Godfather Of Soul*, Brown admits to some knock-down-drag-out fights with members of the troupe over personal comportment.)

As his career took off, Brown's domestic arrangements went through a powerful upheaval. Although he'd left his first wife, Velma Warren, back in Toccoa he continued to visit and she bore him another son and a daughter. He was not a faithful man on the road and more often than not hitched up with the young woman he'd hired to sing with the band. The first woman singer he added to The James Brown Revue was Beatrice "Bea" Ford. She sang 'You Got The Power', the flip side of 'Think', and gave a full-pelt performance in the strong and lusty duet with James which followed the A-side all the way up the R&B Top 20, stopping at No. 14, seven places below 'Think'. Not long before she joined in 1960, Bea had been wife to Joseph Arrington Jr., otherwise known as Joe Tex. They divorced in 1959 and when Bea joined James the defection of affection was rumoured to be the cause of disputation and rivalry between the two explosive soul performers – as if the professional challenge each posed to the other in the South was not sufficient to spark healthy competition. (Five years before his death in August, 1982, Tex said that he thought Brown had started the rumour that he stole Joe's wife. Brown insists that he never knew Bea and Tex had been married.)

When Joe Tex took 'Baby You're Right', a song he had written and thought was perfect for Brown, to a gig in Texas, he was surprised to find Bea making herself at home in James's dressing room but chatted convivially. Brown's confident ballad version of the song, released in 1961, four years before Tex became a fixture on the R&B charts, reached No. 2 (R&B) and No. 49 (pop). By that time Bea had left the Revue and was replaced briefly by Sugar Pie DeSanto who went on to record some fine soul sides for the Chess subsidiary, Checker.

There had been another innovation in the Revue. "One thing we did to make sure of a continuous show was to have two of everything in the rhythm section – two drummers, two bass players, two keyboard players and so on. So our show never stopped. If we broke down there was always somebody who could step right in and keep the thing going."

Ben Bart's extensive knowledge of the business, and the surrogate father-son kinship which had developed between him and Brown, was undoubtedly responsible to some degree for the expansion and style of the road show. "I remember," Jack Bart said, "from time to time my Dad would say 'I think you'd look good with this particular outfit, this suit, this costume. And maybe you should have The Famous Flames stage right instead of stage left, and maybe we should get a couple of girls singing background.' My father was very much involved with him as far as his staging, and some of the way he dressed and things like that. It was strictly a suggestion type situation. It was not 'James, you must wear this or you must do that.' They didn't have that type of relationship."

In fact Bart indulged Brown a good deal as the relationship evolved from stand-in father, to manager to business partner. "There was an incident in Jacksonville, Florida," Byrd recalled. "This was still earlyish days before the real big time, although Ben was with us. So Ben and James sit together on one table and the rest of us were over here in the corner. We had ordered bacon and eggs and coffee, and James wanted potatoes, eggs, a steak and all that. So we had just started eating when trouble broke loose again.

"James is talking all this stuff about. 'You don't know who I am, do you? Ben, tell 'em who I am!' All this is going off. James talked so much that the man brought him two raw potatoes, two raw eggs and a steak that hadn't been cooked properly. Ben was sitting opposite and his was fixed OK. So James hauled off and hit the man, BAM. So, Oh Lord, here we go again.

"Funny thing is, in that instance the man went to jail even though James hit him first. The police came right away and said: 'You can't do this. We don't want this in this town. This man ordered food and he brought all of these people in here to spend money, so you should serve him right.' But I think, if James had been more civil, there wouldn't have been any trouble in the first place."

Despite the improved contractual arrangements and the increased fees and percentages from live shows Bart and Universal were able to negotiate because of the Revue's increased pulling power, Brown was often incensed by the cash commanded by other acts. "There were still a lot of groups out there making a lot more money than us. The Drifters were making good money, for example," Byrd recalled. "I remember on one tour we worked with Dion & The Belmonts. Now we'd had three big hits by then, 'Please, Please, Please', 'Try Me' and 'Think', and we were on 750 dollars a night. Dion and them had one, 'Teenager In Love', and they were getting between fourteen hundred and two thousand dollars a night. And there's only three of them to split the money.

"Now remember, we all worked hard, especially James, dancing, splits, flying around, sweating, working himself half to death. And they strolled on, sang 'Teenager In Love', and walked off again with all that extra money. James was looking at 'em as if he was gonna mug 'em. 'Gimme that money!', you know, like he was gonna snatch it away from them. That was another big argument between him and Ben." (Actually, if this was in the summer of 1960 after 'Think', Dion & The Belmonts had had eight pop hits but only two of them, 'Teenager In Love' and 'Where Or When' were really substantial. However, the story does illustrate a very significant disparity between the financial rewards available at that time depending on the act's race.)

Brown had one more single on Federal, 'This Old Heart', a Top 20 R&B hit, before future releases were switched to the King label. The stage show was burning up but the subsequent singles were inclined towards ballads. Among them was a remake of the Billy Ward & The Dominoes' classical doo-wop song 'The Bells', which was one of the very few James Brown singles to feature on the pop charts but not on the R&B list. This might have been due to its appearance on the main King label, the first James Brown release under that imprint, rather than the R&B biased Federal. Other ballads included 'Bewildered', a rhythm & blues standard which had been in The Cremona Trio's repertoire but made No. 8 R&B and Top 40 pop in 1961; the measured drama of 'I Don't Mind', a No. 4 R&B hit and Top 50 pop hit; and 'Lost Someone', whose verses carried a more melodious appeal before breaking down into a typically wild beseeching vocal supported by the horn and guitar. It went to No. 2 in the R&B charts at the end of 1961 and again crept into the pop Top 50.

All three were long-time stage show staples and shared certain characteristics. The arrangements were trimmed-to-the-bone, cut with the basic road band and, in the increasingly bland pop market of the late Fifties and early Sixties, were searingly emotional vocal performances delivered, without exception, by a man who sounded on the verge of piteous tears or wanton violence born of emotional frustration. These raw expressions of what used to be known as 'the blues' are evolving into a new style, directed both by Brown's use of the ballad form and by the strictly-arranged lines being followed by his band. On stage, he increased the emotional heat to boiling point, wrestling with emotions in hugely dramatic versions of the slow hits.

Brown was also playing Big Daddy to an uptempo style that by the mid-Sixties had developed into hand-clappin', footstompin', head-shakin', hip-snakin' soul music, the sort you danced to like demons rather than smooched to like sweethearts or listened to as lonely as a star-crossed lover. On stage, these uptempo songs – from 1960's 'Think' and 'Mashed Potatoes' to 'Night Train' (1962) – were the focus of the other side of James Brown's showmanship, the master of the new dance. The earliest film and television footage, dating from the early Sixties, shows Brown to be the Michael Jackson of his day but in overdrive. Standing on one leg, he glided across the stage as though on a moving pavement, or he would leap, twirl and shuffle the shoes in a blur of black patent leather.

Not surprisingly, after the success with 'Mashed Potatoes' in the guise of Nat Kendrick & The Swans, Nathan relaxed his views about recording the band on instrumental releases. 'Hold It', credited as James Brown Presents His Band, was the first and a riff from the Bill Doggett hit would form the link he used to segue between songs in the breathless, non-stop Revue that seared across the States as he forged his reputation as the King of the One-Nighters. After one more single as 'Presents His Band', all subsequent instrumental releases were credited to James alone or James Brown & The Famous Flames, which led to the misconception that it was his whole band and not just the vocal group that had the legendary title. Brown was recording so much high-quality material now that King simply could not release all of it for fear of flooding the market again, as they'd done in the months after 'Please, Please, Please' and 'Try Me'.

At this time Danny Ray, the small, slightly stooping, rather sad-eyed man who would become Brown's long-time master of ceremonies, joined the Revue as the singer's personal valet. The precise date was September 19, 1961. "My whole involvement was to be in show business so I started valeting, which I still like doing. [Later on] One of the guys who was MC-ing the show, he didn't make it. So Mr Brown was talking and talking and he kept looking for this guy. Then he said, 'Well, since he's not here, you do the show'. And he stepped inside the dressing room and closed the door. I said:

'Oh God, I know he really didn't mean that'. He opened the door again and said: 'I'll see you on stage'. I was just thinking, my mind was going and my knees is shaking and everything. I never did anything like this in my life. I'd always watched someone else do it. It was a little struggle the first time but I said: 'I got to go and buckle down and really get serious about what's going on'."

His first date as MC was at a place called Streets in Maryland. "We were working a skating rink. I will never forget the place. The first time I stood there in front of a band, a big band, you feel like they're going to blow you off the stage. You feel like your knees and everything was sort of jelly." The new MC got his act together quickly and his introductions became a much mimicked part of JB's performance. "James Brown showed me a lot of things about the business and sometimes I think 'Wow, this guy's a hard man to work with', but at least he wants it right because he understands when people pay the price of a ticket they really want that and giving that to people is really something that you should always do."

He also recalls vividly his inauguration into that great spectacle known as The Cape Routine. "The first time we got that together was in Baton Rouge, Louisiana, and he did it with a white Turkish-style robe. He was coming off and turned around and come right back and threw it off, and [the audience] went wild and he'd come back to the mike. It got so that it was worked into the show. I love doing the cape, and when they say 'What's your favourite tune with James Brown?' 'Well,' I say, 'it has to be 'Please, Please, Please'."

Danny Ray stayed with James Brown through many of the later defections by musicians, and witnessed their not infrequent returns to the fold. He has a partial view of the Hardest Working Man. "Being together that long, you learn to think alike in a lot of things. You get to know one another's moods and what have you. And once you see someone with the determination to make sure things are right become an institution in the business, you can't help but follow and play as much of a role as possible."

Earlier in 1961, Brown had decided to respond to the improved record sales and the ecstatic response his live show was consistently getting, by broadening the scope of his stage performances. The Revue took shape as he expanded the band to 10-pieces. The central axis of the group was still J. C. Davis (sax), Roscoe Patrick (trumpet), Les Buie (guitar), Hubert Perry (bass), Nat Kendrick (drums) with Brown, Famous Flame Bobby Byrd or Fats Gonder playing keyboards. Now he boosted the horn section with the addition of a slim, quietly-spoken old school friend from Augusta, Georgia, St. Clair Pinckney, and Al "Brisco" Clark on saxes, and then Teddy

Washington who doubled on trumpet and trombone. Kendrick and Davis walked out at the end of 1961. Davis became Etta James's bandleader and recorded a few sides for Chess/Argo. Kendrick, meanwhile, his head perhaps turned by the success of 'Mashed Potatoes', tried to build a career as a solo name. Clayton Fillyau took over the drum stool and when Kendrick returned in the fall of 1962, Brown retained both drummers and would later add a third, Obie Williams. J. C. Davis's role as musical director of the band was taken over by trumpeter Alfred Corley and, not too long after, by Al Clark.

He also hired its first chorus line, The Brownies, who had been lured from the safety of their previous employ as The Hortense Allen Dancers. He recruited Yvonne Fair, who had performed with The Chantels, to take over the role established by Bea Ford and Sugar Pie DeSanto. While the James Brown band was down in Miami in January, 1962, Fair recorded 'I Found You' with the entourage, the first and much less frenetic version of 'I Got You (I Feel Good)', which a little over three years later would mark another important staging post in Brown's soul odyssey. Yvonne Fair had another two King releases – 'Tell Me Why' and 'You Can Make It If You Try' – and another James Brown production, 'Straighten Up', which was released, thanks to the Miami connection, on Henry Stone's Dade label in 1963. She was also Brown's main squeeze for a short while and had a daughter, Venisha, by him. It went with the job.

(Yvonne Fair briefly returned to prominence in 1975. When she quit Brown's Revue, she had tried, unsuccessfully, to work as a solo act, and after a brief retirement met Chuck Jackson, with whom she worked on the chitlin' circuit for many years. When she was playing with him at a club in Detroit she was spotted by "someone from Motown" – the company blurb at the time alleged it was Temptations' lead singer David Ruffin, strange how only Berry Gordy's biggest stars ever spotted talent – and she was duly signed by them in 1968. Whether it was a comment on the label's feelings about the wilful Temptations lead or not is a matter of speculation but it took two years for her to get a début single out – 'Stay A Little Longer' on Soul – and by the time 'The Bitch Is Black', her début album, was released, she had spent seven years in the Motown Waiting Room while the writers and producers attended to what they thought or were told were more pressing matters. The album had an excoriating version of 'Funky Music Sho' Nuff Turns Me On' produced by its composer, Norman Whitfield.)

Meanwhile, back at King, Syd Nathan was happy with the way things were going. The hits, which had once been a gentle trickle, were coming in a steadier stream now and no matter what state the rest of his independent empire was in, James Brown was paying the bills. However, James Brown and Ben Bart formed the view that the star did have a problem and it was one of communication, of reaching all of the potential audience. Few of his records so far had captured completely the crackling vitality that had made James Brown one of the most compelling stage performers of the time. And although by the middle of 1962 his records were reaching the broadest of racial audiences so far, he had not penetrated the white market in the same way as other African-American artists.

CHAPTER 6

By the middle of 1962, elemental figures of rock'n'roll such as Little Richard, Fats Domino and Chuck Berry were past their first peaks but other figures popular in the Fifties continued to flourish. Ray Charles, having used his soulful voice in Big Band swing and orchestral string settings, now even more audaciously interpreted 'Modern Sounds In Country and Western Music'. His experiments struck a chord with white audiences. Other acts from the R&B market crossed over big-time that year by virtue of comparatively pallid dance hits, notably Sam Cooke's 'Twistin' The Night Away' and 'The Locomotion' by Little Eva. Two other hits that transcended their R&B origins to climb the pop charts in 1962 outlined the soulful shape of things to come for the rest of the decade. The first was Booker T & The MGs' instrumental hit 'Green Onions', a big breakthrough for Stax Records, the Memphis independent label. The influential house band led by organist Booker T Jones would be central to the development of southern soul in the mid-Sixties not just as accompanists but as composers with Jones, Steve Cropper (guitar) and Al Jackson Jr. (drums) co-writing with and for many Stax and Atlantic artists. In the North, Mary Wells had three Top 10 hits – 'The One Who Really Loves You', 'You Beat Me To The Punch' and 'Two Lovers' – and could genuinely claim that 1962 was hers. 'Punch' had been the first No. 1 scored by Berry Gordy's fledgling stable of labels in Detroit. The impact of Tamla and Motown on the pop market over the next two decades scarcely needs amplifying here.

After months of diligent touring and recording, James Brown's band was at its hottest. In May, 1962, his session in the King studio produced some extraordinarily fervid performances, particularly 'I've Got The Money'. James had produced a version of 'I've Got Money' under the title of 'I Need Love' two years earlier with Famous Flame "Baby" Lloyd Stallworth singing in front of the Band. But now, Clayton Fillyau had taken over from Nat Kendrick as drummer and proved to be a sensational find, laying down a mind-bogglingly busy undercoat of syncopated rhythm at a breath-taking pace in a time when technological assists were limited primarily to the occasional echo chamber and overdub. At the same session he recorded 'I Don't Care', a blasting piece of work that served as an album track, the flip-side of singles in 1964 and 1966 until it was finally stripped down and turned out as 1967's hit 'Cold Sweat', when it still sounded a decade ahead of its time.

With records entering the R&B charts as a matter of course, Brown could fill the biggest arenas available in the South more than once over. The year was shaping up to be one of his busiest, most successful and satisfying yet. Although 'Try Me' had been aired on Dick Clark's *American Bandstand* TV show, Brown did not make his own national US TV début until 1962. At the Tan Playhouse in Philadelphia he was crowned the King of Rock'n'Roll and the nation's dee-jays had polled him No. 1 R&B Singer.

By diligent touring of the roots venues he was ousting pretenders to the throne of the most dynamic live show – notably Jackie Wilson, another former prize-fighter whose performances were always reckoned to be a heavyweight match for Brown's, in terms of athleticism and sheer get-down-on-the-knees-and-scream-oooowee! emotion. "In the early days, he'd do a lot of that kind of stuff, tumbling and going crazy," Bobby Byrd recalled. "But it's a funny thing, after he got big … I guess maybe he figured 'Well, I don't wanna hurt myself because if I accidentally hurt myself I'll be through.' Maybe he had that on his mind. We used to wonder why he wouldn't do it and we'd try to get him to do it. But he never would. Oh, except one time, later on. We was at the Apollo Theater and he got on top of the piano. It was an upright. He flipped off the piano into a split on the floor and then up again. 'Course, that stopped the show. We couldn't do nothing else after that. That was it. That done killed everybody. He had to be helped to the dressing room, but he done tore up the house. He had to slacken up after that."

The phrases 'slacken up' and the Hardest Working Man in Show Business seem anathemas and, after a pause, Byrd has another vivid take of Brown in action. It was at the Five Four Ballroom, one of the big black venues in Los Angeles in the late Fifties and early Sixties. "He and Tina Turner got into a thing there. Ike [Turner] used to watch us a lot. He'd hang around with pencil and pad. We didn't know what he was writing about but he knew what he was writing about. He was figuring these things out. We were all together on this show, and James and Tina got into 'Please, Please, Please'. So they went back and forth with 'Please, Please' and Tina got up on the piano and fly off that piano into a split, while she was into her split, James jumps over her head into his split. Tina was … that woman was something else. Every time James come off with something, she'd come right back at him. He wasn't gonna let her outdo him and she wasn't gonna let him outdo her. Boy, let me tell you, The Flames couldn't do nothing but just get out the way. Ike too. He didn't understand it himself. He said, 'I ain't never seen Tina like this'.

"Tina just had the fire in her eyes that night. She was gonna show this man. But you know James. He's not about to be beaten, especially by a woman. So they were at each other's throat and it was one of the best shows you ever wanna see. The people went crazy. It's horrible that they didn't have no cameras back then to film it all. The world has missed a whole lotta great stuff."

To the young black audience, he was, indisputably, the Soul Messiah, Soul Brother Number One! To James Brown it seemed obvious that anyone who had seen him perform live would be more than happy to hear a record of the fantastic experience in the comfort of their own home, be it ever so humble. Bobby Byrd backed the idea but it appalled Nathan. First, he considered himself to be in the singles business, not the albums market. That was what he knew and what he thought his core markets – they were called race music and hillbilly when he started King – wanted. Although his plant in Cincinnati had the technology to switch from 78 rpms to 45s and 33s in the Fifties, he'd been reluctant to do so. And although Ray Charles, for one, had put out two successful live albums by this time – 'At Newport' (1958) and 'In Person' (1959, recorded in Atlanta, Georgia) – Nathan was not buying. Once again, the label boss and his star act were at loggerheads and, as with the previous major disputes over 'Try Me', Brown called the man in Cincinnati's bluff by funding the live recording himself.

The Apollo had already been the scene of many exceptional James Brown shows, the first in April, 1959, when a fee $200 under the normal rate had been accepted in order to get the exposure. When they walked out half way through the season, literally walked off the stage, out through the auditorium and into the lobby, dragging the audience with them, the owners, the Schiffmans, made up the cash shortfall. (Interestingly, James Brown's later demands for a percentage of the receipts forced the theatre to change its ticket sales policy. Originally, you would buy a ticket and sit there and watch the alternating acts, show after show, until you got bored and left. The first show was at 9am, mostly for the kids. Then came a midday show, a third show at four or five in the afternoon. The work really began in the evening, four shows a night. Acts would play six or seven shows a day for seven days a week. Theoretically, you could stay there all day, from the noon show to lights out if you wanted to. But after Brown and other regular Apollo-fillers began to demand a percentage of the takings the owners decided that the audience would have to be decanted onto 125th Street after each show and a new set of tickets sold for the night's next performance.)

And so here comes The James Brown Revue to the Apollo again for a one-week residency, starting on October 16. When it became clear that Nathan would not budge an inch on the issue of live recording, Brown put up $5,700 of his own money to record there. By the midnight show of Wednesday October 24, the band was as ready as it was ever likely to be and the tracks recorded that night formed the basis of 'Live At The Apollo'. The album set a standard for live soul performance against which all subsequent in-concert albums are measured in terms of the excitement generated by a singer's emotional output, the draining, physical nature of the performance and the band's strong, strict, and very focused playing of the tight arrangements. Add the audience's thrilled and chilled response to Mr. Dynamite's explosive package to these quintessential characteristics of "soul" staging and you get a record which so truly and accurately captures the spirit and emotion of a moment in time that it transcends that moment in time to become the eternal live recording.

"So now, ladies and gentlemen, it's star time," MC Fats Gonder announces in a style not dissimilar to the one he'd used in the same capacity for Little Richard. "Are you ready for star time?" Yaaaay! "Thank you, and thank you very kindly." What follows has become one of the great set pieces in live popular music. "It is indeed a great pleasure to present to you at this par-tic-u-lar time, the performer nationally and internationally known as the Hardest Working Man in Show Business, man who sing 'I'll Go Crazy' [cheers and screams! a fanfare of horns!], 'Try Me' [screams and horns!], 'You've Got The Power, [horns!], 'Think' [screams and horns!], 'If You Want Me' [horns!], 'I Don't Mind' [horns!], 'Bewildered' [a bigger cheer here!], million-dollar seller 'Lost Someone' [real big scream!], the very latest release, 'Night Train' [horns!], everybody 'Shout & Shimmy' [horns!], Mr. Dynamite, the amazing Mr. Please, Please himself, the star of the show, James Brown and The Famous Flames!"

The band sped through the introduction riff for two verses, then at the start of the third the screams in the Apollo tell you that James and The

Flames have mashed potatoed and boogalooed from the wings to centre stage. "You know I feel alright!" he sings and the band gives him a "Yeah!" "You know, I feel alright children" and the band gives him a second "Yeah!" "I feel" – and this final word he takes up and up and down and then finally up and up one last time again, way up to the back row of the upper circle – "awwwwwlright!" They taped 'I'll Go Crazy', 'Try Me', 'Think', 'I Don't Mind', 'Lost Someone', 'Please, Please, Please' and a medley of lesser hits ending with his biggest hit of that year, 'Night Train'.

'Night Train', a No. 5 R&B hit and No. 35 pop hit, had been followed by three more singles in 1962 – 'Shout & Shimmy', a fairly unblinking steal from the frantic dance mode of The Isley Brothers which they worked up when Bobby Bennett, a dancer to match Brown, Byrd and "Baby" Lloyd Stallworth, joined the group. It reached No. 16 R&B and No. 61 pop. A mix of rhythm & blues and jazz, 'Mashed Potatoes USA' is at heart a strong instrumental riff leaving space for a long muted trumpet solo. The vocal is reduced to an aside. Added as an afterthought, the recitation of towns and cities on the band's itinerary (he misspelt his home town) was one of the first times Brown used overdubbing. In the immediate post-Twist era, a new dance craze was concocted on a monthly basis but Brown was faithful to the Mashed Potato. It was, he said, "one of the most dynamic dances in the world because you can just go all over the floor, you can defy gravity with it. 'Cos they saw me do three steps in the air before I hit the ground, three different steps." His final single of 1962, 'I've Got Money', failed to make the R&B charts and just crept into the pop 100. So despite the many reasons to feel good in December 1962, there was a feeling of frustration at the lack of big breakthrough into the pop market. Brother Ray Charles's career proved a vital model again.

After his live albums, Ray Charles had used studio orchestras to broaden the appeal of his music while still holding on to the core listeners. When he switched from Atlantic to the major ABC-Paramount, the process of expanding his appeal had increased in tempo until by 1962–63 he was the biggest-seller in the market. Although Brown and Charles had similar roots – southern, gospel, poor – their styles had developed in markedly different ways but now Brown's career appeared to trace a very similar pattern to Charles's. With 'Live At The Apollo' sizzling in the can awaiting release, Ben Bart suggested to Brown that it might be a good idea to record with strings. On December 17, 1962, Brown, producer Gene Redd, arranger Sammy Lowe, a band of session musicians, a string section and a five-voice chorus assembled at Bell Sound studio in New York. They recorded four tracks including 'Prisoner of Love', a hallowed weepie given an unsparing gospel makeover, and 'These Foolish Things', 'Again' and 'So Long' which with Lowe's string section overdubs on three of Brown's older ballad hits made up the 'Prisoner of Love' album.

Although Brown's recordings had a reputation for immediacy and impact they did not necessarily come together with the speed that that suggested. But this was his first multi-track session, a carefully set-up and meticulous piece of work – there were 15 takes of 'Prisoner' – and the end justified the means. Released as a single in April, 1963, the track gave Brown his first American Pop Top 20 that spring. Certainly the American trades had been rather more sympathetic to this new, superficially sophisticated style. "A tender and very touching reading of the old standard by James Brown and The Famous Flames that could go all the way, like their recent smash 'Prisoner of Love'" was the verdict on 'These Foolish Things', "Stylish backing helps too". A while later, when 'Again' was released, the trades noted that "Brown has a string of 'em on his former label and he's got another romantic side here. Tender reading of the standard."

In May 1963, Nathan finally agreed to release 'Live At The Apollo'. Like Otis Redding's 'Otis Blue', 'Live At The Apollo' was a defining soul album. But even though he'd not had to lay out a penny on recording the album, Syd Nathan still could not see the sense in releasing it. King Records' attitude to albums was at best tolerant unlike, say, Atlantic Records, where the format had been embraced with energy and not a little imagination, particularly for the jazz market. King merely shuffled together a collection of stockpiled filler tracks with little thought for value either to the customer or to the development of the artist's career. Seven James Brown albums were released between January, 1959, and October, 1962. The first was a collection of tracks from singles and B-sides. The next six mixed previously issued tracks with unreleased material. That they were good, of their type, was simply a reflection of the fact that Brown and his band was good at its job. But the albums' sales were not outstanding. By the fall of 1962, James Brown's stature in the African-American marketplace was the equivalent of Elvis Presley's in the white market in 1956. Yet the first pressing order for 'James Brown And His Famous Flames Tour The USA', a 12-cut collection of which six were instrumentals, was for 3,000 mono copies and 500 stereo.

To put what happened next into context, the album charts at the time were full of what would come to be known as middle-of-the-road recordings by stars of Las Vegas or upmarket New York cabaret nightclubs – easy listening music predominantly bought by white 'middle' Americans – plus jazz albums by the more accessible musicians, bossa nova was the latest big swing at the time, unabrasive folk music, albums of Broadway musicals or movie soundtracks or the latest (white) teenage craze, such as the Twist. The few black album-buyers that existed tended to be older and favoured jazz, gospel or MOR. *Billboard* did not deem it worthwhile to start a rhythm & blues albums chart until 1965. So James Brown's album was measured against white MOR releases. While it is true to say that if 'Live At The Apollo' was the only album appealing to a market its sales were likely to be high, it was even more accurate to say that to become that pioneering album, it had to change preferences and habits, influence taste and tap an entirely fresh new marketplace. The financial mould to be broken was significant, for only a very small proportion of the black community could afford the price of an album.

In the record business of the early Sixties, the problems of over-exposure and audience burn-out were as finely argued as they are in the media-saturated Nineties. When fans have seen you in the sweating, all-dancing flesh on stage, argument against the live album went, they will not want to hear you in the sterility of their homes doing the same show without the dances, spins, dips, splits and cape. And if that argument did not convince, there is an extension – if you give fans a live show which they can play in the comfort of their homes every night, why should they go to see you next time you're in town?

These fears proved to be ill-founded in a major way and 'Live At The Apollo' established the rhythm & blues album as a far more profitable item than had hitherto been imagined. Much like the exposure which gave lift-off to a hit single, the album's success came via extensive airplay. Once they'd heard a track, listeners rang their local radio stations to demand to hear more, swamping them with requests. In the end, many stations set aside a regular slot in the schedule to play the complete package once a day. This went on for months. King Records boasted, a year after the album's release, that it had sold 66,000 copies in 11 days and become a best seller in "a few short weeks" – as opposed to a few long weeks? – which was a remarkable claim because the order for the first pressing was only 5,000 and 'Live At The Apollo' did not break into the national album chart until the end of June, 1963. The album's sales performance needed no hyperbole. It reached No. 2 on the *Billboard* national pop chart and was the 32nd best-selling album in America that year. This would not have raised an eyebrow had it been a sweet Nat King Cole or Johnny Mathis LP whose sales would have been boosted by consistent exposure on national television. But this was a raw, privately financed, live recording by one of the most visceral performers of all time whose lack of inhibition on stage still affronted the growing ranks of middle-class urban African-Americans. Moreover, the album was released on an independent label which had no mind to advertise or promote its records other than in the most rudimentary, tried-and-tested way of putting it out and plugging it to dee-jays known to be sympathetic on stations which formatted that type of music and waiting for the orders to flood in, or not, as the case might be.

Perhaps a better barometer of the impact of 'Live At The Apollo' than its 32nd placing in 1963 total sales list is the fact that it was outsold by only one other American album aimed at the youth market that year, The Beach Boys' 'Surfin' USA'. Of course, the three Wilson brothers and their two cousins had the might of a major record company, Capitol, behind them with all that that implied – sizeable advertising and promotion budgets, access to network television, appeal to the white market which had more disposable cash. 'Apollo' legitimised "Live" soul albums and opened the floodgates for a flood of them, notably by numerous Tamla Motown acts either singly or as part of the Motortown Revue and by the rawer soul singers on Stax and Volt, again either singly or as part of label-promoting packages.

The Apollo album of October and string sessions of December, 1962, had given Brown, in less than half a year, a toehold in the white market and preached his gospel so far and fundamentally into the black market that his stature as Soul Brother No. 1 would soon be untouchable. (At first, the nicknames attached to Brown were genuine – the 'Hardest-Working Man', Bobby Byrd said, came from the audience, not the organisation, although the band and local promoters would spread the word that 'Mr. Dynamite' was due in town by leafleting and leaving stickers in restaurant and gas station rest rooms, in phone booths and bars, anywhere to catch the eye – ain't nothin' new on the streets.)

To even further emphasise the way his career in 1962–63 appeared to shadow and seek direction from Ray Charles's move away from rhythm & blues, King released two interpretations of country & western songs – 'Three Hearts In A Tangle', which had been the A-side to 'I've Got Money', and 'Signed, Sealed And Delivered', a song co-written by Syd Nathan and Cowboy Copas. (Copas's 'Filipino Baby'/'I Don't Blame You' had been King Records' first ever release back in 1945.) Fortunately, the style was not considered worthy of further investigation.

Brown's diversity at this time has been analysed by some writers as a lack of cohesive direction. Frustration with King Records and a confidence spawned by Ben Bart's faith and the visible and tangible evidence of the reaction to his live shows, which were breaking house records in black theatres all over as he criss-crossed the States, is a likelier diagnosis for his diversity. Nathan's health, which had not been robust, was again failing. Hal Neely had to all intents and purposes taken over the day-to-day running of the company and even though Nathan, like many of the old independent label bosses, was losing touch with taste in his business's core markets, he still had ultimate veto.

Nonetheless, he was wise enough to allow his most valuable signing a certain degree of latitude. Brown set up his own label, Try Me, to be manufactured and distributed by King, and Jim Jam Music, a song publishing company. James Brown Productions began to proliferate – he already had credits on Federal, King, Dade and other small labels. In the early part of 1963, he produced three sides for Try Me. 'Devil's Den' by The Poets was an instrumental featuring Mr. Dynamite on organ in which the band give their version of the funky small group style which would be a feature of the Blue Note, Verve and Prestige jazz recordings of the mid-Sixties. Brown liked the enormous variety of sounds he could get from a Hammond organ. He had the same one for 20 years, called it The Godfather. The other Try Me singles were by Johnny & Bill – Johnny Terry and Bill Hollings – and Tammy Montgomery. Terry, James's long-time friend, and Hollings had their own spot in the Revue, as by now did Bobby Byrd and "Baby" Lloyd Stallworth.

Montgomery was his latest featured young woman, on and off stage, but as a duettist she would be much better known a few years down the line as Tammi Terrell, Marvin Gaye's vocal partner on a string of romantically upbeat Tamla hits such as 'Your Precious Love', 'Ain't Nothing Like The Real Thing', 'You're All I Need To Get By' and 'If I Could Build My Whole World Around You', among others, before her untimely death in 1970 from a brain tumour. As Tammy Montgomery, she recorded 'I Cried' for Try Me, a sweetly sung Brown/Bobby Byrd pop ballad – with a rap at the end using phrases like "don't make me over" and "any day now" as an acknowledgement that the Burt Bacharach/Hal David productions on Dionne Warwick were an inspiration. As a producer, a bigger opportunity soon presented itself to Brown and the Try Me label. But it was tried and set aside.

It seemed that the business relationship and trusting partnership between Ben Bart and Brown could get no tighter. But it did. After proving himself as the right booker, co-promoter, adviser and unofficial father-figure, Bart decided to hand over the reins at the Universal Attractions agency – at a price – to his son Jack, and Dick Allen, a partner in the company, and leave to manage Brown full-time. "We got into many battles over those years that passed that my father managed James," Jack said. "This was due to the fact that James felt 'why should he pay a booking agency, why should he pay a manager'. If it had been two separate families and our last names had been different, he probably wouldn't have objected. But he felt his money was going into the same pot and we used to get into lots of arguments. I used to fight with my father, James used to fight with my father and I guess [my father] was in the middle. He wouldn't defend my position and he wouldn't defend James's position.

"The relationship between my father and James was like father-son, and I remember James used to call our home many times and I'd answer the phone and he'd say 'Let me speak to Pop', because that's what he'd call him. And deep down I would sort of resent that slightly. But that was foolishness on my part, because the two of them really did have a very close relationship."

In business, Jack felt Brown was "trying to beat me for money, when we were doing our job booking them and they didn't pay us sometimes. So the love between James Brown and Jack Bart and Universal Attractions at that period was not very great. In fact, if it was a marriage, we would have been divorced. But we plodded along and listened to each other's craziness. Then, unfortunately, my father passed away and James came to me and said, 'Look, the two of us don't really get on very well, but I made a promise to your Dad and it seems that we'll have to work out our differences'." That was to be five years down the line. For now, in the fall of 1963, Brown and Ben Bart set up Fair Deal Productions, an independent outfit, and placed the next two releases with Smash, a label under the umbrella of the major Mercury Corporation. Anna King, a young Philadelphia singer who had replaced Tammy Montgomery in the Revue, had a modest pop hit in early 1964 with 'If Somebody Told You' and Bobby Byrd's 'I'm Just A Nobody' was put out. The third release was a King-Byrd duet, 'Baby, Baby, Baby', which was attractive enough to be released in European markets. (The extra distribution muscle a major label was able to offer Brown's productions would not have been lost on him. Brown also knew that as by far the biggest act on Syd Nathan's label, he had a certain amount of leverage there. Yet King could not allow itself to agree to every small demand from its meal ticket. A face-off loomed.)

In the meantime, James Brown's major headlining tour of 1963 was a remarkable package. Essentially, he acted as the main draw for Marvin Gaye, The Supremes, The Temptations, The Four Tops and other breaking acts on Berry Gordy's Tamla and Motown labels. "That was one of the hottest tours," Byrd said of the forty dates that September and October. "Motown was just starting to get played a lot. They were getting pop airplay and they could appear in white gigs that we weren't getting to, but the whole of the Motown roster put together couldn't outdraw James Brown & The Famous

Flames in black venues. They were known record-wise, not working-wise. So I guess Berry wanted to get them across to the black audience by touring with James."

The Detroit labels had only one star who might have upset an Apollo audience as much as James – Marvin Gaye. "Although his records went over to the whites because of the name Motown, Marvin could sing black music good and he was very good looking. He was the most popular Motown guy with the girls. Funny thing was, Marvin didn't dig it. He was into jazz and Broadway stuff and didn't really enjoy performing." So despite the fact of three R&B hits in the previous 12 months – 'Stubborn Kind Of Fellow', 'Hitch Hike' and 'Pride And Joy' – with 'Can I Get A Witness' to follow soon after, Gaye did not give the Hardest Working Man In Show Business serious competition. "Otis [Redding] was like that," Byrd added. "He could upset a house but it didn't make no difference to him, he didn't care. It didn't shake him at all."

After the Motortown joint operation, Brown recorded another "live" album, at the Royal Theater in Baltimore, and went back to the Apollo. The Harlem theater had become his symbolic home and he made New York his actual home when he split up with Dessie, left Macon and bought a house in the St. Albans area of Queens. He would have plenty of time to examine soft furnishings for his new home because his advisers read his "personal services" recording contract with King as covering singing only and suggested he was free to sign to another company and record as an instrumentalist. The result of this contentious analysis was that for much of 1964 Brown's organisation would be as busy in the courts as it was in the recording studio. His recording career might have been stalled by the litigation but it had a momentum as powerful as a James Brown groove and nothing could stop his music moving forward.

CHAPTER 7

The "politicisation" of James Brown did not reach its full expression until the latter half of the Sixties – and a fairly muddled expression it was in terms of consistency and logic. However, by 1963–64, as the hottest African-American act in the black market, he was coming under pressure to speak out on issues of integration and equality of opportunity. After 'Live At The Apollo', he was known to a not inconsiderable core of young white record-buyers. He was a potentially potent ally to whichever political party or movement he chose to support. For the understandable reason of wanting to build a career with continuity, or simply earn a modest living, many artists in America were disinclined to speak out on political and social issues. The precedents of the McCarthy witch-hunts of writers, actors, film directors and producers in the Fifties, to the hounding of Paul Robeson, were recent and vivid reminders of what could happen to artists whose opinions differed from those of the political, industrial and social establishments.

Brown's emergence with 'Please, Please, Please' in 1956 coincided with the first attempts to segregate schools in the South and with the campaigns to force segregation in other public places. Many of the images of those days have become so idealised by film that the raw courage of the frail but determined-looking Rosa Parks, daring to sit in the "whites only" seats at the front of a bus in Montgomery, Alabama, which led to the blacks' boycott of the company there, is hard to convey. Brown's stature grew slowly at first through years of exhaustive touring and the gradual emergence of a unique style on record. The movement against segregation and racial inequality also

81

solidified during those years under the emerging leadership of Martin Luther King. Its soundtrack in the Fifties was provided by folk music, which spoke to whites, and spiritual-based anthems rather than rhythm & blues or jazz. Simply, the guitar and human voice were the most portable and universal instruments for rousing spirits and minds on marches or during a sit-in.

As Bobby Byrd has described it, Toccoa was a fairly benign place compared with many small towns south of the Mason-Dixon line but as soon as the band moved outside this unlikely Eden they encountered their share of troubles on the road. Although relatively few and far between, if you cared to ignore the day-to-day insults to dignity and humanity that segregation and intolerance produce, they were nonetheless powerful enough to leave a mark. Even the first Motortown Revue to swing through the South had been shot at as they hurriedly boarded their bus and they were singers who made records which whites bought. But The Famous Flames' usual concern was to get out of one town and on to the next, find a hotel that would accommodate them, a place that would serve them food, play the show, get paid and get on the move again. Sit-ins at restaurant counters and the freedom rides were on the periphery of this life although Brown has always had a keen radar ready to detect and react to disrespect. And anyway, itinerant entertainers were not thought to have opinions or influence, they were just song and dance folk.

But after his storming success with 'Live At The Apollo', that was a less accurate assumption in James Brown's case. The year was a traumatic one for Americans. In September, a racist's bomb, planted at the 16th Street Baptist Church in Birmingham, Alabama, killed four young black girls – Carole Robertson, Cynthia Wesley, Denise McNair and Addie Mae Collins. On November 22, 1963, President John F. Kennedy, a leader perceived to be steadfastly dedicated to progressive values and ideas by the vast majority of his fellow Americans be they for or against him, was assassinated in Dallas, Texas. It would be impossible not to have some sort of an opinion against the background of murders so obviously motivated by political, social and racist aims. Whether James Brown could yet be encouraged to express it publicly was another matter. It would appeal to his ego but Ben Bart would point out that it was not prudent at that stage of his career. Besides, he had more mundane matters to contend with, like a battle with King.

His final studio session for King under the old contract was on October 23, 1963, memorable for a row between Brown and producer/arranger Gene Redd as well as for the secular revamp of the classical Swan Silvertones' gospel delight 'Mary Don't You Weep' which became 'Oh Baby

Don't You Weep'. Brown, at the piano, leads The Famous Flames, who repeat the title behind his vocal, through six minutes of emotional exhortation, tributes to other gospel-soul singers and acknowledgement of his own recording achievements. It took Brown up to No. 23 on the pop charts in January, 1964 and, with overdubbing, was one of two studio tracks added as make-weights to the live album recorded at the Royal Theater, Baltimore. By now he and Bart had added Try Me Music, a publishing company for which his songs appeared as "Ted Wright" compositions. In March, he recorded a batch of rhythm & blues standards with big band arrangements by Sammy Lowe (echoes of Ray Charles' tactics again) for Fair Deal and placed them with Smash as an album called 'Showtime'. This both capitalised on the success of the 'Apollo' album and, it is hard to not believe, was deliberately designed to damage sales of the 'Live At The Royal' album on King and provoke Syd Nathan's temper, which was about as settled as Brown's. Two singles from 'Showtime', his versions of Louis Jordan's evergreen 'Caldonia' and Guitar Slim's 'The Things That I Used To Do', were mild sellers and, commercially, must have been tremendously disappointing to Mercury.

From April 10 to May 17 he headed out onto the road with an expanded line-up. Fats Gonder was still in the band with Al "Brisco" Clark as em-cee but a new name in the sax section was Nat Jones, who would take over as musical director at the start of the next tour in the middle of May. Jones was from Kinston, North Carolina and, Byrd said, "was a good bandleader and did some good arrangements. He did the first Christmas album for James [1966's 'Christmas Songs'] and James took it all away from him. That hurt him real bad. It truly sent him off the deep end. He had idolised James, he was that kind of a person. And we had tried to tell him, you cannot be close with James because he's gonna turn on you. You're working for the man so don't be always up in his face."

Back in the studio, Brown was recording prolifically. Although comparatively little of the music he was cutting now would be issued in this form, the experiments were the foundations for his progression through soul and into funk during the next few years. In the summer, he recorded the first versions of 'I Got You', 'It's A Man's World', 'Nature Boy', 'Till Then', 'I Wanna Be Around', 'Only You' and 'I Loves You Porgy' for his own Fair Deal Productions company. Some of these were from an orchestrated selection of middle-of-the-road standards, some were jazz-flavoured instrumentals with his own band. The breadth of his ambition is evident when comparing the desire to impress as a "sophisticated" singer or ultra-hip keyboard player, as apparent in those sides, with the naked ambition for a pop hit on 'Out Of

The Blue', an extraordinary and untypical bare-faced shot at a Top 20 teen beat sound.

Of course, Syd Nathan had not been idle all this while and filed suit against Brown and Mercury in April. On October 16 he got the injunction which prevented the singer from recording vocals on Smash. But now everyone knew that King's contract with Brown allowed him, through their oversight, to record as a musician with other labels. By then, Brown had released two Smash albums and three singles, one of which made the pop Top 30 and gave him a first, significant taste of success overseas.

But he couldn't follow it up. During the legal wrangling which surrounded the contract dispute, Brown tried to pressure King into giving him a new contract. Although he subsequently started recording again for the Cincinnati label, he remained technically in dispute with them for several years. In fact, to jump ahead, on January 26, 1967, we find him in New York in the Madison Avenue offices of Shea, Gallop, Climenko & Gould, before Anthony Werner, a Notary Public of the State of New York, for Examination Before Trial in the matter of the plaintiff, King Records Inc, against James Brown, the Mercury Records Corporation, Mercury Records Production Inc and Fair Deal Record Corporation. The sixty-five page transcript of the pre-trial deposition is comprised mostly of exchanges between Brown, who had arrived at least one hour and 35 minutes late, and Martin Shelton, attorney for King Records, with interjections by Brown's attorney Marty Machat.

Shelton first attempts to establish when the singer stopped recording for King. Brown recalls it was 'Oh Baby Don't You Weep'. What year? "I don't remember exactly. The only thing I can remember real good is that I was not getting paid." Which ones? "Most all of them." It is a theme he works into his answers whenever possible. Either he was not paid or he paid for a share of items, like advertisements, that he shouldn't have. He also claims to have no knowledge of the contents of contracts and no clear memory of dates or names from three, four and five years earlier. This from a man acknowledged to have an uncanny memory of promoters, disc jockeys, venue capacities and their exact locations. "I don't take care of the books, I'm just a singer. If I knew about the books I'd be in a better position." At one point, Shelton tried to goad his ego, to get him to admit widespread popularity. "You would say your style is kind of inimitable, wouldn't you?" "I don't understand you. You see I only stopped in the seventh grade." "There is no one in the business like you, is there?" "I don't know because there is a lot of people doing much better than I am."

After discussion about Brown's business relationship with Bart and the setting up of Fair Deal, the inquisitor Shelton then turns to publicity photos and flyers (stickers and posters for displays at venues and record stores). One flyer, for Brown's live albums at the Apollo and the Royal, would be sent by King to record stores, he admitted. "If you buy a record I imagine they would give you a flyer. By the way, this is one of the biggest albums to have ever been recorded and this is one of the albums I didn't get paid for. That album stayed on *Billboard* for sixty-four weeks and went off the charts and came back in." Shelton shows an advertisement in an October 1963 *Billboard* for a James Brown album. Brown says he paid half the cost of the ad. "It's not something that was given to me. I paid half and I shouldn't have paid nothing. It's something the company should have given free and it didn't. I paid half."

Shelton establishes that Brown ceased to record for King at the end of 1963 and started to record for Smash at the beginning of 1964. "I was almost ready to quit singing because I wasn't getting paid." Finally, Shelton gets to the nub – Fair Deal signing to Mercury. Brown recalls a meeting between himself, Bart and a man only referred to as Mr. Irving Green of Mercury Records but, when pressed on the details of their conversation he says: "I don't remember a thing about it." He agreed he signed a five-year contract with King on July 1, 1960. "Well, I wasn't trying to figure out a contract. I was looking at the way a man was being treated. I don't think a man should be treated this way in the United States."

Further exchanges follow. One, concerning why Green of Mercury was in the meeting with Brown and Bart, is worthy of the Marx Brothers. Shelton: "Did you have any discussions with Mr. Green at this point of time other than what you have testified to?" Brown: "What kind of discussions?" "Any kind." "There is nothing I could discuss. What could I say to him?" "I don't know. You had him there. Did you invite him?" "Did I have him there. I didn't have him there." "Who did?" "I don't know who had him there." "He was there, wasn't he?" "That's right." "Did you invite him?" "I'd invite you if you would come by there."

At the end of the interview Brown admits that he got $27,000 from Mercury but none of it before he recorded for them. Brown's performance throughout moves from humble and know-nothing to feisty, combative and self-aware. They adjourn *sine die* after two hours although Brown's counsel doesn't want to. He wants to press on and finish the deposition because Brown is soon off to the West Coast.

Back in real time, the litigious in-fighting of 1964 did not hinder Brown's capacity for work and while in Chicago in June he recorded the first smash for Smash, his third single on the label. By August, 'Out Of Sight' was in the pop Hot 100 and reached No. 24. The record was a giant leap for Brown, and for soul music, and had been kick-started by the expansion in the late Spring of The James Brown Orchestra's horn section under md Nat Jones. Brown had spotted an outstanding but too-young drummer, Melvin Parker, who was still at school in North Carolina when the Brown band passed through. The Parkers hailed from Kinston, same place as Jones. A year later, Brown found the drummer again and hired him. But Melvin would only come along if there was a place for his elder brother, saxophonist Maceo Parker. All of the tenor spots were filled but Maceo had a baritone too.

"I was a music student at North Carolina University in Greensboro," said Maceo, "where I think I was in my second year as a saxophone major. I met [Brown] through my brother … at the time we felt that school was getting a little beyond us so we thought we heard somewhat of a distant calling. We needed something else other than school and we felt that working in the James Brown band would be an answer to this calling. James Brown was the hottest thing back then and this type of music was fresh and I thought it worked hand in hand with what I thought I was about musically."

Maceo had been in 10th grade when he first saw the Brown magic. "It was a mystic kind of thing … it was a magnetism kind of thing where it drew me closer to him and the group and everything. I guess I can say [it was] predestined that I would be part of his show. I knew that I was watching something that I would be part of. It was almost scary." (Bobby Byrd recalls his first sighting of the Parkers as scary too. The Revue had finished its set in a hall in North Carolina and was about to move on to the next date when Maceo and Melvin took to the bandstand before the equipment had been broken down. They blew up a storm, pulling the emptying audience back into the auditorium. They were hired on the spot, says Bobby.)

Although the Parkers stayed for only a little more than a year before Maceo was drafted into the US forces – he was stationed in Augusta, Georgia – the vitality in the rhythm section's playing and in the dynamics of the horn section shifted fundamentally. Rhythm became the predominant factor in Brown's music. Previously, the horn section had helped carry and embellish the melody but on 'Out Of Sight' the horn arrangement of clipped phrases places emphasis on the section's ability to bolster the drive and glide of the beat. And Bernard Odum's bass, taking a lead role, is pulled way up to the front of the mix, his bass patterns springing off the downbeats as well as driving the arrangement. (Rhythm becomes the central element of the song, a change which would become even more pronounced in his next big hit. Gradually, the melodic content was distilled as Brown's voice was recruited as virtually a part of the rhythm section – certainly as much a part of it as the horn section became. Thus some of the later glorious grooves are little more than rhythm explorations on one chord.) By contrast, the flip side of 'Out Of Sight', the more traditional arrangement of the gospel-rooted 'Maybe The Last Time', bids a fond farewell to the old James Brown style. It was also the last time he worked in the studio with The Famous Flames as backing vocalists. From now, it would be Bobby Byrd and whoever was hired for the session although on stage it was singing and dancing as usual for The Famous Flames. He's still the Hardest Working Man In Show Business but Mr. Dynamite is dead, long live Soul Brother No. 1.

'Out Of Sight' wasn't the first James Brown single to be released in Britain but it was the first to be extensively reviewed there when Philips put it out in the last week of October, 1964. Brown's impact outside the USA will be discussed in greater detail later but the reviews give an indication of first impressions. In terminology which appeared to be left over from the Fifties, *Melody Maker* described him as "US idol of many frenzy-lovers" with a "Good solid tight sound in the Little Richard vein." The reviewer thought that, given exposure, it would do well. *New Musical Express* was less hip to the coming sound. Brown "shout-sings a mid-tempo R&B opus with his earthy gravel-flecked voice ... Vocal group supports, but the tune could have been stronger. OK for connoisseurs, but won't mean much here." *Disc*, reviewing both sides, was easily the most impressed, admiring Brown's "sand-blasted throat ... in good form here. He husks the catchy beater in a way which will set your hips moving" and perceptively noted the "excellent sax sound underneath". The flip-side was "a wild squawking performance which rocks steadily down the middle of the road". Finally, and again very accurately, the paper thought it was "a disc the groups will buy, anyway". *Record Mirror* noted a "pounding medium beat with a touch of Rufus Thomas here".

As 'Out Of Sight' made its way up the charts, King's suit against Brown, Bart and Mercury made progress in the courts, the aforesaid injunction in the New York Appellate Court restraining the artist from recording for Smash while the exclusivity of his contract with King was established. Brown had failed in his attempt to keep the suit out of court by negotiating a better deal with King and after this decision refused to record, vocally, for almost a year. Nathan, meanwhile, flooded the market with James Brown singles in 1964. After the hit with 'Oh Baby Don't You Weep', King released seven more singles from the extensive vault of old material, four of them coming after 'Out of Sight' charted. They were reissues, assorted live cuts and cover versions. Brown continued to record instrumentals for Smash.

Despite the variable quality of releases, 1964 ended on a stratospheric high for James Brown. First, he threw himself into even more live work and continued to pick up awards like a man harvesting his new crop. Late in 1964 he was named R&B Artist of the Year by *Music Business* – in the pre-trial deposition a few years later he would dismiss the Award, self-deprecatingly saying that awards like it meant nothing because, he alleged, it could be bought by the artist or record company – and in October, he was presented with New York radio station WWRL's Soul Brother Award – a tasteful trophy about three-feet tall – by dee-jay Rocky G on stage at the Apollo. He also filmed a small clip in *Ski Party*, a 1965 movie vehicle for Fifties pop star Frankie Avalon.

An immeasurably more significant piece of filming was his segment for Steve Binder's extravaganza, the *T.A.M.I.* show, filmed at the Santa Monica Auditorium in California on October 24. Brown was head-to-head with the British beat invasion in the shape of headliners The Rolling Stones. "I know James tells this story but it was so amusing to all of us, I've gotta say it," Bobby Byrd said. "Lesley Gore went and did her little pop thing, 'It's My Party' and something else. And when she came off, there's big drama. Her mother or manageress or somebody is calling out, 'Give her air! Don't bother her now, she's so tired'. For what? Standing and singing a couple of tunes? Now wait a minute, we was about to die and they're making a big commotion over Lesley Gore? That was so funny.

"We were somewhat concerned about the Motown acts because they were getting all the pop play and we weren't. So we were determined to outdo them. But our biggest worry was The Rolling Stones because we didn't know anything about them. Everybody had said, 'This British group is coming over and they're gonna tear y'all up'.

"We talked to 'em afterwards and they said, 'We ain't never had our butt kicked like that. Y'all kicked it to death'. But, you see, what they hadn't understood is that at the beginning we were just as frightened as they were 'cause we'd been told they were hot stuff and we hadn't seen them. We tried to see them rehearsing but they kept 'em locked up. So that really built the thing up. We had pleaded with the organisers to put us between a couple of the Motown acts, we knew we could deal with them. We didn't want to be nowhere near The Rolling Stones. James was as nervous as can be, he couldn't get along with nobody that day. He just wanted peace and quiet with us there, trying to figure out what we're gonna do to beat these unknown boys. But Ben [Bart] told us, 'Just do what you been doing. Don't change a thing'. And that's all we had to do as it turned out, our own show like we always did it.

"The Stones' big mistake was they came out of their dressing room to see our rehearsal. That did it. From then on they were jittery. Apparently they told Mick, like Ben told us, 'Just stick to your normal thing'. But when they followed us, Mick jumped out and started to try to do what James did. That was definitely a mistake, he hadn't got it. Still, they went over OK and we all ended up as friends.

"After the show, James and Ben tried to find out whether we could do anything with them, a tour or a couple of shows or something. It would have been good pop exposure for us. 'Cause after that show James had stardom, I'm talking about true stardom in his eyes. He wanted to do anything with anybody that had anything going. He figured he could beat 'em all. But the Stones' fella told Ben, and we were all standing there so I heard him, that it would be bad business for his boys. He said he had to pull them together to get their confidence back 'cause we had wrecked quite a bit of their thing."

As history relates, the Stones were soon back on track and Brown was soon back on King Records. He had a spruced up contract and a track which heralded a new epoch in African-American music.

CHAPTER 8

It is customary in biographies of important – and even the less important – figures in post-War popular music to interrupt the story every so often with a bulletin on the state of the marketplace in general. Who was doing well with what style, who were the comers, what was on the way out. In the case of James Brown, from 1964 for the next 10 years this exercise in compare-and-contrast is of use only to show how utterly different, how rhythmically and melodically of a different planet, his style had become in comparison to anything else in the wider world of popular Western music. Analysis of the pop charts is of little help. In the second half of 1964, when 'Out Of Sight' was hot, the American No. 1 spot on the charts was shared by pickled crooner and movie star Dean Martin, TV western star Lorne Greene, WASP teen heart-throb Bobby Vinton and British beat bands The Animals and Manfred Mann (with covers of black American originals). The dominant act were those apples of Berry Gordy's eye, The Supremes, who had three Number Ones in the last four months of the year (and a fourth in January, 1965) and they were clean and gone. On record, Gordy's mushrooming empire in Detroit gave the Sound of Young America a blackbeat backbeat. On stage, his tastes inclined towards voices and presentation that could slide from the Apollo to the Copacabana, the music business's first Buppy.

The appeal of James Brown's music had nothing to do with any of this. His career was further down the line and it was his instinctive ability to connect with and express the African-American experience that gave him strength in his market and kept the music virile. He was not making music to reach out to a wider audience. The wider audience was coming to his music. His lyrics during this period – before the more overt sloganeering and social commentary of the late Sixties and early Seventies – are rarely discussed, but in the mid-Sixties, at the time of his move to St. Albans, Queens, there is a clear switch from the language of love common to southern soul music to hipper, streetsier phrases that drive and give energy to the cadences of urban street talk. Witness the very title 'Out Of Sight'. It was the start of the period in which LeRoi Jones, later known as Amiri Baraka, would call Brown "our No. 1 black poet", countering Bob Dylan's assertion that Smokey Robinson's graceful metaphors and similes made him America's Number One poet. The gradual absorption of phrases like "out of sight" into the lexicon of white music and language was no new thing – it was hip to the tip and had been happening since the jazz age. But by the mid-Sixties the world had turned and jazz, rhythm & blues and rock'n'roll were being superseded by yet another seismic shift in music, this time powerfully informed by British musicians exporting their interpretations of African-American music back to the United States. James Brown, by rhythmically digging deeper into his roots and, in his lyrics, using the tougher street expressions from the northern urban world in which he now made his home, set soul's standard for matching hard rhythms and hip words. We'll hear them later in the chapter, most other writers and singers would not catch up until the early Seventies.

Brown's burst of relentless productivity in the mid-Sixties coincided with a hardening of attitudes over the long-simmering political and social issues in the United States. Unlike the smiling sounds created at Motown – even Smokey Robinson's bittersweet ballads left a little glow in the heart as well as a tear in the eye – or the grittier love songs cut at Stax and Atlantic, Brown's music caught and threw back at the African-American audience the energy and fire of its desire for change. By 1964, the "war" over segregation had been won. Well, on paper at least. President Lyndon Baines Johnson, in the White House since the assassination of President Kennedy, had signed the latest Civil Rights Act, drafted in 1957 and 1960 and designed to protect the rights of black men and women to vote. But in large areas of the South, few had registered and even fewer had been encouraged to do so.

Selma, the seat of Dallas county in Alabama 50 miles to the west of State capital Montgomery, had a population of 27,000 with a few hundred registered black voters. Administered by aggressive white county officials who put every obstacle in the way of voter registration, the town was focused on by Martin Luther King's Southern Christian Leadership Conference, and the Student Nonviolent Co-ordinating Committee, as the proving ground for the campaign for a federal voting rights statute. For once, the local police played it softly so King virtually forced them to arrest and jail him. National publicity quickly ensued. When a civil rights protester was shot and later died in nearby Marion, the leaders decided to march from Selma to Montgomery in tribute. On Sunday, March 7, 1965 the 600-strong procession wove through Selma, leaving it by the Edmund Pettus Bridge to cross the Alabama River. Waiting on the other side of the bridge were heavily armed state troopers, county sheriffs and other local police. When the marchers did not immediately turn back, they were gassed, shoved to the ground, clubbed and forced to flee from the hooves of the horses of the mounted police. The television pictures of the police's heavy-handed reaction, and Martin Luther King's call for a larger march in Selma, spurred the federal administration into pushing through the legislation the movement had sought. Two weeks after the first march had begun, the second got under way with considerable National Guard and FBI protection. Four months later the Voting Rights Act was signed.

Amid the celebrations there were reasons for cold, hard reflection. In February, 1965, Malcolm X, the former Black Muslim who had left Elijah Muhammad's group to propound his own radical ideas, had been assassinated on the orders of his former leader. In the summer of 1965, tension in the urban ghettos, which had been flaring up intermittently for two years – Birmingham, Alabama (1963), Harlem, NYC and other cities (1964) – erupted in a larger scale riot in the Los Angeles suburb of Watts. From this point, the focus of the black movements moved swiftly away from the rural areas of the South to the huge, stifling urban centres of the North, tinder boxes kindling the anger and frustration of the younger generations. It did not take much to ignite them.

James Brown's dispute with King and the consequent 11-month lay-off from new releases, with only old tracks dusted off from the shelves and put out as new by Nathan's company, meant that he had overhauled his band and style when he returned to the studio. The title 'Papa's Got A Brand New Bag' spoke nothing but the whole truth. It was cut in an hour at the Arthur Smith Studios in Charlotte, North Carolina in February, 1965. Maceo played the tenor and baritone sax solos, Melvin created a fresh syncopated spin on the drums and it was the first session for Jimmy Nolen, the inimitable guitarist who'd be fundamental to James Brown's sound for many years. The previous Christmas, Les Buie, who had taken over from Bobby Roach in 1961 and featured on 'Lost Someone', 'Out Of Sight' and the 'Apollo' album, among many other sides, quit. The band was in Los Angeles and their tenor saxophonist Eldee Williams recommended Nolen, who'd led the band he was in before joining Brown. Nolen had actually played behind Brown when the singer guested on a talent show headlined by Johnny Otis, the guitarist's boss at the time, at the Oasis Club in Los Angeles. There was no audition, Nolen was hired and standing on stage next to organist/md Nat Jones who was calling the changes. Nolen remembered it as "smooth, frightening, unforgettable". In an interview published in *Guitar Player* magazine shortly after his death in 1983, Nolen tried to describe the typical James Brown recording process. "Mostly all of his hit records he's thought up in his mind, as far as lyrics and a general idea of how he wants his rhythm to go ... You just get there and you strike a groove ... Sometimes you might work half a night on one tune until you get it the way you want it, and you record it, and most of the time it's a hit."

"During those times it was hard to really figure out exactly what the boss is doing or what he's thinking," Maceo said. "Sometimes he'll call and dictate a rhythm and say to the drummer 'You do this' and horn players, 'Do this', and bass player, 'Do that'. He would do it and it would all gel together. And we don't know whether we're going to make this into a song later or whether we're going to the studio tomorrow or what have you. But we knew most of the time, when he came up with an idea or a rhythm it clicked and it sounded good and it made us all feel good. And we knew that somewhere down the line he was going to have us in the studio and it would be another hit."

The version of 'New Bag', recorded after a long bus journey, was based on an ad-lib in one of his shows. In its original form, it was audibly slower than the record as released. Brown's confident, opening shout, "This is a hit!", was snipped off from the start of the track and the tape was speeded up before the disc was mastered. "When I recorded 'Papa's Got a Brand New Bag', that was a new formula to music; jazz licks with a gospel overtone, which has no musical concept where you can actually write it," Brown told Cliff White. "You just kind of take it and move it, because I can just take one chord and make a thousand variations from it. That's the difference with soul music and the blues, that's why I could never sing blues, because I don't want to sing something that kept me in one bag." While it's true that the roots of most of his horn players were steeped in jazz training and background, the emphasis of the music on 'New Bag' moved to rhythm. "His previous tunes were more or less a lot of blues," Jimmy Nolen said. "It was either slow or real, real fast. That was the first tune that he ever just dropped back with and set it in the pocket. He came up with that laid-back music, and that started a whole lot of different groups and musicians going in that vein."

The horn section either hits crisp and clean on the first beat of alternate bars or punctuates the first off-beat of each bar with a three-note curlicue. Maceo's solos, particularly the baritone, are dedicated totally to accentuating beats and adding syncopations to the rhythm. "I gotta get to where I can swing and I can't swing," Brown said before starting the original recording. "Lotta words in there …" Which is true enough but the lyrics are scarcely demanding, a mix of Sixties dance crazes – the Twist, Boomerang, Mashed Potatoes, the Jerk, the Fly, the Monkey and so on – recited urgently and connected by hip phrases – "ain't no drag", "dig the crazy scene", "ain't too hip", "dig the new breed". "I'm gone, so long," he sings at the end of the slower original version, "If you don't think I'm gone, follow me. Goodbye, I'm gone."

And gone he was, way up the pop charts when the six-minutes-plus Parts One-Two-And-Three take of 'Papa's Got A Brand New Bag' was edited down to just over two minutes, given some echo, cleaned-up, speeded-up and released on K5999 in July, 1965. There was nothing remotely like it on the market. If 'Out Of Sight' gave James Brown a toehold in the white market, 'New Bag' planted both feet squarely in it. Bobby Byrd remembers the racial mix of their audiences changed all over the States as the record crept up the charts. Brown eloquently describes his usually successful efforts to integrate the audiences, once he had outgrown the smaller club venues, at his shows in theatres, cinemas and larger auditoriums, even in the South, in his autobiography and it requires little expansion here. If the theatre owners or promoters wouldn't play ball, he would not go back to the venue or work with the promoter again. He was a big enough attraction to dictate terms now and he wasn't afraid to use that muscle to integrate audiences, if only for the few hours they were at his show.

With 'New Bag' – a No. 1 R&B hit and No. 8 pop hit – the sparring between Brown and Syd Nathan was at an end. The owner of King Records had been ill for some time and was convalescing down in Florida, which had been part of Brown's frustration before the row. Although Nathan had wanted a hands-on input into the running of the label, he no longer had the reserves of energy necessary to keep the business moving forward. After 'Bag', he left Brown to pick and choose his own releases. And despite the lack of new releases – or perhaps because of it – Brown's road work had increased in value. During the period his fee for a night's work had increased from $3,500 to $5,000, quite a price for 1965.

After picking up a gold disc for 'New Bag' in December, 1965, he won the only Germmy open to "soul" records in the National Academy of Recording Arts & Sciences (NARAS) Awards in January, 1965. His, perhaps, was the most "in touch" award of an organisation almost completely out of touch with contemporary popular music and which had given too much power to Nashville in order to get the country & western caucuses to join the fold. C&W artists and writers were given six categories, R&B had one. Roger Miller got 10 nominations; Bob Dylan, quite an influential figure at the time, got none; nor did The Beach Boys or The Rolling Stones, who had both dominated the American charts. And The Beatles, whose nominations included the album 'Help!' and the song 'Yesterday', won nothing. In the context of these astounding decisions, the victory of Brown's 'New Bag' over Wilson Pickett's 'In The Midnight Hour', Sam Cooke's 'Shake', 'My Girl' by The Temptations and 'Shotgun' by Junior Walker & The All Stars seemed like the result of a real competition. (By the end of 1966, Nashville-dominated NARAS had even infiltrated and won in the soul category. Although Brown was up for the award again with a superb soul ballad, Ray Charles won with 'Crying Time', his interpretation of a country song. Brown would not win another Grammy until 1986.)

'New Bag' was no accidental achievement – Brown's next release, out in November, 1965, did even better, topping the R&B charts again and rising to No. 3 on the pop lists, his highest-ever Hot 100 placing. 'I Got You (I Feel Good)' was a reworking of 1962's 'I Found You' with the leader taking over the vocal role from Yvonne Fair. He had refashioned the song during one of the Smash sessions in 1964. Now, with the 11-month new-release purdah shattered by 'New Bag', he went back into the studio in May, 1965, at Criteria in Miami, and cut the definitive version with his enlarged group, imposingly renamed The James Brown Orchestra. Again, the horn section's work in each verse is to share the load of driving the rhythm – they and bassist Bernard Odum play virtually the same lines – and elsewhere Odum, drummer Melvin Parker, guitarist Jimmy Nolen and the nine-piece horn section (three trumpets, four tenor saxes, alto sax and trombone) play as one instrument.

Between now and the summer of 1966, the Orchestra continued to evolve quickly as he hired experienced blues and jazz players such as trumpeter Waymond Reed, saxophonist Alfred "Pee Wee" Ellis and drummers Clyde Stubblefield and John "Jabo" Starks, who had been in Bobby "Blue" Bland's band from 1959 to 1966. His music demanded skill and discipline and he knew that good new players bring good new ideas. When a visionary musician is experiencing a burst of productivity he might, as Coleman Hawkins once advised Miles Davis, hire young musicians because they'll defer to what you tell them to play. The jazz trumpeter, though, took players who would add something of their own to his suggestions. This is the way that Brown's music developed in the second half of the Sixties. And what did these seasoned musicians think of Brown's band and music when they considered joining? Well, the money was good if not exactly generous and the work was regular and plentiful. The fines were perhaps a bit stiffer than you would find elsewhere and the routines? "Pee Wee" Ellis, a jazz player who scarcely knew who Brown was at the time, learnt them by standing at the side of the stage and watching the horn section work for the best part of a week. It was like watching a dancing drum and bugle corps, he memorably said. And, of course, he could use their skill and professionalism to realise his ideas. When it came to co-writing, members of the horn section have said that Brown's instructions were little more than grunts which they would "translate" into sounds that a listener could recognise as music. It was a style which gave the players a lot of latitude in how they interpreted his ideas.

As well as hiring new players, Brown expanded the show in January, 1966 with a new set of dancers from Lou Parks Parkettes to bring it up to a 40-strong troupe. In addition to the 16-piece band and dancers, the featured artists were Elsie "TV Mama" Mae, Bobby Byrd, James Crawford, a singer from Atlanta who James had produced for Mercury, and Vicki Anderson, a young singer from Houston, Texas, who would remain an integral part of the show for many years. Although still at the peak of his athletic powers on stage, he used the Revue format to conserve his energy ready for the nightly physically-draining finale.

In between the two big hit records, Smash had issued an instrumental version of 'Try Me' backed with a similar take on 'New Bag', which reached No. 34 on the R&B charts, No. 63 pop and, in the early part of 1966, King released a single which coupled live versions of 'Lost Someone' and 'I'll Go Crazy'. Both sides made the lower reaches of the Hot 100 but by February the band was back on the big money with the release of 'Ain't That A Groove', much more of a romp than the two, tightly-marshalled studio singles before it. 'Groove' was recorded in New York with his musical director Nat Jones and a studio band which included Bernard "Pretty" Purdie, and a rather too well-enunciating vocal group, The Jewels. When he sings "Hit me band!", they do but not as wildly as would his own musicians. The cats sound like they're reading in a way his Orchestra never did. But they swing.

While 'Groove' was scampering up the charts, Brown crossed the Atlantic to make his first European trip to England and France, a short tour for live shows and television appearances which will be dealt with in more detail in the next chapter. The trip gave rise to one extraordinary rumour, started by

Brown's own organisation, allegedly at Ben Bart's suggestion. Brown, went the whisper, was actually travelling to Europe to undergo a sex change operation and on his return would plight his troth to Bobby Byrd! Despite the amount of heavy pancake make-up Brown was wearing on stage at this time, the rumour was so absurd that it was (a) obviously a joke, (b) a deliberate plant to ensure he got some publicity while he was out of the country. The real reason the rumour was started, Brown said in his autobiography, was to make Bobby Byrd better known. Surely making a hit record with The Famous Flames would have been a simpler tactic and a lot less far-fetched or liable to get him a heap of unwanted adverse publicity? Even in the swingin' Sixties, there were some aspects of the sexual revolution that were less easily accepted than others. Actually, Byrd said, it was done to pull in more customers at the box office. But, again, (a) they were SRO wherever they went and (b) what kind of gawping customers were they hoping to attract?

On his return to America, manhood still intact and Byrd still as little or as well known as before, Brown played his first gig at New York's Madison Square Garden. Previously, his dates in the Five Boroughs had been at the Apollo in Harlem or at the Breevort which stood on the corner of Bedford Avenue and Fulton Street in Brooklyn. His first appearance outside these two black venues had been WMCA's Easter show at the Paramount Theater. But the MSG gig was a big step up in terms of prestige amongst his audience and peers and another significant move into the white market.

To anoint the date – March 20 – the magazine section of that day's New York *Sunday Herald Tribune* ran what was probably the first piece of any substance on him outside of the black press. Many of the experiences described have become familiar to journalists down the years. Writer Doon Arbus is kept waiting outside and inside his house – "part castle part hacienda" – on Linden Boulevard in St. Albans, Queens, the same house Reverend Al Sharpton hung around at as a kid of 15 and 16. Count Basie lived in St. Albans, too, but you would never mistake his and Brown's house. (A couple of years later, a piece written by UK soul enthusiast James Hamilton also gave a thumbnail sketch of the detached house on the Linden Boulevard corner plot, the initials JB set in the lawn now invisible from the road because of a seven-foot-high black fence. Hamilton described the house as small in size but flamboyant in appearance, built in a style that mixed Baronial Hall and Scottish castle with conical roof and turrets. By now a miniature moat, with rowing boat, had been added. A huge black awning stretched over the front of the house to warn-off sightseers.)

The sparsely furnished den reminded Arbus of a gymnasium, most of the furnishings were black. Many of the windows were one-way glass so that he could watch the world but it couldn't see him, and much of the furniture and carpets was covered in plastic "as if the whole house were being preserved against the hazards of being lived in, as if it were being prepared for a great future as a museum." She wore soft slippers to go into his bedroom for the first part of the interview. He wore his hair in curlers in preparation for that night's show in Virginia Beach, Virginia, and suggested she call him James which will be a big surprise to anyone who's done business with Mr. Brown since.

There were two Cadillacs and a Stingray in his garage and the writer persuaded him to let her fly down to that night's show despite his strong misgivings about a white woman travelling with a party of black men and women in the South. She was given a hotel room a short route march away from the suites of James Brown and entourage. In the interview, he is already seen as a great hope for the entire black population of the United States, an inspirational leader by deeds but one who felt the pressure and said he experienced a certain sense of loneliness.

Not at the Madison Square Garden concert the piece was promoting, though. One can imagine how pumped-up Brown would have been for the show. Mr. Dynamite, Soul Brother Number One, worked 15,000 fans into a frenzy and *Time, Newsweek* and the *New York Times* headlines screamed it loud. On the night of the concert, he drove back up Manhattan Island to the Apollo to pick up his second WWRL Soul Brother Award. He was presented with an NAACP Award by its figurehead, Roy Wilkins, in Washington. His tour continued, taking in one-nighters in Houston, Texas; Augusta, Georgia; Florence, Alabama; Milwaukee, Wisconsin; Pittsburgh and Philadelphia in Pennsylvania, and Cleveland, Ohio, before arriving back in the Big Apple for another season at the Apollo towards the end of May. In his autobiography, Brown says that when he collapsed at the end of one of these shows the theatre's doctor recommended an intravenous solution drip to rehydrate his body after performances because he was losing so much fluid and salts during the energetic stage act. The needle marks, Brown said, led some to believe mistakenly that he was taking drugs. He wasn't, yet. To reduce the likelihood of further illnesses brought on by exhaustion, Brown bought a nine-seater Lear jet in August to fly him between dates. Most of the rest of the entourage continued to use the tour bus.

Between the stage shows, he'd made the first of two appearances in 1966 on the *Ed Sullivan Show*, at the time one of the premier pop TV programmes in America. His brief, explosive performance – complete with cape act – totally overshadowed The Supremes, Sullivan favourites since their breakthrough in 1964. The presenter introduced his guest as the graduate of a tremendously hard upbringing "but always singing a song". If the précis of Brown's life reduced him to a humble stereotype, the energetic performance blew it to bits. After excerpts from 'Papa's Got A Brand New Bag' and 'I Feel Good', he swung into a stomping 'Ain't That A Groove' complete with his new dance invention, the 'New Breed Boogaloo' (actually this was a subliminal plug for 'New Breed', his latest instrumental on Smash), before cooling down to the ballad, 'It's A Man's World' and the finale of 'Please, Please, Please'. In the short, on-camera exchange of pleasantries after the performance, Sullivan clearly doesn't quite know what to make of Brown's show, though he must have been aware of its impact on the audience. To Brown, the exposure given by those two Sullivan Shows was invaluable and a rave review of the first in *Variety* signalled that the business establishment had taken note too.

While in Chicago in June, 1964, before the dispute with King had come fully to the boil, Brown had recorded a first version of a song he co-wrote with Betty Newsome, his girlfriend at the time. "Betty Newsome was my girlfriend," James told Cliff White, "and we were riding along in North Carolina and she said, 'You know, when I look around I see a man who has done a lot of things, a man who did this and did that.' And I said, 'You know, you're right.' And when she kept on laughing and talking, I started thinking. And riding along in the car, I wrote the song 'It's A Man's World' but I let her have a piece [of the publishing] because that is where the idea came from." When Brown's dispute with King had been settled, 'New Bag' kept the label solvent and 'I Got You (I Feel Good)' had raised his stock sky-high. He re-recorded 'Man's World' in New York with a band that mixed members of his road orchestra with session musicians like drummer Bernard Purdie working on a Sammy Lowe arrangement written quickly to the blueprint of the original acetate. By heightening the song's sense of drama and using the dynamics of the orchestra to the full, Lowe's arrangement turns a good ballad into a platform for a vocal of great impassioned belief. He also added a 'Man's, Man's' to the 'Man's World' [the film *It's A Mad, Mad, Mad, Mad World* was current] and would later also claim that his ruminations on the problems in the Middle East were an inspiration for the song. In the mid-Sixties, notwithstanding the rise of the Black Muslim movement, it seems unlikely that African-Americans were much exercised by the problems in the Middle East – there was enough happening on their own doorsteps. Clamike Music also questioned the provenance of 'It's A Man's, Man's, Man's World' when they contested copyright. The record, released in April, 1966 was a No. 1 R&B smash and peaked at No. 8 pop.

King continued to flood the market with Brown's music – in 1966 they put out 13 singles, including three Christmas singles, and four albums while Smash added to the stockpile with two instrumental singles and two albums. Even accepting that no-one was making music like this – compared, say, with the innumerable impersonations of Motown, Atlantic and Stax sounds available on smaller labels – the volume of vinyl seems excessive. His next hit after 'Man's World' signalled a willingness to address harder political issues. Recorded at the Arthur Smith Studios in Charlotte, North Carolina in August, 1966, 'Don't Be A Dropout' was something of a musical regression in order to make its point more widely accessible. A straight ahead, post-Motown four-four snare drum snap drives a poppier melody with the horn section martial in its precision, hints of Otis Redding's phrasing and a wink at Curtis Mayfield's arranging. The importance of the record lay in its lyrics. Stay in school kids, sings Brown, because "Without an education, you might as well be dead". He began to promote the Stay In School campaign during the 1966 West Coast tour in July and August. He made speeches in schools and at the Watts Center in Los Angeles, and after the single's release in September he received a citation from Vice President Hubert H. Humphrey for his work in encouraging children to complete their education. He still touches on this theme.

He was now genuinely All-American. Appearances with artists as deeply rooted in the entertainment establishment as Sammy Davis Jr. and Frank Sinatra were in the diary, alongside a note to attend the James Meredith Rally in Tougaloo, Mississippi along with 20,000 civil rights campaigners. Meredith was the rather reluctant hero who had enrolled at the University of Mississippi in 1962, with the assistance of the National Guard, breaking education segregation in the State. On June 5, 1966, he started the "March Against Fear" from Memphis to Jackson, Mississippi to persuade people to register to vote. On June 6, Meredith took a shotgun blast in the back. The act of cowardice had the immediate effect of temporarily uniting the major black organisations, such as the Student Nonviolent Co-ordinating Committee (SNCC), the Southern Christian Leadership Conference (SCLC) and Congress of Racial Equality (CORE), with a fierce sense of purpose to finish the march begun by Meredith. Stokeley Carmichael of the SNCC wanted the role of whites in the mass march to be played down. Roy Wilkins of the NAACP and National Urban League (NUL) leader Whitney Young wanted everyone involved and, when Martin Luther King would not support them, left the meeting. The march went on. Carmichael was arrested by State Troopers in Greenwood on June 17 for attempting to pitch a tent in the grounds of a black school. At the city's park that night,

3,000 turned out to protest and Carmichael, who had been released from custody moments before, addressed them. His acutely angry speech included the words "Black Power", a potent, meaningful, evocative slogan ever since. The march and its culmination was considered by many participants and observers to be the great turning point for a movement which had negotiated so many critical stages.

Brown, meanwhile, jetted to Cincinnati straight after the final "Meredith March Against Fear" rally to play a dance. He was up at New York's Waldorf Astoria to pick up the National Association of Radio Announcers' (NARA) Golden Mike Award as top R&B singer and by October was in the White House to meet Humphrey and set up a programme of speeches and campaigns with the politician on the Stay In School initiative. Later, he announced that he would set up a scholarship fund from the proceeds of the million-selling 'Drop Out' single.

In the same month, he returned to the *Ed Sullivan Show* and although Brown did not play 'Don't Be A Drop Out' – the show's organisers wouldn't let him, he alleged – there was mention of the Stay In School programme over a picture of Humphrey. Brown, wearing a snazzier spangly, sequined jacket with his bow tie, compared with the formal black suit and tie of his first appearance that year, led the way through a medley of 'I Feel Good' and a tremendously quick 'Papa's Got A Brand New Bag', into a spellbinding 'Prisoner Of Love', then 'Please, Please, Please' and 'Night Train' with some of the steps that the very young Michael Jackson will have gazed at and imitated. The Stay In School programme gave Brown a much higher political profile and the great and the good, eager to continue representing their voters in the Senate and the House of Representatives, found a useful new way to court the black vote – get the blessing of Soul Brother No. 1. Back at the Apollo in November, 1966, he was joined on stage by Nelson Rockefeller, New York's Republican governor, and the State's senator, Jacob Javitz, though he said in his autobiography Rockefeller's walk-on came as a complete surprise. He would have plenty of time to get accustomed to being used by the political establishment.

A surprise of a far nastier sort awaited. A concert at the Municipal Auditorium in Kansas City was halted after fans rioted. Police stopped the show, according to Lieutenant Maynard Brazeal, because obscene dances were allegedly being performed on stage. The band blamed the police for the fracas which followed. Before the show, Brown had followed his long-held practice of persuading the authorities to integrate the concert audience. The concert was going fine, nearing its climax when a black teenager jumped on stage and started dancing. According to Bobby Byrd, when a white kid did the same the police grabbed him and threw him off. His girl-friend jumped on stage and started hitting the police and mayhem ensued. The report in the *New York Times* – "'Soul' Concert Ends In A Teen-Age Riot" – speaks of 20 arrests, one woman stabbed, another cut by broken glass, several police with minor cuts and trouble inside the Auditorium last-ing no longer than 20 minutes while most of the 8,000 audience streamed out. Outside, the disturbances continued as "bands of youths continued to roam the downtown area" smashing shop windows, turning over refuse bas-kets and throwing missiles at passing cars. Sceptical that the police started the riot by provocative behaviour, the *New York Times* pointed out that "Mr Brown, as part of his act, wails, 'Do you love me, baby?' and invariably teen-age girls wail back: 'Yeah, baby, yeah.' At one point in his act, the girls are encouraged to rush onto the stage and rip his jacket off. They invariably do." Another version of events at the time suggested that the riot was sparked by a locally organised and judged dance competition held during the intermission in the show. Although Brown had not even appeared on stage when the mêlée began, he was blamed and banned from further gigs in the Kansas City area. In his autobiography, he gives "credit" for the riot to the gyrations of his women dancers whose exposed bodily hair inflamed the passions of impressionable young men in the audience.

Nothing could take the gloss off the leaps and bounds Brown had made in the years 1964–66 as a bandleader and singer, as a businessman and as a spokesman who had the potential to achieve something positive in social issues for African-Americans.

CHAPTER 9

Time to take a break from James Brown's relentless drive for megastardom in the USA and examine his emergence as an international artist. "England was a hard market for me to crack," James said. "I came over here and we did a show called *Ready Steady Go!*" Earlier, we touched on the minimal impact he had made outside the United States up to 1965. As mentioned in an earlier chapter, 'Out of Sight' had been favourably reviewed by a very few music journalists in October, 1964. Before that, *New Record Mirror* had run a profile of the singer on October 26, 1963 in their series The Great Unknowns. Brown was Unknown No. 16. Not as inimitable as Bo Diddley, writer Jes Pender began, or as insistent as Jimmy Reed, as arresting as John Lee Hooker, as raucous as Ray Charles "but he is, without doubt, the wildest of our time". Mention is made of the preamble to Great Unknown No. 16 to illustrate the touchstones against which he was being measured by music writers on the eastern side of the Atlantic. By then he'd had a few UK releases – 'Please, Please, Please' was the first, then a four year gap until Parlophone picked up 'Think'. 'This Old Heart' was leased by Fontana for the UK, a gap then until 'Shout & Shimmy'. London took on the King catalogue and put out 'Try Me' and 'These Foolish Things' and were deciding on a release date for the 'Live At The Apollo' album. Pender thought it a shame that the most exciting artist in the USA at the time "is ignored even by most of the R&B enthusiasts" in Britain. His appeal was not limited to specialists as was that of Reed or Howlin' Wolf. "Perhaps, as in the case of Ray Charles, we will catch on when his singing and crooning transcend his squawking and crying." Hmm.

Brown's international assault did not begin in earnest until the so-called British invasion of the USA was in full spate. The transatlantic influx of British beat groups in the mid-Sixties, was matched in the United Kingdom, and Europe, by the biggest invasion of American performers since the Second World War. Instead of GIs, the shipment this time was singers and musicians. After years of being starved of the Real Thing, Britain, and London in particular, was inundated with American rock-'n'rollers, rhythm'n'blues performers and soul stars.

The turnaround was a direct result of the British Musicians' Union tit-for-tat policy, which stipulated that foreign musicians could only play in Great Britain if their country of origin gave work to a British musician for roughly the same amount of time. This was meant to protect the jobs of musicians in orchestras and dance bands. In popular music terms, it meant that if you send us your prime beef we'll send you our offal. For many post-War years – the late Forties, the entire Fifties and the early Sixties to name but a few – America sensibly reasoned that they could well do without the sort of popular music being produced by the British Isles. Even at this distance we can imagine that a request along the lines of "Give us Elvis Presley, Little Richard, Jerry Lee Lewis, Fats Domino, Buddy Holly and Ray Charles and you can have Tommy Steele, Adam Faith, Cliff Richard and, um, er, Russ Conway and Eden Kane" will have elicited one of two answers. "No" or "Who?" And so while the American industry sensibly reasoned that it could live happily without the majority of pale imitators, stiff-necks and sadsacks that made up the vast majority of the British pop industry *circa* 1954–62, it also meant that Britain rarely got to see the genuine American originators. Some blues and jazz acts brought succour, but these were isolated spots of rain in the parched, cultural desert.

However, the success of The Beatles and The Rolling Stones in opening up the American charts and market for young British acts changed all that. And Britain still managed to sell them tat! We got the Stax/Volt packages with Otis Redding and the entire Memphis clan and we got Motown tours featuring the pride of Detroit such as The Temptations, The Miracles with Smokey Robinson, The Four Tops, Martha & The Vandellas, The Supremes. They got Herman's Hermits, Freddie & The Dreamers, Billy J. Kramer & The Dakotas and The Dave Clark Five! Strange thing was, they seemed to like them. Anyway, the music scene in Sixties Britain was primed to hear the real thing. When they got access to the music press, most of the UK acts – notably The Beatles and The Rolling Stones – willingly gave credit to the black American singers and groups who'd provided inspiration and much good material to cover and learn from. In terms of hearing the records, the ultra-establishment music policy of the BBC largely favoured indigenous UK product but Radio Luxembourg and American Forces radio had specialist programmes which played rhythm'n'blues and burgeoning soul music. The jazz club scene in London had found profit in running blues and rhythm'n'blues nights which led to specialist rhythm'n'blues and soul clubs opening up in the capital and around the country. In continental Europe, restrictions on visiting musicians had been less rigorous and Paris had long been a haven for disaffected African-American jazz musicians, so the openness to developments in black music was already established.

When The Rolling Stones returned from the USA having recorded the *T.A.M.I.* show, they embarked on a brief crusade to get James Brown's name more widely known. Mick Jagger, being the one the UK Press wanted to talk to, did most of the unpaid promotional work. He told *Record Mirror* that "When we heard that we were topping the bill, going on just before James, we couldn't believe it. We tried for two days to get it changed round but it was no good. I mean, you can't follow an act like that." Jagger and Keith Richards had been to the Apollo previously and been hauled on stage to take a bow, Richards said. Bill Wyman described the act, accurately and in some detail. "Halfway through he does a heart-failure bit, and falls to his knees. The three guys who sing behind him put a drape over him and move him slowly to the edge of the stage. Suddenly, he throws the drape away and raves into the mike, and the audience go completely berserk. He sometimes does this four or five times in one show." Wyman said you could put Jerry Lee Lewis, Little Richard, Chuck Berry and Bo Diddley on one side of the stage and Brown on the other and you'd only have eyes for JB. They met him again in Louisville, Kentucky, Wyman said, and the American had suggested a tour together. "We told him he could keep that idea." Too much pressure.

There was also much interest in the UK press about Brown's non-performing entourage – the hairdresser, the valet, a tailor, a road manager, a driver for the £14,000 luxury coach, a personal driver, a bodyguard, a publicist, a secretary – and his wardrobe, information doubtless supplied by that publicist. In any 30-day period, Brown gets through 120 shirts. "Cotton Picker Brown Drives A Cadillac Now", *Melody Maker* had reported deliriously in October, 1965.

The majority of the British writers likened Brown's massive popularity in the USA with the all-markets crossover achieved a few years earlier by Ray Charles. Guy Stevens, who later reactivated the Sue label in the UK and re-released 'Night Train' when Brown visited in 1966, (he would go on to produce Mott The Hoople and other UK bands for Island Records), was particularly fulsome in the pages of the *Record Mirror* (December 9, 1964) predicting that 'Night Train' would do for JB what 'Hit The Road Jack' had done for Charles. He was not quite on the money. Then again, almost all of the bands which played on the mid-Sixties rhythm'n'blues and soul scene and had a horn section played 'Night Train' so it received a very widespread airing, if not always in versions which Brown would have approved of or, indeed, recognised.

Well, the unpaid publicity machine worked, to an extent. Promoter Arthur Howes wanted Brown to tour and showed a film of his performances to a group of managers from key Top Rank theatres around the country. They declined to have such a wild and potentially inflammatory performer in their halls. In the end, Brown was booked to appear on *Ready Steady Go!*, Independent Television's Friday night pop show. The whole of the March 11, 1966 programme was to be devoted to his show and he would play his first UK dates for Howes immediately after in north east London at the Walthamstow Granada on March 12, and in the north east at the Newcastle City Hall the following day before flying to Paris to play at the Olympia on March 15. (The Newcastle date was cancelled and replaced by one in Brixton, south London.) He was bringing a smaller than usual band – eight musicians and two singers – but the plane tickets were still costing £2,500.

In the run-up to the dates, journalists who had not seen Mr. Dynamite perform, grappled with the Brown phenomenon much as they had been struggling to convey his act. *New Musical Express* had reports from both sides of the Atlantic – in the UK John Wells watched a promotional film of four songs from "Blues shouter James Brown" and predicted "one of the greatest sensations of the year" when he eventually appeared. From the USA, the paper's correspondent, Ann Moses, who despite an uncomfortable habit of calling everyone "boy", was entranced by "James Brown. Such a plain name – they call him Mr. Dynamite". Like all of the other writers, she was transfixed by his movement and dancing – gyrating as though electrically charged, feet slithering as though on ice. Interviewing him in Hollywood, she got the barest minimum of biographical colour and compared his original poverty to the 500 suits and hundreds of pairs of boots he now owned, all designed by himself, as the profilers of the time repeatedly pointed out. She asked him what he felt like when he performed. "It's the only time I'm completely free and I feel very thankful." Roughly 20 years later, Michael Jackson, using different words, would say similar things about the control, comfort and safety of being on stage. But, Brown added, "I wanted to show that any man, regardless of race, colour or creed could be something if he tried." Took guts, he said. "Ten years ago I created a monster and it turned out to be a good monster." What made up the monster, Moses asked? His answer was unexpected in its priorities. First, unusual hair. Next, shoes and clothes which are different. Then, the singing, that's different too. He works hard, he said, and he's a businessman. Great music but unusual priorities. This was going to be a voyage of discovery indeed.

By the spring of 1966 and Brown had enjoyed two Top 30 British hits – 'Papa's Got A Brand New Bag' and 'I Got You (I Feel Good)', on the Pye International label – and he was a huge, huge favourite among Mods, the teenage movement of the Sixties which made rhythm'n'blues and soul, blue beat and ska its soundtrack. But he also had a sizeable following among the older, rock'n'roll fraternity. The live shows blew everyone away except Cathy McGowan, the young co-presenter of *Ready Steady Go! (RSG)*, and the somewhat narcissistic self-appointed "in-crowd" attracted to the Rediffusion studios. "The show was awful," she told the BBC's *The Story of Pop* almost a decade after the event, indignation and disbelief still resonant in her words. "He just couldn't produce the sound. It was terrible." She went on in like manner, adding that the only reason that he'd been given the show was the hysteria built up by the Mods. Everyone had been writing in demanding that he appear, everyone the producers spoke to wanted him. "When he actually did his numbers, the Mods didn't like him … when they actually came there to the studio to do it live … something went."

Other contemporary accounts disagree with this verdict, though all admit the live show was far better than the TV version – it was ever thus – and one doubts that the *RSG* engineers had ever had to cope with a sound similar to Brown's band, even though he'd brought over a smaller orchestra. Second, the majority of British teenagers were actually far more attuned to the less aggressive Motown Sound, which had its own *RSG* Special a year earlier, than to the tougher, brassy sound and wildly demonstrative performance of James Brown. "That was a hot show," Brown recalled, "and they didn't put me on camera but they were shooting me on music." The Beatles, The Animals and The Kinks were in the audience, which might possibly have distracted the young groovers. "They were watching me perform and they couldn't believe it because we got the people in a frenzy. The next day I got a bad write-up, they said it was a bloody show because they could never see the people act that way."

This was reference to the typically tabloid news story the following day in the *Daily Mirror*, "Pop Singer's Mock 'Fits' Shock Viewers" which reported "scores of viewers" phoning in to complain about his "disgusting behaviour" in feigning a series of heart attacks and recovering in a frenzy each time. "I realise that the English people are reserved and may be astounded by James's act," Ben Bart told the *Mirror*. "It is a completely new act, and I suppose you can't please everybody with it. But James had had 32 hit records in succession and a million sales are not unusual for him."

George Melly, a blues and jazz singer and art collector and expert who does a nice line in Bessie Smith, also went to see the *RSG* recording and wrote about it in the *Observer* and, without the benefit of hindsight other than a few days' reflection, was as sniffy as McGowan, though in more lucid phrases. At their essence, his objections were to the use of gospel phrasing in a blues format. "The whole gospel spirit is against the wry poetic realism of the blues." But he is very warm about Brown's energy and application to the stage show and was inclined to lay the blame for its tepid reception in the studio at a door other than Brown's. Namely, the crass attempts to warm-up the crowd before transmission by haranguing them, which in those days of comparative TV innocence would be as likely to get a young audience's collective back up rather than encourage its wholehearted participation. Grinning response to cue cards was not yet the norm. Lastly, Melly laments Brown's influence on The Rolling Stones, formerly blues enthusiasts now seduced by the siren soul.

Pop writer Peter Jones was at the reception organised to introduce Brown to the British Press. Due to start at 6pm and end at 7.30pm, Brown arrived at 7.20pm having been delayed by his hair dryer, which needed an adapter. Jones interviewed Ben Bart instead. "He has a truly magnetic personality," Bart offered, "There is nobody quite like him in the States. The real honest truth is that he likes his work, feels lost when he's not making contact with an audience."

They'd delayed visiting Britain because the singer needed a couple of more UK hits but the pressure from British fans had been enormous. In the States, he was earning between $15,000 and $20,000 a day, Bart claimed, or up to $125,000. "So taking pure money, you can be sure that we're dropping a lot of money but we figured we owed it to the British fans. The people who buy the records deserve the chance to see James working."

As a jobbing drummer at the time I'd been keen to see Brown but found myself working that evening – at the Carousel Club in Farnborough if frail memory serves – but Bill Millar, respected author of fine books on The Coasters and The Drifters, inveterate diary-keeper and letter-writer saw the show from a knowledgeable fan's perspective:

Walthamstow Granada, March 12, 1966. Two houses, 6.30pm and 9pm. The queue between houses stretched for ever. The James Brown Band opened both halves – blue silk suits, fancy hair styles, The Famous Flames and bandleader Nat Jones in black. Introduced in the Apollo style, Brown strode on, short, with a huge shock of hair – maybe he was right about his priorities! – dapper in a gleaming brown suit with pink and blue lining. The bright colours of the show made an unexpected spectacle.

The sound was a constant barrage but the hits were recognisable and his version of a 'Prisoner of Love' all but stopped the show dead. Europe, let alone London or Britain, had seen nothing like it. After impassioned verses and distraught choruses, many delivered after he'd dropped to his knees in emotional anguish, Brown stood up one more time and left the microphone, slowly wandering the stage from wing to wing, repeating pleading screams of 'Prisoner of Love' and variations thereon. He was answered, unamplified, call-and-response style by The Famous Flames, "Prisonerrrrr-oflove!". Soul Gospel had come to downtown Walthamstow. The audience was absolutely silent during this. Spellbound. Brown's dancing, too, had them agog as he did the splits and dips and zoomed across the stage on one leg as though on skates. A taste of the mock heart seizures and the Great Cape & Collapse Routine had been picked up from the TV and the tabloids (the *Daily Mirror*'s disapproval ensured that both shows were sold out). As another, and final, tradition, he flung a set of cuff-links and a tie into the audience and shook hands with some of the crowd at the front. By then they were crushed up against the stage for behind them all was sweating, seething pandemonium. The rest of the audience, dancing in the aisles, clambering wildly over the seats to get to the front, had gone barmy. There was sporadic fighting between the theatre's bouncers, the police and the audience until Brown returned to play on, well past the curfew of the theatre's licence.

Keyboard player Pete Wingfield, later of The Olympic Runners, a solo hitmaker with 'Eighteen With A Bullet' and noted UK session musician and producer, was also at the gig and wrote about it with a friend in a fanzine called *Soul*, then in its third issue. He and his chum got quite poetic, as was the crusading way of fanzines. That was the effect James Brown had on folk as they strained for expression to convey his impact. "It hardly seemed possible that his diminutive figure, clad in a distinctively styled dark red suit and 'dancing shoes', could contain such a vast soul; perhaps it couldn't, for his soul burst out of him in great clouds reacting wildly with the audience; the result 'pure dynamite'. The whole audience leaping to their feet, raving, screaming and clapping. One was hardly conscious of jumping over several rows of seats into the aisle." The writers were "left with the rather depressing feeling" that they "cannot hope to see anything better" in their lives. The Brown show went on to Paris where cerebral reviewers compared his orchestra to those of Count Basie, Jimmie Lunceford and Cab Calloway but without soloists of the calibre of Lester Young.

Back in the USA, Brown had a chance to give *R'N'B World* his own version of events in Europe. In England, he said, "Nobody knew me. I wanted to leave." As history tells us, he didn't. "During the show, we went non-stop. They might not dig me at first, but they have to dig me eventually ... when we hit the stage, we started cooking. When we finished the kids rushed the stage. The Bobbies couldn't stop them." [Interesting how he apparently picked up this quaint terminology for the local police.]

In Paris, they were impressed with the fact he did a whole show so energetically. "They said I was Superman ... I'd try French, a few words, and they'd see that I was trying. And when I'd shake their hands, I couldn't get loose."

CHAPTER 10

By the end of 1966, Brown, crowned as an international star on the strength of one highly successful European tour, was emerging as a spokesperson and a role-model at home. The political interest in his hit 'Don't Be A Dropout' started to raise his profile and his image as a ferociously determined and hard-working man who had succeeded against ludicrous odds was the epitome of the American Dream. And he had plans to expand his business interests. His music, too, continued to evolve at breakneck speed although his instinctive, unique take on music which was forging a new style was not quite so readily recognised as something apart from the ordinary soul stream. Although his music could never be as viscerally exciting on record as it was on stage, the energy generated by the swing-like drive of 'Ain't That A Groove' or the sheer straight ahead power of 'Money Won't Change You' or the syncopated boogaloo groove of 'Bring It Up', which was a compendium of JB and other soul licks of the time, were in a new bag, to borrow a phrase, moving along significantly different lines from other popular music. Its integral energy, its fire, urgency and passion was an accurate reflection in music of the state of hearts and minds of much of the black community as the civil rights movement continued its struggle, and life in the ghettos simmered on.

The four songs mentioned above were all co-written by Brown and his most flamboyant bandleader, Nat Jones. In Chapter Seven, Bobby Byrd thought Jones's mistake was to think he could get tight with his employer. A revealing cameo in Doon Arbus's piece on James Brown in the *New York Herald Tribune*, found Jones called into the boss's dressing room after the show in Virginia Beach to take instruction on a new intro to 'I Got You'. Do it his way, James said, and it would have real Soul. But what is Soul, Jones asked. [It was always spelt with a capital "S" in those days.] You know, shouted James, it's feeling. "Yeah, yeah, I know," Jones replied. "But remember that time we was talkin'? You and me? About Soul? About what it really is?" Jones would say no more in Arbus's presence. Brown said much as he likes Arbus, he had to agree with his bandleader. The Meaning of Soul was too deep to discuss in front of an outsider. Jones wanted private time with the boss. (Of course, 30 years later the exchange reads like a tremendous put-on, but in 1966 the word Soul signified rather more than the label a marketing man has hung on style of music. As well as a certain type of emotionally committed singing, it was the spiritual heart of a people, something like "the essence of blackness".)

After riding the roller-coaster from 'Out Of Sight' to 'Bring It Up', Nat Jones quit the band at the start of 1967 on the first night of a season at the Latin Casino in Cherry Hill, New Jersey. The dates introduced Brown – successfully, he broke attendance records – to the swisher end of the American nightclub scene. Shows were recorded at the venue over a weekend, and then edited, pumped up with echo, released on King in May, 1967 as the 'Live At The Garden' album. The daub on the sleeve was meant to represent Brown at the Madison Square Garden, which made the live album a touch misleading as well as fairly tame by comparison with the Apollo albums. Jones returned briefly in late 1970 to record the 'Hey, America' album but to all intents and purposes his swift exit before the Latin Casino recording marked the end of the road between Brown and his most demonstrative md. The singer called all the shots and left his bandleader little room for manoeuvre, but Jones had helped to fashion a fearsomely tight and well-drilled unit, able to blow up a powerful storm and snap into a new groove at the slightest signal or call from Mr. Dynamite.

There were so many good players in the band that choosing a replacement was not hard. What was required was an evenness of temper, something which his next three bandleaders all shared. Alfred "Pee Wee" Ellis, a skilled, serious jazz tenor saxophonist from Rochester, New York, had – indeed, still has – a calm, equable demeanour. In the context of Brown's music, Ellis was much better able to interpret his wishes carefully and pass them on in a form that musicians could understand quickly and clearly. He had joined the band in February, 1966 and was already doing the arrangements for Jones. Just before recording another take of a tune called 'Let Yourself Go' after hours at the Latin Casino, Brown told drummer John "Jabo" Starks, who had taken over from Clyde Stubblefield after a couple of run-throughs, to hit the snare whenever the singer grunted "uh uh". The accents shift the physical emphasis of the music from feet to the hips and the interplay of Jimmy Nolen's chicken-scratch guitar chording and the horn section's interjections as the trumpet and saxes shadow box further developed the style started on 'Papa's Got A Brand New Bag'. It's a final building block in the house Brown built called Funk. Immediately, every soul singer and his drummer got their "uh uh" in synch and within a year, maybe two, the device was reduced to the level of Genuine Soul Cliché, right alongside crude impersonations of Otis Redding's "gotta-gotta" and Wilson Pickett's scream, Brown would experience this sort of imitation to a far more damaging degree, professionally, in the Seventies.

'Let Yourself Go' and, before it, 'Bring It Up' kept Brown and King Records in the R&B Top 10 and pop Top 50 in the early part of the year, but, the odd reissue apart, the Smash deal ended that year after two more singles and albums. Although he had genuinely wanted to leave King and would have been delighted if any one of several attempts by major labels to buy out Nathan had succeeded, the link with Smash had won him a better deal and more autonomy with King. His production of other artists continued in number though few of them charted. But in early 1967 he released a sparky duet with Vicki Anderson, a remake of 'Think', which created a good buzz.

The demands on Brown's time were now many and his schedule was frantic. A brief resumé should give some idea of its pace, bearing in mind that he was still maintaining a pounding live date itinerary as well as recording his own material and producing others at every opportunity. In January, 1967 he was appointed co-chair, with world heavyweight champion Muhammad Ali, of Hubert Humphrey's Youth Opportunity Programme, reporting directly to the Vice President. As part of the programme, he announced an initiative with the National Association of Radio Announcers to distribute *Don't Be A Dropout* campaign badges and literature to dee-jays and young people nationally. By March, he was negotiating a multi-million dollar deal with Ali. The plan was for Brown to be on the undercard of Ali's next fight. The singer wasn't preparing to pull on the gloves again, he was fit but not that fit, instead his show would replace other bouts as prelude to the main fight at future matches of the heavyweight champion of the world. (This deal, and the Youth Opportunity Programme, were quashed when Muhammad Ali refused to be drafted in the US Forces, was arrested and stripped of his heavyweight title.)

Since the fracas in Kansas City, his live shows had been signposted by State and County authorities all over America as potential flashpoints. To add to the continuing racial unrest, which was likely to explode at any time, the protests against the war in Vietnam were accelerating. Officials at all levels were getting, and had reason to be, twitchy. A date at the Baltimore Civic Center was cancelled on the orders of the city fathers, fearing a repetition of the trouble in KC, and of a riot which blew up after a previous James Brown show in the city. Ben Bart hired a huge tent in which to stage the gig at a fairground outside the city but the county authorities followed the city's lead and slapped a ban on Brown. Yet way down south he played the first-ever integrated dance in Shreveport, Louisiana and it went off without a hitch. In May, 11,500 turned out at Madison Square Garden to see Brown, with new singer Marva Whitney making her début, Joe Cuba's sextet and gospel group The Mighty Clouds of Joy. When he topped the bill there 14 months earlier, nervous advisers had insisted that he add white acts like Len Barry, Lou Christie and The Shangri-Las to the bill. Now, he grossed $55,000. It was a different act, if not quite another new bag.

Brown was now 34 – the Apollo had staged a special birthday party for him on May 3 – and fixing to admit to the ageing process. He had said he wanted to take a break in the early part of the year. To the James Brown fan base, this bulletin became an announcement of retirement, one of several during these years. The offices of James Brown Productions at King in Cincinnati were inundated with letters of protest and pleas to reconsider, baby. His diary for April stayed pretty empty. The occasional vacation did not lessen the demands of the physically punishing live show, which drained so much energy and fluid from his body that he still needed that intravenous top-up. The non-stop barrage of eye-bulging dance moves and lung-bursting singing remained. Had to stop. He'd been doing over 300 shows a year for the best part of a decade-and-a-half. It was time not to slow down but to spread the load. He restructured the show into three separate vocal shifts to give himself clearer, longer breaks from the action (previously, he would join the band as an instrumentalist for the first half and then sing for the entire second half). Moreover, by adding a regular touring string section of three, unheard of in pop music, let alone rhythm'n'blues or soul, and a segment in which he sang interpretations of less physically demanding "standards" he was able to turn the heat down. (In the "old" shows, he could by no stretch of the imagination cruise through intense ballads such as the intense 'Prisoner of Love' or 'Lost Someone' or 'I Don't Mind'.)

He previewed the new style on NBC TV's *Johnny Carson Show* on June 8, singing 'That's Life' and 'Kansas City'. (A version of 'Kansas City', the Jerry Leiber and Mike Stoller blues standard, had been a hit for Brown that spring.) He taught Carson a few James Brown steps and danced off to open at the Apollo the next night. During that stint at the legendary theatre, he was presented with a plaque for selling his millionth ticket there. The live show was tailored for quick adaptation to the Apollo or a venue like the Flamingo Hotel in Las Vegas, where he played a three-week season in July, outdrawing Woody Allen, Jimmy Durante and Johnny Carson. Then he took the Revue on a big swing along the West Coast. Well aware that not all of his fans could afford the big ticket prices he was now able to charge, he stipulated a 99 cents ticket price at outdoor concerts that summer so that "poor kids and drop-outs can catch the shows that they usually cannot afford, and get the message".

The move to embrace Las Vegas was at one with the aspirations Berry Gordy had for his top acts at Motown. It was the way in which African-American entertainers comparable to Brown – Sam Cooke, Ray Charles – had progressed but, in retrospect, it was ill-advised and short-sighted. The older audience in Las Vegas was not likely to provide him with a long-term fan base. The soul artists at Atlantic and Stax, by contrast, were being fêted in earnest by the young, white rock audience. Otis Redding's show-stopping reception at the Monterey Pop Festival in 1967 brought him quick, massive acceptance by white rock fans in the United States, and appearances in Europe on the Stax/Volt Revue soon after helped him shoulder aside Brown as the most popular soul singer in the UK. Which seemed totally at odds with what was in the new grooves because Brown's music was now taking its last big stride into this thing called Funk, 'Cold Sweat'.

Groove on an arrangement of 'I Don't Care', faster than the ballad version recorded in 1962, and pulled from the vaults by King in 1964 during the dispute with Brown and Mercury, and stay on it. Have "Pee Wee" Ellis write horn parts – he thought them up wandering around a music store in Cincinnati, he said – and groove some more. The rhythm section emphasises hard on the first beat of alternate bars. At that one moment, every eight beats, guitarists Jimmy Nolen and Alphonso "Country" Kellum, bassist Bernard Odum and drummer Clyde Stubblefield snap together and then fly off to do their own do on the syncopated rhythmic boogaloo. It was finished in two takes at the King Studios in Cincinnati. Not for the first time, Brown had changed the ground rules. A new rhythmic feel, jazzier, but the horn parts are minimalist. Brown's singing, too, was freer, building gradually to a screaming climax after the solos. These give an insight into how his music was being put together in the studio and rehearsals at this time. They'd get the groove going and see where it led. "Maceo, c'mon now, brother, put it where it's at now," he sang-spoke introducing Parker's sax solo and interjected "uhs" and exhortations throughout the break. "Let's give the drummer some," he memorably yelled, before Stubblefield's loose but funky breaks.

Maceo had come back from the Army. "Ironically, I was stationed in James's home town, Augusta, Georgia. 'Papa' was really hot at the time and I was somewhat of a star in the Service because everybody knew that I was a saxophonist on the record. I stayed in two years and went right back with the group in 1967," Maceo said. He was to leave and rejoin a few times after that. "He gives you room to go out and try certain things, but he's always waiting with open arms if it fails for you to come back. It's almost like you always have a home. Go out and try little things and all that of that, but if it does not work out, come on back. You can't beat that."

'Cold Sweat' was at No. 1 on the R&B charts for three weeks in the summer of 1967 and on the R&B lists for 16 weeks, his biggest record since 'Papa's Got A Brand New Bag'. It reached No. 7 on the US pop charts. It's a hard, solid sound, upbeat and frantic but totally in control and aware. "I think what he tries to relate first of all is a happy type of feeling," Maceo explained. "Forget your troubles, come on, get happy sort of thing which I suppose can be said about most music. Most of his recordings are fast, which is going to create some type of 'let's get up and dance' type of feel. When you get up and dance, you have a tendency to forget your troubles somewhat. And love, I would have to say he would want to project a certain amount of love in his songs, in his music. Togetherness and things of that sort."

His next singles picked up and ran hard with the advances of 'Cold Sweat'. Back down in Atlanta, Georgia, he cut 'Get It Together', almost 10 minutes of blisteringly paced, intricately meshed new funk. Advising one and all to get their acts together like he and his band's got its act together, Brown calls for an instrumental line from each of the main players, conducts them through accented beats a-go-go, exhorts them not to play so much, to think 'Cold Sweat' (i.e. cut the music to the minimum). "If you hear any noise," he says halfway through, "it's just me and the boys," a line around which George Clinton would some years later build the song 'Mothership Connection'. By the end, Brown's asking the studio engineer if he's got enough, fade the tape, he's outta here. Back in Cincinnati at the end of October, he recorded 'I Can't Stand Myself (When You Touch Me)' with The Dapps, a white band including bassist Tim Drummond, who would later go on the road as the first white musician used by Brown on stage, and guitarist "Fat" Eddie Setser. And, yes, you can tell the difference. The rhythm is jerkier, doesn't have the flow of his regular band. Nor would you expect it to. These guys had not honed their JB chops for months solid with the leader. All the same, the record, slowed down from the original studio take, was a No. 4 R&B hit on a double A-side smash with the blistering 'There Was A Time', which went one place higher. The record's sales were helped by a blitz of national small screen appearances in the early months of 1968, on *Hollywood Palace, Happening '68* and *American Bandstand* and syndicated shows such as *Woody Woodbury* and *Merv Griffin*.

Shortly before he left for his second, and much more extensive European tour in September, 1967, Brown was presented with a citation from the President's Youth Council Opportunity programme for his part in securing over 20,000 jobs for ghetto youngsters that summer. He took his complete 42-strong entourage for the transatlantic trip in late September and October, took in Berlin and Frankfurt in Germany, on to Copenhagen, Denmark and finally on to the Paris Olympia in France. Whatever the language, the review was a rave. On his return to the States he went back home – or to the Apollo, as it's also known – and broke house records. Again. In November, he used the pages of *Jet* magazine to voice his anger that he could not get permission to fly to Vietnam and play for the troops. Three weeks later he announced permission had been granted for a trip in the "early spring". However, because of an escalation in military activity in the spring of 1968, the trip had to be postponed until the summer.

Nineteen-sixty-seven ended in terrible tragedy, a harbinger of many more grievous losses the following year. Otis Redding, ostensibly a competitor, was killed in a plane crash on December 10. In strict business terms Redding was a rival, but he was a sweet man for whom no-one had a bad word and the singers had shared a common, tough upbringing in Georgia. A pall-bearer at Redding's funeral in Macon, James was mobbed by fans who tore off his coat. Police brandishing night sticks had to rescue him. On his way to the private burial rites which were held at the Redding ranch, Brown was stopped at the gates. A guard, under orders to admit no-one unless they had an invitation, listened to the singer's explanation as to why he'd lost or mislaid his. "Who's James Brown?" the lackey cried. "Can't get in!" Brown turned around and drove back to Macon.

The following year was an extreme confusion of wild success on record, solid and profound expansion of business interests, tragic losses, and triumphant exhibitions of the great power he was able exert over a large proportion of the African-American population. The sort of mixed social and political messages that typified both his unease as a spokesman for his people and the opportunism of the white career politicians who came sniffing round this very obvious and potent vote-catcher.

On record, 1968 could scarcely have started better. After the double-sided triumph with 'I Can't Stand Myself' and 'There Was A Time', he released duets with Bobby Byrd ('You've Got To Change Your Mind') and Vicki Anderson ('You've Got The Power'), giving Byrd and Anderson the B-sides, and then shot to the top of the R&B charts with 'I Got The Feelin'', a ballad version of the show tune 'If I Ruled The World' on the B-side. Cut in Los Angeles, 'Feelin'' also sold extremely strongly in the pop market, reaching No. 6, his highest placing since 1965's 'I Got You'. A band arrangement of tremendous sophistication, 'Feelin'' was driven by the waves of energy and pace generated by Clyde Stubblefield's drumming, furiously syncopated in the busily controlled style for which The Meters' Joseph "Zigaboo" Modeliste would be known, and by Bernard Odum's bass playing. The horn section chips in brief accented phrases to mesh gears with the rhythm section in a polyrhythmic structure, the aural interpretation of a perfect mathematical equation. Brown's role as focus of the track is all but wholly usurped by the band. His lead vocal has to fight for space and attention. The track was one of the last Odum recorded with Brown before The Dapps' Tim Drummond became the first-ever white band member in the James Brown Orchestra.

The funk grooves gave both the drama and the loose drive to frame lyrics now based solely on black street phrases, black speech patterns, black vowel sounds. The messages had universal application but the language was very specific and as natural as Brown's post-process hair would be.

In business, the soul star's ascendancy was uninterrupted, though the seeds for setbacks were sown. He moved to new New York offices at 850 Seventh Avenue and was beginning to expand his business empire. In August, 1967, he had bought a controlling interest in attorney Gloria Toote's TNT Records, which had been part of Tru-Glowtown Records. Don Gardner's 'Let's Party', recorded before the deal, was the first release under the label's new owner but Brown was soon at the TNT Studios to record new material on the singer. Moves into business outside the specific recording and manufacture of discs started with the purchase of radio stations, paying $75,000 for a bankrupt country and western station in Knoxville, Tennessee and relaunching it as WJBE (it stood for James Brown Enterprises) in January, 1968.

A month later, he offered between $377,000 and $500,00 for WRDW in Augusta. The city's largest station, outside which he shined shoes as a child, would not start operation until the spring of 1969 following protests from other station owners in the city. He became the first African-American entertainer to own his own studio. Gregory Moses, one of Brown's business managers, who was made vice president of the radio operations said it was "a business [Brown] knows". The singer announced that both stations would be run as R&B formatted operations with an integrated staff headed by black administrators. Two experienced radio men from a Houston station were brought to the knoxville daytime station – Al Gardner as general manager and programme director Al Jefferson. As Moses told Billboard at the time: "It was a good investment. We hired the best dee-jays we could get and spent a lot of money on new equipment." It was the start of an attempt to build a chain of seven JB stations. He bought a third, WEBB in Baltimore, but there were to be no more links in that particular chain, though in 1973 he claimed to own five.

Later that year, appearing on the NBC-TV show *Tonight*, Brown gave a fuller explanation of the thinking behind his move into radio. Poles ran the Polish newspapers in the USA, Germans ran the German language papers and Italians ran their own sheets. Blacks, he told host Johnny Carson, were the only racial and ethnic group which did not control its own media (although they had some well-established newspapers and magazines) and he called for the immediate transfer of R&B stations from white into black hands. (He estimated that of 500 black stations operating at that time only two, apart from his, were black-owned.)

In the spring of 1969, he opened the first of a projected 150 "James Brown Gold Platter" restaurant franchises, which would be spread throughout the United States and Caribbean. It was not a new idea, entertainers from country singer/movie cowboy Roy Rogers to gospel singer Mahalia Jackson had launched fast food chains. His partners were E. Raymond Smith, the Macon car dealer who'd befriended him early on, Leroy R. Johnson, a lawyer and State senator from Atlanta, and Herbert L. Parks, former head of an Augusta insurance company. A million dollars was raised by selling 200,000 shares of stock to the public, Brown owned 55,000, or 8.2 per cent. The base would be back in Macon, Georgia, the menu to include fried chicken, collard greens, corn bread, fried catfish, sweet yams, black-eyed peas, buttermilk biscuits and 'tater pudding. "If our food don't make you feel good, you ain't got no soul" was the challenge. His public statement, reported in *R'N'B World* at the time, gives an idea of the fine line he was trying to draw in demanding equal rights without inflaming intolerance. "I am an advocate of black power but not of black separatism. In my business operation I am stressing the opportunity for black to move ahead and to be involved in business operations." His new company was "an inter-racial organisation. We have both white and black in our executive offices. I feel that anything that excludes whites is a perpetuation of what we've had all along and which I am strongly against."

The Gold Platter company would also be a food packaging firm and would give training to minorities.

By September, 1969, 11 franchises had been sold with 25 more in preparation, but Gold Platter Inc lost $480,000 in its first fiscal year and by July, 1970, had moved out of the fast food market into convenience stores. Twelve stores, some retaining the name Gold Platter, others operating under the name Penny Pantry and They Do Well. Alas, they didn't.

A month earlier, Miss Mary Brown, then 20-year-old former president of the Sacramento branch of the James Brown fan club, persuaded a Californian court that the singer was the father of her son, Michael Deon Brown, who, she claimed had been conceived in a San Francisco motel room in 1968. Although Brown did not deny being in the hotel room, he denied being the father. But he agreed to pay $500 a month for 20 years towards the boy's upbringing and Ms Brown's $2,700 legal fees.

Later that year, he unveiled plans for James Brown "Black & Brown" Trading Stamps, along the lines of Green Shield stamps, to be available through black and white outlets. His face would be featured on them. He began to use other products to sell records – box tops from Cold Power and Axion detergents could be exchanged for free James Brown records. In fact, almost all of these excursions into the wider world of business were to end in failure. "In the early Sixties I defended the Afro-Americans," Brown said. "I knew that they were just not trained to do anything at all. I mean, they don't know anything about real management. At that time, it was fashionable to be black. At least, it would give you an identity because one day they would call you coloured, next day a nigger. So when I got the radio stations, I made a mistake in hiring black managers rather than managers who happened to be black, not knowing that they would have to know the administrative end of it and they made a mess of things."

On March 5, Syd Nathan, the founder and owner of King Records and the man who, albeit reluctantly, gave Brown his first chance on record died in Miami from a heart attack. At retirement age, he'd been very ill for some time, his liver had deteriorated badly and he was slowly becoming paralysed from the waist down. The funeral, which Brown attended, was three days later and soon after he tried to buy Nathan's company but the family named Johnnie Miller as its new boss. A week later, *Jet* magazine ran a piece about Brown's separation from Deidre, his second wife. (A young woman named Florence Farmer had been installed at his St. Albans home in New York and he produced a single on her, 'Living Legend Part 1 & 2' for King's Bethlehem subsidiary. On the road, the Revue's singer from Kansas City, Marva Whitney, Marvellous Marva as she was also known, was his companion.)

Mid-March he played the Apollo, only two shows a day this time, and took the band and his dancers on to the *Tonight* TV show hosted by Sammy Davis Jr. On March 29, he filled in the part of the gap in his schedule left by the postponed trip to Vietnam with a short visit to the Ivory Coast to play and tape a TV spot in the West African state's capital Abidjan. The country's government paid $70,000 for the one-nighter, fares for his 35-strong entourage included. "This is the heart. The core is there," he said after his return. "When I got to Africa, I had my own thing. I found in music we were in a depth they weren't even in. Maybe I didn't go far enough into the bush country to find out more. The people didn't even see me before and they knew who I was."

Almost a month to the day after Nathan's death, on April 4, Dr. Martin Luther King was murdered at a hotel in Memphis. After the battles for integration in the south, King had continued to fight in more general terms for a reassessment of American values. He blamed the lack of progress on the domestic issues of racism, poverty, disenfranchisement and militarism at the door of the White House's obsession with the Vietnam War, which was increasingly seen as unnecessary, immoral and unwinnable. A year earlier, to the day, King had made his most acerbic anti-war speech at the New York Riverside Church. He had been organising the Poor People's Campaign, a multi-racial effort to unite the rural and urban poor in demanding better education, health care, housing and more jobs which would help them to be less dependent on welfare, such as it was. The basic demand was that Government deflect expenditure from the Vietnam War to this arena. By the spring of 1968, the Campaign strategy had taken shape but recruitment was slow. King broke into his schedule to join a protest in Memphis over pay and union recognition for 1,300 sanitation workers. Black militants, ill-disposed towards King and the non-violent organisations he represented rioted, leaving one dead. Concerned that his efforts were so easily undermined, he returned to the city on April 3 to attempt to lead a peaceful march the following day, despite death threats from white extremists. He was accustomed to those. He made his last great speech at the Mason Temple in Memphis in which he virtually predicted his own assassination and finished the oration with the poignant, ringing passage "I've been to the mountain top". He'd looked over and seen the promised land. "I may not get there with you" but "as a people" they'd get there.

As word of King's assassination spread that day, shock and then anger spread like a flashfire. There was no doubt, cities would burn. Brown, in New York, went on New York's WNEW TV station as a studio guest for two hours appealing to everyone "to cool it". He had a date at the Boston

Garden the following day. That city's mayor, Kevin White, a Bing Crosby and Frank Sinatra fan, was watching *Gone With The Wind* when he was told about the assassination. He wanted Brown's concert cancelled. It was a potential flashpoint, he reasoned. Nonsense, said black city councillor Tom Atkins, but it would become a flashpoint if it were cancelled. Atkins and Brown negotiated a deal with WGBH TV to broadcast his show live. When Brown went on radio to advise kids not to rampage in the streets but to stay at home and watch his show, there was a flood of returned tickets – why pay when you can watch for free? The city agreed to refund Brown lost revenue.

Footage of the show reveals an intense performance, simmering with nervous energy and a visible tension. At one point a black youth jumped on stage to dance. Cops threw him off. James stopped the performance to calm tempers. But while 110 cities burned, Boston and its black area of Roxbury remained eerily quiet. Everyone was home watching James Brown. Mayor White appeared on stage, introduced by the singer as "a swingin' cat". (According to a local Boston TV news documentary, *Our Times*, screened to celebrate the 20th anniversary of Brown's intervention, White planned to renege on his promise to compensate the Hardest Working Man and leaned on the Garden authorities to forgo their share of the proceeds under the threat of raised taxes. Barney Frank, a city official, remembered $100,000 being taken from a kitty raised by local businesses to fund Brown's concert. On camera, Brown says the city "only gave me $10,000". Tom Atkins became a civil rights lawyer. Asked for his views on Mayor White, Brown said he's "still a swingin' cat". White, similarly prompted, called Brown "a snake oil salesman".)

"The government, city-wise and state-wise, knew somehow that James Brown was a strong force as far as entertaining and getting people together," Maceo Parker recalled. "And it was the same chaos, I mean total chaos all over following the assassination of Dr. Martin Luther King." But Brown's show "put a curtail on the riots and running around and looting." It was one effective curfew. "It worked. We performed our regular show at the auditorium and it was videotaped and shown on late night TV. He was so hot at the time that people just said, 'Wow! James Brown's gonna be shown on TV, so we'll just come from the streets and we'll stay home and just watch it'."

News of Brown's success at quelling riots travelled. On April 6 he flew to Washington DC, the city hardest hit by rioting, to talk to the capital's youth, advising them too to stay home. And then he flew down to Memphis for Martin Luther King's funeral. His advice was carried on national TV by the news networks and in the most upmarket newspapers such as the

Washington Post, in articles and editorials about Brown's effort and his importance in getting the message of non-violence to black youths was recognised and praised. On April 10, Brown was cited in the Congressional record. In May, the Mayor of Washington presented him with the keys to the city and he attended a White House dinner given for the Prince of Thailand by President Lyndon Baines Johnson and met again with Hubert Humphrey. "Thanks much for what you are doing for your country," the place card read. He continued to raise funds for black charities with a huge benefit at Soldier's Field, Chicago, in aid of SCLC and other black organisations but not everyone was quite so impressed.

Couple his known affiliation with Humphrey with his cosying with LBJ and the Establishment to get the profile of the man who'd be some way down the Black Panther's playlist. He dropped even further down two months later when he flew out from Kennedy Airport on June 5 to entertain the US troops in Vietnam (for three days) and at bases in Okinawa, Korea and Japan. Cancelling $100,000 of bookings, he took his full orchestra for the two-week tour of duty but on the final leg into Vietnam he was allowed to take only a seven-piece band. The day before he arrived in Saigon, the Viet Cong launched their heaviest rocket attack on the city sending in 35 rounds of 122mm rockets. He played the Tan Son Nhut Air Base – it was hit by 10 rockets in the morning and by two James Brown shows in the afternoon – moving on to play shows at the Phon Rang Air Base and Long Binh, 15 miles north-east of the South's capital. After a final show at Bear Cat he flew to Okinawa to rejoin the rest of his band. Throughout the trip he'd been angered by the less than courteous treatment. He thought he was being messed about from day one and it was because he was black. "We're back into the left-handed world again and we're going to have trouble, problems, the rest of our lives." But, like Maceo, Brown thought the trip worthwhile. "Prior to leaving [Brown's band in 1969], one of the highlights I think was performing at the Vietnam thing," the saxophonist said. "I had the pleasure of going over with James Brown to do what we could do, trying to lessen the confrontation and give the soldiers a sense of wanting to do what they could to end the thing and come on home. We did regular shows and it was very, very hot. Transportation was not up to par but we knew that under those conditions, we could endure somehow."

He flew back into Kennedy Airport from Tokyo at the end of June, gave the authorities back in Vietnam heavy grief about their treatment of him and went off to prepare for the Soul Festival he was headlining at the Yankee Stadium three days later. It was a disturbing performance. Not because he opens the first half with standards such as 'If I Ruled The World' and 'That's Life' – yes, he was singing them waaaaay back in the Sixties, their appearance in the set is not a new Nineties, Viva Las Vegas phenomenon as some younger fans might imagine, and young writers certainly do imagine – but because the explosive second half goes so awry right at the finish as the crowd pours onto the baseball diamond. He persuades them back to their seats once, twice and just when it seems all might be fine a transvestite leads a final invasion. He had lost control. Brown, initially at a loss for words, eventually pulls himself together. "I fought all my life and still I must fight. We went to Vietnam to show a black man could have self respect but I'll tell you … tonight is my last night. I'm finished with the stage and that's it. I've been looking for an excuse to leave, but if I'm going to do these … I can't take it no more." The crowd filed out of the Stadium in silence.

At the end of July, he appeared at a Watts rally for Humphrey and endorsed the vice president's campaign to win the Democratic nomination for the Presidency. After another mishandled and manipulative event reported less than scrupulously by newspapers and TV, Brown found himself explaining his reasons for backing Humphrey, if not apologising for them, because of the inaccurate reporting of the public meeting. "I think [Humphrey] was one of the finest humanitarians that ever lived," Brown said much later." 'The Happy Warrior' we called him, and that was the reason he never got elected President, because he was too nice and real for people. After I recorded 'Don't Be A Dropout', he and I worked together and I campaigned for him very proudly because he was a great man."

At a show in the Oakland Auditorium the night before the meeting in Watts, he had taken time to rap to the audience. "I don't know what's going to become of this country … but there's only one cat in the country who can stop the war – the cat in Washington." A reason to get close, to have the man's ear. "It seems that some of our people think that James Brown's a Tom – but Tom has been dead a long time. After tomorrow, you won't hear James Brown talk this way anymore because I don't want any black man to feel I'm fighting him. After tomorrow, I'm going back to singing, dancing and telling kids to stay in school."

If his moods appeared to veer from the strongly, and most typically, egocentric to the unusually despondent and confused, the live shows in 1968 were extraordinary. A tape of a show, recorded in August, 1968 at the Memorial Auditorium in Dallas during this red-hot spell, must rank as one of the great unreleased live albums of all time. The band was in astonishing form as one track, an absolutely blistering version of 'There Was A Time', released on the 'Star Time' CD box set illustrates. But the whole show is a classic, including the MC's introduction from the stage to the colour brochure. He even tries to elicit a round of applause for it.

Between the burning shows, Brown further tested the militants' ire with the concurrent release of two singles – 'Licking Stick-Licking Stick', recorded a little over a week after Dr. King's murder and released as King's first stereo 45, and 'America Is My Home'. Bearing in mind the anger of the times, this affirmative and proudly patriotic statement can be interpreted as astonishingly bold or ill-timed and very foolish. 'Licking Stick', much the bigger hit, was co-written with Byrd and "Pee Wee" Ellis as a vigorous and unyielding post-'Brand New Bag' funk groove with slice-of-African-American-life lyrics. (Said stick was a switch irate mothers sent misbehaving offspring into the backyard for when a beating was in the offing; the appearance of a lickin' stick in any novel of the American South is obligatory; urban equivalent – papa's belt.). 'America Is My Home', by contrast, was a personal rumination on the good things in life that Uncle Sam had to offer. Until it was recalled, the record looked to be heading for hit status but, considering the high standing in which he was held on the streets, the backlash against him from the young and increasingly vocal black militant movements was prodigious.

Brown's problems with the uncompromising black power organisations came from his apparent cosiness with the formal, elected government establishments in the White House, The Man, and his own patent lack of strategy, philosophy or agenda over and above the betterment of James Brown Inc and the example of self-advancement through hard work and application of talent which his success provided to others. As he emerged as a role model for millions of impoverished African-Americans his profile nationwide was raised. His utterances and record releases came under closer political scrutiny. His high profile demanded a political acuity that he found difficult to express. Most of his statements could at best only be interpreted as knee-jerk reactions to events. His philosophy of life in the United States became a roller coaster ride.

Rather than his rumination years after, the record of what he was thinking at the time is informative. (British tabloids in the late Sixties were less inclined to invent quotes than you may think and took a more sympathetic, less cynical view.) "Black power?" he said in 1969. "I don't like the word 'power'. Respect is what I want, the opportunity for black men to become a race. The Negro race is not a race, it has no identity. I don't want to be a Negro. I'm a black man and because I'm black, I want to become 100 per cent a man. I'm doing what I have to because, again I say it, I'm black and I want opportunity for black people. I don't want to arrive at the start of the race to be told that it started two minutes ago. I want that we should all come out of the starting traps at the same time."

He gave the African-American Press of the time a spin that varied only slightly. "I am attempting to spread black power through ownership," he said of his organisation. "I want to show blacks that they can do it. They can be constructive if given the opportunity to spread out." He added: "It's bad that the whites are unaware because they are causing many disastrous thing to happen ... We have to stop saving face and start saving the country. How long will a man take this and continue to like what is happening? It's not a question of black or white, it's a question of what is right!" He was asked what black was to him. "I'm black as a man. This is my colour. There is a lot of depression, disbelief and weariness that goes along with this colour. But I know I'm going to make it." And, as he told the *Afro American* newspaper, "I'm black but I'm a man too. Nobody tells me what to do. I know I'm blacker in my heart than any man." His fans seemed to agree. One, waiting at Kennedy Airport to greet him on his return from Vietnam, told a *Village Voice* reporter: "James is for black people more than Stokeley [Carmichael] – he's never been to jail – that Stokeley's just a big put on. [Adam Clayton] Powell? He's a phoney! All he tried to do was impress the white man with his big yacht and all."

The riots and trip to Vietnam focused attention on Brown as never before. All through June and July, his face was on the cover of magazines – *Jet, Tan, R'N'B World, Jazz & Pop* and *Soul Illustrated* – and he was featured in *Newsweek*, the *New York Times, New York, Look*, and the jazz magazine *Downbeat*. The inks were impressed by his stature, perhaps, but muddled by facts: during 1968 *Rock'N'Roll Songs* magazine said he was 31-years-old, *Afro American* settled for 34 and *Village Voice* gave him 38. This was celebrity indeed. His birthday cake that May had 35 candles. He was a regular TV guest on programmes like Johnny Carson's *Tonight*, NBC-TV's early morning *Today Show* and the *Merv Griffin Show*, twice. The second Griffin show was taped outdoors on 115th Street in Harlem, an estimated 10,000 kids looking on from tenement windows, roof tops and the streets. ABC even repeated *Ski Party* on the strength of his minor appearance.

To publicise the June 9 screening of *James Brown Man-To-Man*, a one-hour special produced by David Wolper for Metromedia, the *New York Times* ran a piece by Albert Goldman, later best-known for spit roasting Elvis Presley and John Lennon. The special featured Brown performing at the Apollo in March and walking the streets of Harlem and Watts discussing the issues of the day. It was raved over by *Variety* and subsequently syndicated to 20 TV outlets after transmission on Metromedia's five outlets. "Talk about your Black Power," Goldman began, "Take a look at James Brown, Mister." To whites, he asserted, Brown was still "an off-beat grunt, a scream at the end of the dial". To blacks, "he's boss." In similar of-the-moment language, Goldman recalled Brown's calming of the riots much as the Bible notes Christ calming the storms on the Sea of Galilee. This was a "cat with a pushed-in face, a hoarse voice, a bag of tunes that sound alike and an act that is nothing new for the black vaudeville stage," roared Goldman. "But there you have the genius of James Brown. He is the greatest demagogue in the history of Negro entertainment." Near the end, the colourful and affirmative piece insisted that "he teaches us the meaning of the phrase 'black is beautiful'." Within a month, Brown was teaching the world another phrase.

'Say It Loud – I'm Black And I'm Proud' was recorded in Los Angeles on August 7, 1968 and released less than two weeks later. Pretty quick by late Sixties' standards. "Brown socks the message home with a steady and solid beat," *Billboard* said, "and should prove a hot sales winner for both pop and R&B markets". It sold 750,000 in the first two weeks and shot to No. 1 R&B and No. 10 pop. The impact was more profound than chart-placings. Brown did not overnight metamorphose from the pariah of black militants into their official entertainment spokesperson but the simple and effective slogan, chanted by kids hauled in off the streets, gave a voice and direction to black demands for education and equality of opportunity. It sat well with the clenched fist. "As far as the black man's concerned, he's not even born yet because a man isn't born until he has his rights ... Don't make me equal, I can't survive on equality. Even if I'm not ready, get me into college," he advised *Newsweek* before the record came out. "We need leadership, we need education, we need hope." "It's more than a record," he explained to *R'N'B World*. "It's hard for a man to get himself together if he can't take pride in himself."

Of course, some commentators saw 'Say It Loud' as a clarion call to the ramparts and suggested Brown the Peacemaker had turned to inciting mayhem. "I can't see how they can be so unaware of the English language. Just listen to what I was saying," he commented much later. "I never said anything about destroying anything, I thought about building character and principles, but I think the uneducated people thought I say 'Watch your bad self'. I say, 'Watch your sharp self'. I mean, you're together, the fact that you can overcome with no help. And they took it another way and they took pride in anger. They celebrated into anger." But he did have his hair cut short to a natural. "Well, I cut my hair during the Sixties because of a movement trying to stop some of the racial overtones. I had long hair and I cut it off and a lot of my friends got mad until I grew my hair back."

Bob Patton joined the James Brown organisation as a record promoter at this moment. Born in Georgia but raised in Ohio, Patton had been a disc jockey, a trade which meant he often bumped into Brown. One day at his station, WDAO, in Dayton Ohio, the jock took a call from the singer. Work for me, said Brown. Between 1965–68, Patton worked for both until the station told him to choose one or the other. He was making $30,000 a year with Brown and $18,000 with the station, an easy choice to make. "When I first went on the road promoting James's records, I went out one week with 'America Is My Home' and came back out two weeks later with 'Say It Loud, I'm Black And I'm Proud' and we got them both played. Most of the black stations and some of the white stations too. Some argued with us about 'Say It Loud'. That was the turning point of making James a 'black' artist. Before that he was considered R&B.

"What he was actually saying was 'If you're black, be proud of it just like if you're white be proud of it'. The record says stand up and be proud of who you are, 'cos then you can smile and talk to anybody. That was his logic and it was a pretty good damn logic I thought. Unfortunately, Rap Brown and all those militant guys took it as their song and people started thinking it was a militant song only."

Patton confirmed the story in Brown's autobiography of death threats to the singer, allegedly by militants – a hand grenade left outside the door of his hotel bedroom. The next night, Patton said, Brown cut 'Say It Loud'. Another time, "we were playing in New Haven and the Muslims showed up. This was when the Muslims were looking over their glasses. In fact, Charles Bobbit [a James Brown manager] was a Muslim at the time. He and I were starting to get along because he found out that even though he was raised one way, I was the guy who would go out and bring in the goods, get the bookings and bring back the right amount of money. The disc jockeys would be happy when I was in town. I actually take care of business and be straight. Same with Alan [Leeds].

"These Muslims came back stage and wanted to know why they hadn't had the show to promote. So James looked at them and said, 'I'd love to let you promote but my manager won't let me.' Mr. Bobbit and I are standing there and James points to me. So I was the one that had to take the blame on that. James left the room." Patton and the Muslims sat down and made a deal on the next engagement in New Haven in four months' time. "We came back and made more money, made more profit, but I'd worked it out with them as a business and they were fine after that. But I said 'We're not going to give you charity. There's no reason for a black man to suffer because of black organisations. He started with poverty, he doesn't have to go back to poverty to work with some groups that are not going to help anybody. I wanna see the programmes you got started, that you're gonna help the people with'.

"We did the same kind of thing with the Panthers in LA. KGFJ would not play our records because they wanted fifty per cent of the show. So James sent me down to the Panther headquarters in Watts and I talked to Rap Brown and Huey Lewis. I'm from Ohio, I wasn't smart enough to know that it was bad. But I walked in there with my three-piece suit and they knew that I was either a pimp or a gangster or something. Wasn't long after the riots and they knew I was coming. James had called them. When I walked in the door, they said 'Mr Patton, how are you?' I sat down and told them the problem about the station not playing the records. I said 'We'll do you a show. We'll give you 20 per cent of the show, five per cent in cash and 15 per cent to food programmes to anybody you tell me as long as it goes to the people.' They looked at me and said 'Well, why don't you just give us the 20 per cent?' I said 'Because I want to show that you're doing good.' And we agreed on it and within an hour the Panthers had a line around KGFJ. Fifteen or twenty minutes later it was sounding like James Brown's radio station. We sold out, about 10 or 12 thousand, and did the food programme."

A year earlier, The Beatles had been telling the world 'All You Need Is Love' but not too many blacks fell for that one. They heard Brown though and others quickly picked up the riff. Black awareness songs were not new, Curtis Mayfield's aspirational 'We're A Winner' came out in January, 1968 and after 'Say It Loud', had another hit with 'This Is My Country'. By the end of 1968, even Motown had reacted by addressing a black family issue in The Supremes' 'Love Child'. Larry Williams' 'Wake Up (Nothing Comes To A Sleeper But A Dream)' on Venture and, on King, Hank Ballard's 'How You Gonna Get Respect (When You Haven't Cut Your Process Yet)' gave their own twist to the message.

'Say It Loud' was notable for another change. Tim Drummond, the band's white bassist, had caught hepatitis in Vietnam and had to be replaced. "When I first joined the group," said "Sweet" Charles Sherrell, "I was actually hired as a drummer. Then James found out that I could play a couple of instruments." When Drummond took sick, Sherrell took over. "The actual first recording that I played on was 'Say It Loud – I'm Black And I'm Proud'. We cut that out in California, about five o'clock in the morning." Another major recruit about now was the definitive James Brown trombonist, Fred Wesley, from Mobile, Alabama, home of drummer John Starks. A jolly man, Wesley was another frustrated jazz musician in a tight funk suit.

Good cook, though, and his spreading girth over the years suggests he enjoyed his own culinary skills.

Midway between the recording and the release of 'Say It Loud', on August 12, Ben Bart died of a heart attack while playing golf on a Long Island course with Jack, his son. Brown and his manager had had disagreements and once, briefly, severed the business relationship but the singer has never been slow to acknowledge the debt he owed Bart. "I was going through a transition period, because I was a leader and Mr. Bart and I were not having problems," he said of a time shortly before his manager's death. "He said 'You'll outlast them all, James.' I said, 'Why do you say that, Ben?' and he said 'Because you're intelligent.' I didn't understand what he meant but he meant that I knew how to do things, knew how to put it together. I knew when not to argue, argue for a point and once the point had been made then forget it."

Jack Bart took over the reins. In the beginning the relationship had not been as amicable between them as it had been between his father and Brown. "The first three or four years, James and I battled consistently, constantly, and we had many, many differences and we used to get into shouting matches. I wouldn't talk to him for a while because I was young and felt I owned the world and I could do whatever I wanted, and James sort of felt the same way. And he was the artist and I think he had more of a right to take that position than I did.

"But over the years we sort of understood each other and gained a mutual respect for each other. And I noticed that our arguments became less and less and I would learn things from the man – not that I would really admit it and run up to him and say 'Yes, you're right, I'm wrong.' But deep down I knew that the man had a lot of good qualities and really knew the business, not only as an entertainer but also as a businessman. He was very knowledgeable. And as the years passed and we got closer and closer, he said that almost everything that he knew, my father had taught him. So, in a roundabout manner, what I learned from James Brown was really my Dad teaching me but through James Brown."

After Syd Nathan's death and an unsuccessful bid to buy the label which had been surviving on his hits alone for half-a-decade, Brown was forced to sit back and watch King Records pass through various hands for the rest of the year. Hal Neely had been with King since 1958 and as vice president had been an effective buffer between the headlong express train that was James Brown and the implacable terminus named Nathan. He wrote the sleeve notes for 'Live At The Apollo', he'd tried to buy out Nathan at the beginning of the Sixties, shortly before Brown signed with Smash, and in

October, 1964 became vice president and general manager of Starday. On Nathan's death, he had an option to buy King and on October 1, 1968, Starday bought out King and its publishing companies. Neely became president of Starday-King. A little over a month later, on November 10, LIN Broadcasting, who owned a string of radio stations, bought Starday-King and by 1969 had moved its headquarters from Nashville to New York City. Neely remained in Nashville but was dissatisfied with the deal and bought back the music assets he sold to LIN, which the contract allowed him to do, so that he now owned Brown's past and present masters and his personal services recording contract (i.e. his future recordings), which was due to run into the next decade. Brown's advisers began to sell him the idea of moving to a new company, Polydor, a German label strong in Europe (it already distributed King in England and Germany) and keen to break in the United States. He was not a willing buyer.

A third death, between Nathan's and Bart's, hit Brown every bit as hard. Little Willie John, the singer headlining when Brown made his début at the Apollo in April, 1959, died in Washington State Penitentiary on May 26, 1968. He'd been found guilty of manslaughter two years earlier after stabbing a railroad worker in a fight in a café in Seattle. A precocious talent with a poignant, aching voice, Little Willie John had been appearing on stage since he was 11 and, at 14 sang with Count Basie. He joined King a year before Brown and the two of them, along with Hank Ballard, provided the label's bread and butter during the late Fifties and early Sixties. The hits dried up after 1961 and the rest of his life mirrored the unbearable sadness of his songs. He drank heavily, sported knives and a gun and his career was all but derailed before he stabbed his victim. Brown recorded the touching tribute album 'Thinking About Little Willie John And A Few Nice Things', released in the run-up to Christmas, 1968, along with the LP 'A Soulful Christmas' (his eighth album of the year) and three Christmas singles including 'Santa Claus Goes Straight To The Ghetto' and 'Let's Unite The Whole World At Christmas'. There were a lot of releases but after 'Say It Loud', his 1968 records were determinedly lacking in controversy. The immediate follow-up, 'Goodbye My Love', was his first soul-ballad single for two years and had been in the can since September, 1967.

But he was soon back developing the hard funk groove with 'Give It Up Or Turnit A Loose', credited to Charles Bobbit, who joined as a valet in 1966 when 'Don't Be A Dropout' was riding high, and recorded in Miami in October, 1968. It was a hit in January. Brown's own tough demand, 'I Don't Want Nobody To Give Me Nothing (Open Up The Door I'll Get It Myself)', recorded in Atlanta with a memorably insistent Sweet Charles bass

line. The locations those sides were cut at give some indication of the con-
tinuing punishing touring schedule he was forcing on himself and the band.
Twice a year along the West coast, a sweep through the South, two or three
seasons at the Apollo and huge stadium events – almost 40,000 for a con-
cert at the Yankee Stadium in New York in June, 17,000 at Madison Square
Garden with the Count Basie Orchestra and Ramsey Lewis Trio as support.
Themed as "Black & Everybody's Proud", this extravaganza included Vivian
Whitted, the reigning Miss Harlem, reading a poem, and, in the words of
Soul magazine, "a show of models representing the various types of black
beauties". "I know where I've come from and I know who put me there,"
Brown said. "I'm a man identifying with himself. I'm not protesting." He
later played some one-nighters with Basie, a brass blast.

It seemed that every city he visited now had a merit award or citation to
present, most of the shows had part of the proceeds donated to a local or
national black fund or charity. Every day was James Brown Day. He
appeared on TV quiz shows and filmed a pilot for a projected small screen
series. In January, 1969, passing through Hollywood on a tour of the West
Coast, he set up a film production company to shoot his life story.
Scheduled start was April or May. By March 1, Dick Clark Productions
were talked about as film-makers for the project, shooting to start in May or
June. Within a month, negotiations seized up and were postponed indefi-
nitely. But his productions for other acts – notably Marva Whitney's duet on
'You've Got To Have A Job' and some "Pee Wee" Ellis instrumentals – were
every bit as cookin' as Brown's own sides, if not quite as commercially hot.

After a year as eventful as 1968 – veering wildly from the triumph of
huge shows and big hits to the deaths of King, Bart, Nathan and John,
threats, insults and disputation from black militants, honours and garlands
from black charities, citations from cities he saved from burning, thanks and
notice from politicians of all stripes – Brown heeded the call of rural tranquillity and decided that New York was not really the home for him and
moved back to Augusta, Georgia. He'd decided to get back with Deidre.
Reaching half-way to three-score-and-ten affects some people that way.
There were other motives. He told *R'N'B World* that people in the North
seemed nice but you never knew what they were thinking. In the South,
you knew what they were thinking even if it was nothing but bad news.

But you rarely knew what James Brown was thinking. Having supported
Humphrey in the Presidential race, he jumped ship almost as soon as the
invitation to headline Richard Nixon's inaugural ball in January, 1969
arrived. Soul Brother No. 1 was in deep trouble with black organisations of
differing militancy now. "I went to ask [Nixon] for a national holiday for

Martin Luther King and I told him there was a lot of unrest and it was because of non-recognition. And I believed if they gave Martin Luther King a national holiday, it would ease a lot of tension. He said he was thinking of something even greater, he was thinking of a monument." Brown said he liked Nixon and felt he got respect from, and was given freedom by, Tricky Dicky. Bobby Byrd said the band's pulling power was hit so hard by the leader's affiliations to Nixon's cause that they were eventually forced to downgrade their new bookings from huge auditoriums to smaller theatres and clubs. Brown's appeal certainly waned but it was not solely due to his vacillating political affiliations. Like many other African–American artists, he began to suffer from the inherent fickleness of the pop market. To reduce history to the most simplistic interpretation, the huge outdoor festivals reached their apogee with 1969's Woodstock, rock replaced soul and "Sock it to me JB" was replaced by "Tune in, turn on and drop out" or "Say it loud – I'm stoned and I've … forgotten what else I was going to say. Or who I am." Record-buyers, radio stations, the business, all followed.

In July, 1969, his show wrapped up that year's Newport Jazz Festival, which featured such ardent devotees of swing, be-bop and cool jazz as Jethro Tull, Led Zeppelin and Ten Years After. Anyone hearing a note of jazz in that lot presumably either won A Very Big Prize or was directed to the Red Cross tent. In fact, Brown was recording some jazz things at the time with the Dee Felice Trio on King's subsidiary Bethlehem and his horn section, which could swing as well as play funk, was certainly attuned to the demands of hard bop.

When in doubt, a wise man once said, have a man come in the door with a dance tune in his head. In this case, the man came through a revolving door. In 1969, James Brown released an instrumental, 'The Popcorn', quickly followed by 'Mother Popcorn', 'Lowdown Popcorn' (another instrumental), 'Let A Man Come In And Do The Popcorn – Part 1' and, shortly after, 'Let A Man Come In And Do The Popcorn – Part 2'. They ran out of popcorn soon after so, sadly, there was no 'Christmas Popcorn' record, one of the great missed opportunities of pop, not to say popcorn, music. They're all good dance records, frenetically funky, syncopated and "up", accentuating the positive without the overt political demands of 'Say It Loud', 'I Don't Want Nobody To Give Me Nothing' and others. He had, he said, got rid of his string section at this time "to get to the hard core of soul music." In fact, he said, it had become so primitive and that was one of the reasons he'd let musical director Nat Jones go. "I do 95 per cent of the arranging myself and it works itself out. I got to a point where I found I could do it all myself."

In common with these artefacts of the Great "Popcorn" Outbreak of 1969, his other hits that year – 'Soul Pride', 'World' and the instrumental 'Ain't It Funky Now' – were evidence of a magnificent flying machine of a band with its own integral drive and each component thoroughly in tune with the working of the other and with the mind of the driver. Or maybe not. Just because a band is playing slick and fine does not mean that it is a happy band. In March, 1970, celebrating another, if smaller, hit with 'Funky Drummer' and preparing to hit the stage in Columbus, Georgia, the band demanded a pay rise and, according to his autobiography, held Brown to ransom that night. No pay rise, no play. Maceo has said: "We wanted a few changes that James didn't go for. He didn't want to change the concept [that] he dominates everything, it's always his music, his writers, his everything. And we wanted change. He didn't want change, so we left." Cash or control, whatever the precise circumstances of the split, no bets who came out ahead.

CHAPTER 11

James Brown, stranded down there in Columbus, Georgia, had a show to play and no band to play it with. Fortunately, there was no shortage of up-and-coming bands, musicians, arrangers and writers very familiar with his latest work, his newest direction. In the deepest South, in New Orleans, The Meters' syncopations sprang from the indigenous Crescent City's style and music base but that rhythm section's polyrhythmic playing could lock into Brown's funk groove. From San Francisco, the first hit of Sly & The Family Stone, stars of Woodstock, gave funk an early infusion of rock populism and pop melody, but the base metal he used was mined from Brown's hits. Sly's good-time hits – 'Dance To The Music', 'Everyday People', 'Hot Fun In The Summertime' – blasted onto the airwaves at precisely the same time as Brown's lyrics started to use his own life's struggle for respect and control to speak far more specifically of African–American experience in general. Even Motown, the Sound of Young America, preparing to move operations from Detroit to Los Angeles, took funk on board thanks to the thundering productions of Norman Whitfield. Towards the end of the Sixties, the defining jazz trumpeter Miles Davis was looking for another new beginning, a way back into the black market. According to his autobiography, he was listening to little else besides James Brown, Jimi Hendrix and Sly Stone. He liked the way Brown used guitar, he said. By the early Seventies, his listening had been distilled further to Brown and Karlheinz Stockhausen. 'On The Corner', a 1972 album universally reviled by jazz critics, used some of Brown's techniques, notably aggressive dominance of the groove and vamping long and hard on one chord. There's little suggestion that Davis's use of

Brown's funk techniques got him back tight with black audiences but Herbie Hancock certainly heard what Davis was trying to do and, with a greater emphasis on melody, gave a clearer definition to the new jazz-funk on 1973's 'Headhunters'.

Meanwhile, back in Columbus in March, 1970, Brown had rung Bobby Byrd at the King Studios and told him to get The Pacesetters on the first plane out. A local Cincinnati band, The Pacesetters had been invited to King by A&R man Charles Spurling. He was also a singer and was looking for a band. The group went in, rehearsed, cut a couple of demos and a recording engineer recommended them to other King artists. "The next thing," bassist William "Bootsy" Collins said, "we were recording for everybody." With young Bootsy – he was scarcely past 16 when The Pacesetters began making a noise at King in 1968 – was guitarist Phelps "Catfish" Collins, Bootsy's elder brother by seven years, and drummer Frank "Kash" Waddy. They first worked on Hank Ballard and Arthur Prysock records and then a Bill Doggett session. They toured with singers such as Ballard, Erma Franklin and Chuck Jackson. Brown had taken notice of them when he was having difficulty with his second-team, The Dapps, who he sacked and replaced with The Pacesetters, dubbed The New Dapps. The first demo they cut, Bootsy said, was 'More Mess On My Thing' in September, 1969. Very soon after that, the core of The Pacesetters became James Brown's newest front line band, The New Breed. The name didn't last long; they became The JBs.

Not all of the orchestra had quit. Bobby Byrd rejoined from his studio-bound job and moved over to keyboards, drummer John "Jabo" Starks sat his ground. But the horns – Maceo, Pee Wee, Fred Wesley, Richard "Kush" Griffith, Joe Davis and Eldee Williams – had gone along with guitarists Jimmy Nolen and Alphonso "Country" Kellum and bassist Sweet Charles. In came Bootsy and Catfish and a horn section of Clayton "Chicken" Gunnells and Darryl "Hasaan" Jamison (trumpets), and tenor saxophonist Robert McCullough. Extraordinarily, they picked up the funk where it lay and moved it along, fast and in a very short space of time. The first line-up of The JBs was with the Hardest Working Soul Brother No. 1 In Show Business barely a year but the sudden infusion of youth and energy galvanised the leader in that time. In return, he exhibited to the younger musicians unexpected reserves of patience which members of his former orchestra would have been hard-pressed to recognise. He was able to put behind him the politicking of the Sixties and get "back to singing and dancing and entertaining the people".

"There was a guy with James named Dave Matthews that really helped me a lot. He did a lot of arranging. Like, he would write out strictly for myself and my brother," Bootsy explained, "plus I had the attitude of 'I wanna learn how to do this'. I don't know nothin' about the studio. He really taught me." With Brown, the relationship was "like a father and son, especially with me 'cos he knew I was young and I dug it 'cos I never had a father that rapped to me." (William's father ran off soon after he was born leaving Nettie Collins to bring up her two sons and a daughter, Brenda.) "But I was also doing a lot of listening and learning and checking him out 'cos he was, like, number one."

Indeed he was, and so were The JBs with virtually their first effort. In the space of one year, the new breed re-energised Brown's music – accelerating the process of moving from a horn-based sound to a more guitar-dominated funk, back to the fundamental predominance of the rhythm. In that year, he cut an extraordinary sequence of hit tunes including 'Get Up (I Feel Like Being A) Sex Machine', 'Super Bad', 'Talkin' Loud & Sayin' Nothin'', 'Soul Power' and 'Get Up, Get Into It And Get Involved'.

'Sex Machine' wasn't an entirely new hit at all, more a dramatically refashioned version of 'Give It Up Or Turnit A Loose' after The New Breed had played around with the song, which was credited to Charles Bobbit. (One of the ways Brown got around his difficulties with the IRS was to credit his songs wholly to members of his staff or family who might have been marginally helpful in writing the song, thus reducing the income which could be attached by the IRS.) 'Sex Machine' gives the 'Give It Up' groove extra zip, energy and immediacy to match the urgency of the street language. Although the new arrangement focused strongly on the rhythm section, Brown played a thunking piano solo in 'Give It Up' and singing is given a conversational counterpoint by Bobby Byrd's vocal. "We were playing a gig in Nashville, Tennessee," Brown said, "and I wrote 'Sex Machine' because we were saying 'Get up, get on up'. We were saying that in a jam and I saw people respond to that, so I came back and I wrote a song on the back of a poster. We finished playing in Nashville, we packed up real quick and went to the studio and we cut 'Sex Machine' the same night. 'Cos that's really the time to record. When we finish playing over the show locally, we could go straight then and do a session and really do it a thousand times better than we could do if we had to get in the studio and get warmed up to do it." (In his autobiography, Brown said he recorded most of the 'Sex Machine' album at the Bell Auditorium in Augusta but the song itself was cut at the Starday-King Studios in Nashville.)

"The riffs I wanted to write [for 'Sex Machine'] I couldn't get my fellows to play them because they were so fast. You see, a bass player couldn't play those kind of things a long time ago because they just didn't have that concept of playing. A guitar had to play those kind of riffs, you know, and the bass player the basic riff. Then Bootsy came along and he could play those fast riffs and I got all my fast parts from him."

Because of their tender years, Brown was less dictatorial in manner at first. There were fewer fines, if any, for the younger band although the work was every bit as disciplined and exacting. The orchestra had been allowed a certain musical latitude – that was how the more co-operative pieces of songwriting were achieved at rehearsals and recording sessions – but he was more generous with his praise in the studio for the new band's efforts. The tapes of the sessions are full of his words of encouragement.

On the road, however, he soon discovered that the new horn section was less accomplished than the bassist and guitarist. At first, he used pick-up trumpet, sax and trombone players on the road and later he persuaded some of the battle-hardened veterans to sign up for further campaigns. Fred Wesley was brought back in as musical director to reorganise the horn section, saxophonist St. Clair Pinckney, who'd been 'Live At The Apollo' a decade before, and drummer Clyde Stubblefield also rejoined. They were also more accustomed to the rigours of touring, the long, long bus journeys, everyone in his or her allotted seat.

In the 1970–71 shows, bassist Bootsy stood impassively still, laying down those solid funk foundations, driving the rhythm, and concentrating on Brown's signals. Phelps Collins' guitar took a little more space with a long solo in the segued 'Brother Rapp'–'Ain't It Funky Now' – Fred, Bootsy and Brown himself, on organ, blew too – during the first half of the show. His performance of the ballad 'Georgia' mingled the rich and the raw. Near the end, in his effort to reach for a top note, he swung back from the microphone and ended the line on a scream greeted by a cheer from the audience. He blew a kiss before the next line started and when at the end of the song he asked "I wanna know does everybody feel alright!" the "Yaah!" was huge.

After Vicki Anderson sang a brief set in that big, expressive voice, her husband Bobby Byrd stepped up to the microphone: "Are you ready?!" he shouted three times. Three times the answer came back, an intelligible booming noise approximating to: "Yaaaaah!" "Ladies and gentlemen, it's Star Time!" In the Sixties, many acts tried to duplicate this introduction but none succeeded in building the pitch in quite the same way, the intensity growing as each line was interspersed with the band's fanfare, echoed by the audience's cheer. "The man who sang 'Try Me' ... 'Black And Proud'! ... 'Let A Man Come In'! ... 'Ain't It Funky Now'! ... 'It's A New Day'! ... So let the Brother Rapp! ... While we do the Sex Machine! ... I said, while we do the Sex Machine! ... 'Cos we got Soul Power! ... We Get Up, Get Into It and Get Involved! ... Ladies and gentlemen, here he is. The greatest entertainer in the world. Mr. Please, Please himself. Hardest working Jaaaames Brown!"

With a roaring blast of funk, Brown stepped out and slid straight from the pace of 'It's A New Day' into the passion of 'Bewildered', a formidable ballad performance which built unbearable tension and eased the temperature down again as simply as lowering a gas flame. Almost without notice, they snapped into 'There Was A Time' as Brown did some impossibly fast steps and then, on one leg, seemed to slide and glide across the stage like a man in stockinged feet skating on a well-polished floor. Unrelenting, The JBs cracked into 'Sex Machine', freshly exciting. They took it to the bridge – a phrase Brown virtually trademarked to get the band into the middle eight bars, or any linking passage, of the song – where Byrd took a break from his relentless recital of "git on up!" and did a boogaloo of his own. Not bad but not bad enough to upstage the leader. Back at the verses, Phelps Collins took a long guitar solo and he and Brown and Bootsy did the dance as the tremendous piece of funk powered to a finish. Into, then, a medley of Fifties and Sixties hits.

The James Brown stage performances of 1969–71 had in them most of the group and individual moves that would fill the sets of soul and funk groups for the next decade-and-a-half. Certainly his footwork influenced the prime African-American male artists in the way they did their thing – Michael Jackson's Moonwalk is here, so too is the way Prince organises his bands, rhythms and performances. In the scheme of his evolving show, the set now had more to-and-fro between Brown and the crowd in its latter stages where previously his audience was simply picked up by the segueing and pacing of the songs and the sheer, non-stop power this generated.

The JBs Mk1 had learned fast and when in the spring of 1971, two weeks after their one and only European tour, Brown said he was letting them go there was no animosity. It had been that rare thing – symbiosis in showbusiness. Bootsy: "I was 17 and it was like he was telling me to do one thing and when you funkin', you kinda resist. Funk is resisting. You know, 'Hey! Lighten up!' Plus that was during the days of acid trip and the band wanted to come out front and here's a cat kept saying 'be cool'. And we already had a band together and it was kinda hard for us, at first [to stay in the background] but I say 'No, 'cos I wanna get outta here, I wanna be on the road with James Brown' So it was a give and take thing. See, a lotta time we would be in the studio just playing and he knew we'd be tripping, so a lotta times he wouldn't even come round. He'd just be in the engineering room watching us and have the tape on while we jammin', y'know? And the next thing we know we hearing it on the radio! It was kinda neat.

"Mainly what he'd do with us was he'd come in and start a rhythm thing and then wait and see what we came up with. Before we got there he'd tell each person his part but when we was there he'd get a rhythm and then listen and see what I'd come up with to go with that, and then he'd listen to my brother and see what he'd come up with and next thing you know everybody's 'Yeah! This Is It! Lights! Cameras! Action!!'." But despite this communal composing style, which was rarely credited or rewarded with publishing, there were no hard feelings on splitting, though there is some debate as to whether Brown sacked them or they quit. "Like I said, in the acid days the bands wanted to be out front, no more backing up singers," Bootsy recalled. "We just wanted to be out 'cos we knew we had a thang. We knew the band was a smash and was tight and always together. All I had to say was 'We got to go' and everybody knew it."

During that 1971 European tour, Brown and The JBs had seen British girls wearing a new fashion item – hot pants. The skimpy shorts pointed the way ahead for both careers. The former JBs threw off their formal band suits and became The House Guests. Uniform: long boots, scarves, hot pants; Music: funk. Not surprisingly, they attracted much attention including that of Mallia Franklin, who recommended them to her friend George Clinton and was later rewarded with a place in Parlet. Bootsy's Rubber Band was just around the corner. Meanwhile, Brown and Bobby Byrd were very much pre-occupied with the hot pants they had occasionally worn on stage and put their heads together on a song about the early Seventies answer to the Sixties' miniskirt. Throughout the first half of the Seventies, every risible lyric, like 'Hot Pants (She Got To Use What She Got To Get What She Wants)', would have its opposite in a heartfelt anti-drug tirade or sober exposition of a specific social problem. He'd taken a battering over some of the stands he'd taken and never quite understood why. Superficially, a song like 'Hot Pants' is a voyeuristic leer but scratch the surface and there's a slice-of-life description of a cash-strapped woman's struggle to get by, not that Brown could remotely be accused of being in the vanguard of a progressive sexual political movement.

Not all of The JBs had quit. By the time 'Hot Pants' was recorded, survivors Fred Wesley, the musical director, St. Clair Pinckney (sax), drummer "Jabo" Starks, second guitarist Hearlon "Cheese" Martin and percussionist Johnny Griggs had been joined by bassist Fred Thomas, guitarist Robert Coleman, Jimmy Parker (sax) and Jerome "Jasaan" Sanford and, later, Russell Crimes on trumpets. This was the core of the band that recorded the next few hits. The rap 'Escape-ism' had given People, Brown's own label launched through and distributed by the Starday-King set-up, its first chart success in June, 1971 and 'Hot Pants' took him back to the top of the R&B charts and into the pop Top 20. But continuing pressure from his advisers encouraged Brown to leave King and sign with a European company keen to break into the American market.

He had been with the companies formed by Syd Nathan for 15 years, four-and-a-half years on the subsidiary Federal and from mid-1960 until mid-1971 on King. His relationship with Nathan had been almost entirely adversarial. The label-owner might have appreciated the bottom line on the balance sheets produced by Brown's records but he never understood or liked the music. From 'Please, Please, Please' through Brown's self-financed 'Live At The Apollo', Nathan did not believe. But the singer's reliability as a hit-maker, the fact that in the Sixties he was King's only regular and substantial hit-maker, had convinced Nathan to let Brown call his own shots, choose his own releases. That and Nathan's failing health. After the label boss's death, Brown continued to have his own way. On Nathan's death and at least once afterwards he tried to buy King but had met with resistance. When the label was sold to Starday and then on to Lin Broadcasting, it ceased to be a small recording company equivalent of his private fiefdom and he decided to move on. If his relationship with Nathan and King had been prickly, the next deal was, for Brown, a descent into hell. The new record company didn't entirely have a ball either.

Brown's last five-year contract with King had been signed in 1966. At the time of signing it guaranteed him $78,000 a year payable at $1,500 a week against a royalty of 5 per cent of suggested retail on 90 per cent of net; a bonus equal to 40 per cent of all royalties from record sales; 10,000 free records for promotion of every new single and 500 promotional albums, any extra at discounted prices. His publishing was through several outlets. Dynatone, he owned 50 per cent, King owned the other half; Golo, split into equal thirds between him, King and Bud Hobgood; CriTed, split in half between King and a trust set up for his son, Teddy Brown; and Tan Soul, split 45 per cent each to Brown and King with the remaining 10 per cent held by Nat Jones. With further and very considerable income from live dates, which soared during this time, and production deals on other artists under The James Brown Productions umbrella, he was not at all badly set up.

His management structure had altered over the years. Ben Bart, increasingly unwell, had relocated to a houseboat in Miami from where he acted as a consultant. After his death, and Brown's move back to Georgia, Greg Moses took on the advisory mantle and Charles Bobbit, the former valet, became day-to-day manager. Bob Patton and Buddy Nolan continued to look after the bookings and Alan Leeds joined as an assistant doing publicity, later working as tour director and booking manager. Bud Hobgood, credited as a co-writer of 'Get It Together', 'Let Yourself Go' and its extension, 'There Was A Time', had been running things in the studio but he died in September, 1970 after a brain haemorrhage. He was only 34.

In July, 1971 Brown announced that he was signing a five-year deal with Polydor Records. The German company had set up in America in 1969 but met with little success. Signing the biggest, most important black artist of the day would give them a real presence in the market. (Polydor would later buy Mercury, so they had access to Brown's Smash material.) His attorney, Jack Pearl, and Hal Neely, former president of Starday-King, both encouraged Brown to sign with Polydor, who already worked his records in many territories outside the United States. In his autobiography, Brown claims that he thought he was signing to a company owned by Julian and Roy Rifkin, not realising they had only a production deal with Polydor. In the end, he was happy with the "very favourable" deal thrashed out by Neely, which included a big advance and a good level of autonomy – his own offices, artistic control – within the corporate structure.

At the time the deal was announced, he had two People singles on the American charts – 'Hot Pants' and 'Escape-ism' – and they'd be used on future Polydor albums. He was due later that month to celebrate the ninth anniversary of 'Live At The Apollo' with a return visit to the Harlem Theater to record 'Revolution Of The Mind – Live At The Apollo, Volume III'. On the surface, the new deal was beneficial all round. Polydor got a consistent flow of US hits – Brown's first nine singles for them all made the Hot 100 but the highest placing on the pop charts was only No. 18 ('Get On The Good Foot', July, 1972) although his stature on the R&B charts didn't waiver with 'Good Foot', 'Make It Funky', his first Polydor release, and 'Talkin' Loud & Sayin' Nothing' all reaching No. 1 and 'I Got A Bag Of My Own' (3), 'There It Is' (4), 'King Heroin' (6), 'I'm A Greedy Man' and 'Honky Tonk' (both 7) selling big. In the period summer 1971, to winter 1972, Brown furnished Polydor with 10 consecutive R&B Top Ten hits. A duet, 'What My Baby Needs Now', with new singer Lyn Collins was by his lights moderately successful. Soul Brother No. 1 would soon become the Godfather of Soul and he expected bigger back-up from a big corporation. As he saw it, he was not getting it. If it had been there, he reasoned, he would have had better penetration into the pop market.

It is worth looking at the R&B hits that reached No. 1 on the American pop charts in 1971–72. All, bar three, were ballads or soft in tone. The

Temptations' 'Just My Imagination', 'Family Affair' by Sly & The Family Stone, Al Green's 'Let's Stay Together', Roberta Flack's 'The First Time Ever I Saw Your Face', 'Oh Girl' by The Chi-Lites, Bill Withers' 'Lean On Me', Michael Jackson's 'Ben', Chuck Berry's novelty 'My Ding-A-Ling', which was only a small R&B hit, 'I Can See Clearly Now' by Johnny Nash and Billy Paul's 'Me & Mrs Jones'. Of the uptempo hits, Isaac Hayes's 'Shaft' was a movie theme which gave it extra exposure far beyond the promotion budget of any record company. Which left The Staples Singers' 'I'll Take You There' and The Temptations' 'Papa Was A Rolling Stone', the only two R&B hits with an aggressively rhythmic base to crossover big in two years. The Jackson 5 were creaming off the youngest record-buyers, the maturer albums of Marvin Gaye ('What's Going On') and Stevie Wonder ('Music Of My Mind', 'Talking Book') were giving Motown a hip and more thoughtful image, R&B bands were experimenting with Hendrix-based guitar in a funk context – notably George Clinton's Funkadelic, soon to be joined by Bootsy and Phelps Collins and the post-Motown Isley Brothers on their own T-Neck label. Philadelphia International was developing orchestrated soul, Isaac Hayes and Curtis Mayfield were pioneering black movie music, Al Green, from the Southern church, and Barry White, from the orchestra conductor's rostrum, were establishing themselves as soul's new kind of "love" men.

These changing times did not affect Brown's sales. He had always been a law unto himself and, since 1964's 'Out Of Sight', a trendsetter, not follower of fashion. There were some strong hits left in Papa's bag. But the pace of his life since 1956 had been phenomenal, relentless performing with an exhausting stage show, incessant rehearsal, a remorseless need to write and cut hit records to keep the business's wheels turning, endless travel and touring. The inability of Polydor to translate his R&B smashes into pop hits of similar stature quickly rankled and he was worried that the company did not know the black market at all, a legitimate concern. He kept Syd Nathan's company going, virtually single-handed, since the early Sixties and reigned as the undisputed king of King since 1965. He expected similar control and respect at Polydor, only with bigger bucks because it was a bigger operation. They were getting immediate street credibility; he would get more money, better international presence and continued artistic freedom. Because they didn't understand the black market, he retained Bob Patton as his own records promotion man. "Back in the Sixties, when [Brown would] get mad, he'd tell us 'Next thing you know I'll have to drive the bus! Gotta do it all myself, gotta do everything!' Actually, he taught his staff well when he wanted to.

"When James hired me, he actually had me go down to Miami and stay with Ben Bart for a month. Ben liked talking about the business. He gave me a list of phone numbers, who to talk to, and he called some people for me. At the time, James was still supposed to be paying him 10 per cent of everything he made. Ben was getting ill by then and he died not too long after." Patton's first job had been co-programme director of WRDW in Augusta but complaints from other local stations stopped the licence coming through quickly so Patton went on the road to promote Brown's shows. Then, because King didn't have a record promotion staff, Patton went to the radio stations too. He was also Brown's booking manager.

"We'd map out a basic routing and then I'd call and find out which buildings were available and go ahead and book them. Ninety per cent of James's personal appearances, either Alan [Leeds] or I booked 'em and we promoted them in-house. We'd buy the advertising, I'd go in and get the disc jockeys, hire them to put out posters and cut the radio spots. If it was a small town and there wasn't a real black station, we'd cut the spots ourselves, Alan and I both came from radio." [Leeds met Brown in Richmond, Virginia by hanging around the shows. His father ran a department store in town. "Alan was a strange kid for a Jewish kid," Patton said. "Instead of running with the group he was supposed to, he was out hanging with the blacks. He only dated black girls and he's since married two!"]

"We did a thing at the Soul Bowl in New Orleans in 1970. James and I, we hired Ike & Tina Turner, we had Pacific Gas & Electric, Junior Walker & The All Stars, Isaac Hayes as co-stars. And Ike [Turner] hated James. They wouldn't have done it except they were getting $12,500 and I gave 'em $15,000, and Isaac was getting $15,000 so I gave him $17,500. We made $500,000. James was going to give me 10 per cent. I got $500."

Not that Patton was doing too badly. "In the end I was Booking Manager, Promotion Director and Office Manager at the same time. In fact, when he went to Polydor I had the same titles except I was also National Promotional Director for James Brown Product at Polydor as well as being Promotional Director for King Records, so I had four salaries for a while. And I collected on all of 'em except from James Brown!" Patton's position at Polydor was a sore with the company from the start. "James insisted on having someone to promote his product exclusively to get it started and then supposedly Polydor's people would jump on the bandwagon. It's kinda strange the way they did it. James called me into New York and I came in the office." Jerry Schoenbaum, then president of Polydor, and Mike Betchy, his promotional director, were there too. "James tells 'em: 'As quiet as it's kept, one of the reasons that 'Hot Pants' is crossing over to all the Top 40 stations is Bob Patton. He's head of my promotion and he's in the contract,

I want him to promote my product with your people.' So James left the room and Jerry and I talked. I don't think Jerry liked it too much that I was pushed on him. So he called in the promotional director and said, 'Mike, this is Bob Patton. The only thing he's trained for is the same thing you do, so work with him. So you can guess how well that worked."

Indeed. Patton recalled that he went out with the next record, 'Make It Funky', which was also the first Polydor release, and got airplay on the number one station in Los Angeles, which persuaded Denver, Detroit, New York to follow. "In one week I got 'em seven major Top 40 stations on James's new record. I call back to Betchy. He says, 'Let me know when you can get anything else.' I said, 'Wait a minute, my job is to get it started and in one week we're already on the black charts and we're ready to break pop.' He said, 'You don't understand, James Brown is a black artist.' They didn't think of crossover back in '71. They could never understand James Brown's potential as an all-round artist. They knew he was a legend in black music back in the Sixties."

In order to get as full a picture as possible of his prickly relationship with his new label, it is essential to look at the dealings as a whole. This will mean getting ahead of the story somewhat but it will form a useful backdrop against which his imminent artistic decline can be seen. By April, 1972, Brown was firing off a memo to Polydor: "To all white people this may concern." "Goddamit, I'm tired," the memo began. "It's been a racist thing ever since I have been here." It continued in a sustained vituperative attack on the company's staff for its racism and inability to understand or sell black music. In spite of the fact that he was less than a year into the new contract, he wished someone could buy him out. The typing is all in capital letters; the tone indignant and angry. Polydor had complained about the number of people he brought into the offices, he countered by suggesting they hire some black staff. "Leave me the fuck alone," he raged. "I am not a boy but a man, to you a black man" before ending with some racist taunts of his own.

Five years later – half-a-decade of gradual, inexorable decline in sales apart from one bright flickering with 'The Payback' band in 1974, of which more later – there was still friction. By now, Polydor was but a part of the even bigger PolyGram Record Group, president Irwin H. Steinberg. On a tour of US military bases, a comedown in itself, he took time to wire Polydor's US chief Eckart Schnabel with complaints about promotion and the poor availability of his records, accusations of discrimination and a threat to sue. His position at Polydor was tenuous. There were restraining notices against James Brown Publications in respect of unpaid bills from Metromedia, *Billboard* Publications, Hertz Corporation and KVC Inc totalling almost $25,000. By the end of December, 1976, Polydor estimated that unrecouped balances paid to James Brown as an artist, a loan made to him and with respect to James Brown Productions totalled $1,514,154. Neither party was very happy.

At the end of November, 1977, Brown wired Polydor from Augusta with the exciting news that he had just recorded a new hit record and would like $25,000 for Christmas, signing off: "The fight is over, your friend". Under no conditions was the money to be sent, insisted PolyGram's chiefs. Indeed, by mid-January, 1978, they had taken steps to impound his aeroplane which, his lawyer wrote, would result in his client doing "everything in his power to make life miserable for you". In the summer, the company ordered an informal audit of Brown's affairs because of (a) management changes in its own financial areas in the preceding years and (b) the singer's deteriorating financial affairs which meant that litigation by a third party was a strong possibility. The company was covering its back.

In August, 1978, Brown appointed as his manager Larry Myers who arranged a tour and, on his client's behalf, demanded a new 10-year recording contract and moneys to pay off all of Brown's debts, which, he told Polydor, were between $4m-$5m but might be settled for $2-$3m. The company reported a neat twist: the new commission would be paid direct to the new manager (i.e. not via Brown). Polydor kicked around the idea of how to get good new product out of the singer – it had deteriorated in quality and quantity since 1976 – such as a payment for each album, additional to a budget for the LP. Only part of royalties would be used to pay off Brown's considerable advances and loan debt to Polydor, some would go direct to the singer as an inducement to come up with another good record. They discussed making a loan to Brown to pay off his creditors.

Another year, another manager: Robert Bray, president of Celebrity Management Inc in Nashville. He rejoiced that Brown had been persuaded to use an external producer on his next album, the singer's latest self-productions had been lazy, at best, totally misguided and out of touch at worst. He'd accept $50,000 cash, a $75,000 budget, Polydor to share in the producer's fee up to two per cent, and after 150,000 copies 25 cents per album to be spent on marketing and promotion of Brown and the album. Great news, the company thought, but there were some problems. There were long-standing garnishments – notices served on Brown to seize money belonging to creditors – which prevented Polydor giving money to him outside previous contracts; the $50,000 to include the producer's fee; fine detail about royalty disbursement; Polydor to administrate the production budget.

Soon after, Brown, Bootsy and George Clinton were working on a new

JBs album, one track of which was played to Polydor. An album written and produced by Bootsy and George Clinton for Brown was discussed but never materialised. It might have been his salvation. By the end of February, a much more toe-in-water deal had been struck with Brad Shapiro who had agreed to produce two sides on James Brown in March for a fee of $5,000, to come out of Brown's royalties. If all three parties agreed, an album would follow with Shapiro getting an extra $15,000. In the end, Brown did two albums with Shapiro – 'The Original Disco Man', which included 'It's Too Funky In Here', and 'People'. The first album was not spectacular and certainly broke no new ground but 'Let The Boogie Do The Rest' had the vocal power and rhythmic drive of old and 'Women Are Something Else (It's No Longer A Man's World)' was a brave, if foolish and tactically inept attempt at reassessing his Sixties hit. The Miami-based producer, who had previously cut albums with Millie Jackson and Wilson Pickett, was a conservative, Southern choice but with the romping.'Too Funky' he seemed to have revitalised Brown's career on record. "When we cut [it] I was mesmerised by his raw sense of rhythm … man, I just got out of his way," Shapiro told Harry Weigner. The Muscle Shoals band – drummer Roger Hawkins, David Hood (bass), Barry Beckett (keyboards), Jimmy Johnson and Larry Byrum (guitars) – had recorded many classical soul albums including Aretha Franklin's Atlantic sessions. They knew their way around funk and gave him the bottom and drive he needed. However, the way 'Too Funky' later evolved on stage into a plodding, mundane dance work-out, speaks for how little there was to the basic song.'Disco Man' sold 175,000, which ranked with his best figures for Polydor, but 'People' did not even break into the Top 75 R&B chart.

The completion of the first tracks with Shapiro had encouraged CNM's Robert Bray to exhort Ekke Schnable to kiss and make up with Brown. He was confident that they had a hit single, Bray could handle Brown, they should get on and record the rest of the album and get it out. If not, other companies were offering upwards of $300,000 for James's signature. Soon after, Brown sent a telegram to Schnabel likening their relationship to a tempestuous marriage. Polydor had his support forever, he telegraphed.

In October, 1979, while Brown was recording tracks for 'People', Larry Myers contacted Polydor and said Brown wanted to negotiate release from his contract, which had 18 months and three albums to go. He would deliver 'People' and record a live double in Japan ('Hot On The One', 1980). Polydor were stuck with their old problem. Court orders from Brown's many creditors amounting to roughly $700,000 prevented them from paying him revenue from his releases and they knew not to expect product from him until he got some cash. A record business Catch 22. Polydor was catching flak not only from James Brown himself but from the black community, outraged that the Godfather of Soul was being prevented from receiving royalties because of unrecouped advances now totalling $1.5m. They suspected Polydor of the sort of Hollywood-style creative accounting that can keep blockbuster movies, like *Forrest Gump*, in the red. There was no evidence to support this.

Interestingly, the debit balance had remained steady since 1975 when new management had taken over his affairs. The $1.5m was spent and not recouped between 1972–75. In the years after 1975, his records had sold about 120,000 mid-price and with foreign earnings and publishing balanced his advance against royalties account for that period. But the company found him a particularly time-consuming, demanding and confrontational artist who took resources away from artists they thought had greater potential and were keen to develop. International income on his new records was in free-fall. They would be glad to say adieu. If the live double was full of old songs – what others were there? – sales would be better for that one double than for three single albums with new songs.

Now that Polydor had secured his back catalogue and could exploit it to recoup advances paid to him since the original 1972 contract, terminate that deal and concurrently offer him a new contract through a third-party company not owned wholly or in part by Brown, thereby avoiding his four or five main creditors, everyone was happy. They offered him $175,000 an album.

And what, precisely, had been Brown's thinking during this time? On November 8, 1979, accompanied by his lawyer, William Kunstler, he held a press conference at the New York Sheraton Hotel at which he called for a complete accounting of his credits from, and debt to, Polydor since the first contract started. He wanted to start again either by renegotiating or cancelling the contract. "Why should I have a deficit with my record company? I'm one of the most popular artists in the world, so why should I have to suffer financial deprivation." He singled out some Polydor executives for sweeping allegations, particularly Irwin Steinberg. "For some reason [he] doesn't want to see me succeed in this business. He is out to destroy me financially, and has done so systematically for ten years."

Brown's lawyer compared his client's case to that of the Watts-based Drummond Distribution, a black subsidiary of Seagram Inc, the drinks firm. There had been a dispute over money and support from the parent company. Kunstler settled by sitting down with the companies to look over the books and contracts together. He felt sure similar agreement could be reached between Brown and Polydor. A representative of Polydor management, Rick Stevens, said he'd be glad to go over the financial records and Brown launched into a tirade about the budget for his previous album. "After all the time I've been in this business, to have to make a record for $25,000 was an insult to me." (He agreed that Stevens had persuaded his masters at Polydor to double the budget.) "They know my records will sell a certain amount no matter how much advertising money they put into it, so they never bother to promote me like they should," Brown went on. Joe Medley, a former Polydor marketing manager, spoke up to back Brown's claims that the company gave a lower priority to R&B in terms of promotional budget. And Polydor knew that, no matter what, he was good for a certain sale that would recoup a clearly-defined advance.

Polydor, Brown and his advisers were still negotiating into the fall of 1980. The record company was on the verge of pulling out and Brown, with Hal Neely back on the scene, was asking for the five-album contract to be modified to a one-album deal, for $175,000, plus four one-album options. To give an idea of how little Polydor executives knew about the history of James Brown, one had scrawled on a memo detailing the negotiations lack of progress: "Hal Nealy [sic] had absolutely nothing to do with any of Brown's success! FACT!!" Having revealed conclusive ignorance, he went on to say that he thought $150,000 for one album was sustainable but he'd prefer to drop Brown altogether.

Like any big corporation, PolyGram, Polydor's parent company, has a significant staff turnover and the reasons for and conditions of old loans are obscured as employees move on. By the Spring of 1981, the parent company had begun to wonder about repayment of a half-a-million dollar loan made to Brown which should have been repaid in 1979. In addition to the loan, interest was now over $800. The advice from executives in place when the loan was made was to write it off. Suing would bring them nothing but grief from the black community. Instead, they should consider a huge push on the back catalogue of forty or so albums because the loan could be recouped against royalties – i.e. all sales would go straight to Polydor. (The web of contracts and debts was tight-spun and entrapped even innocent parties, such as Lyn Collins, Maceo Parker and The JBs who had been signed to Brown's subsidiary label, People. The acts were given a separate accounting by Polydor but the main label's agreement to distribute People had made Brown the sole payee. They paid him advances and royalties, he was supposed to pay the acts. Which is what Polydor told them when they went knocking on the wrong door.)

Of course, Brown was by no means the only African-American artist to become hopelessly embroiled with major recording companies. There have been many similar examples of culture collision over the years and Mammon was only ever likely to emerge as the victor. The decline of the great Southern independent label Stax can be traced to the distribution deal it struck with CBS at, coincidentally, roughly the same time as Brown was moving to Polydor. The Hardest Working Man's funkiest acolyte, George Clinton, got into a dreadful financial tangle when he set up Uncle Jam Records. Only part of the blame for these fiscal disasters can be placed at the revolving doors of the corporations. Bad advice and straightforward graft played their part. Damage from within and without.

After talking about the specifics of James Brown versus Polydor, the conversation at the New York Sheraton Press conference had stretched out to encompass a wider theme – systematic discrimination against "the charismatic black" by white American big business. Brown had felt "targeted" as a black American long before he ever signed with Polydor – by the discriminatory laws of his youth, by the Internal Revenue Service and by the Federal Bureau of Investigation, by the subtler forms of non-legislative discrimination – and it was a feeling that had ample opportunity to fester and grow. If he, the biggest-selling African-American artist of the Sixties, an abidingly popular live draw, could get into such deep financial waters, what hope for the rest? But it was precisely because he was the biggest, that he was a prime target for abuse and misuse from the outside and from within.

CHAPTER 12

James Brown's back catalogue was shifted to Polydor on July 1, 1971. Soon after, despite a previous assertion that he'd stick to singing, dancing and entertaining while steering well clear of politics, he endorsed President Nixon's re-election campaign. Not surprisingly, he took a lot of flak for siding with Tricky Dicky again, particularly from African-American organisations, but although his concert attendances dipped they were soon back up to or near previous levels. For that, he had to thank a super-tight and reliable new show, more hits in the first flush of success on a new label and the amount of work he was getting outside the USA. To this day he has a large, loyal audience base in Europe, many African states and Japan. As the new JBs evolved in the early Seventies, many musicians from the old James Brown Orchestra came back into the fold. Saxophonist St. Clair Pinckney, bass player Charles Sherrell and singer Marva Whitney had left four months before the rebellion in Columbus. Of the others, Fred Wesley went back to Los Angeles but had been hired again as musical director to bring some cohesion to the ex-Pacesetters on the road. He brought Pinckney back too and by the time of their final European tour were again an excellent live, as well as studio, unit.

Maceo Parker and the rest of the horn section, the guitarists Jimmy Nolen and Alphonso Kellum, bassist Bernard Odum and drummer Melvin Parker, signed to House Of Fox and recorded an album, 'Doing Their Own Thing', as Maceo & All The King's Men. The label's owner, Lelan Rogers, claimed that Brown paid dee-jays not to air the record but it's unlikely that the small independent had the distribution set-up to be able to deal with a hit. The group recorded a second album, 'Funky Music Machine' on Excello, and broke up in the late spring of 1972.

As the musicians came and went, so did the other members of staff. "When I decided to leave him," Bob Patton recalled, "James would go through your expense account. He wouldn't really read it, he'd just say 'Well, I won't allow this one, I won't allow that one'. He'd usually do it when you were out on the road, the other side of the country. So you'd have to agree with him or you didn't get home. That's why I started buying rings. I always wear three gold rings, I never wore gold before. So I know I can always hock 'em and get home! James has never said 'I'm sorry' to me. He has said 'You're the one who can handle this problem, I need you back.' I quit, probably, 16 times and was fired 18 times and missed about three weeks pay in the first eight or 10 years. He'd be prepared to say, 'Welcome back' but he'd never, ever say he's sorry. He had to feel like he had to control people. He would try to get Alan [Leeds] and I against each other, or Bobbit and I, or Alan and Bobbit. Divide and rule. You could never get him to be human except when you're one on one. Then, now and again, he'd be James, be OK."

"One thing about James," Maceo said, "he might not always like it but he understands why you might want to try certain things of your own. And if it fails for you, he's waiting with open arms for you to come back. It's almost like you always have a home. You can't beat that." Indeed you cannot beat it so one by one they rejoined it. (Maceo rejoined in 1973 and Melvin returned in late 1975 or early 1976; Jimmy Nolen stayed until shortly before his death from a heart attack on December 16, 1983. St. Clair Pinckney, Charles Sherrell, Fred Wesley all came and went. But even outside the James Brown compound, there's a good chance they're playing together. Fred and Maceo, of course, worked as part of George Clinton's Horny Horns and, well into the Nineties, were touring and recording with a movable feast of former Brown sidemen and singers. The cachet of having been part of the great driving wheel known as The James Brown Orchestra, The JBs, or the most recent incarnation, Soul Generals, backed up with that enormous body of work, is an extremely persuasive entry on a musician's CV.)

The returning players bound together into arguably his last great band. After 'Hot Pants', the last King-distributed single on People whose lyric was made for Joe Tex or Rufus Thomas, Brown used the slower funk grind of 'Make It Funky', which would be split into four parts across two singles, to launch his Polydor career and recorded 'Revolution Of The Mind – Live At The Apollo Volume III', all in July. Good work

Eeeeeeeooooooooow!! As the years passed and the waist spread, the Hardest Working Man In Showbusiness showed few signs of slowing down in May 1985. (DAVID CORIO/REDFERNS)

Everyone had to have one in the 1980s
– James gets funky with a portable Moog.
(DAVID CORIO/REDFERNS)

Give the drummer some! (DAVID CORIO/REDFERNS)

Jerry Lee Lewis, Fats Domino and James at the inaugural Rock and Roll Hall of Fame induction
at the Waldorf-Astoria Hotel, New York City, January 23, 1986. (BETTMANN/CORBIS)

Back on the road again. (LFI)

With new wife Adrienne to announce
a "Live One Night Only" Warner Brothers
pay per view concert in 1991, as he resurrects
his career after release from jail. (LFI)

Hands down – with Adrienne again as he joins
the Hollywood Walk of Fame, January 5, 1992. (LFI)

Taking care of business at his home office in Augusta, September 1995. (TONY FRANK/SYGMA/CORBIS)

Indestructible James Brown on-stage at V99, August 1999. (LFI)

Still a man's world: the doting father with one of his daughters. (LFI)

With Lenny Kravitz after they'd performed together at the Vogue Fashion Awards in New York, October 20, 2000. (REUTERS/CORBIS)

In court again under cross examination at Los Angeles Superior Court, July 2002. (REUTERS/CORBIS)

With his final partner, Tomi Rae Hynie at the Grammy Awards February 13, 2005. (LFI)

Looking fit and well nine months before his death, with Tomi Rae Hynie and their son James Brown II at 'Keepers of the Dream' gala dinner at the Sheraton Hotel, New York, April 6, 2006.
(ARNALDO MAGNANI/CONTRIBUTOR/GETTY IMAGES)

But looking a little tired and weary three months later at the Tower of London, July 4. (LFI)

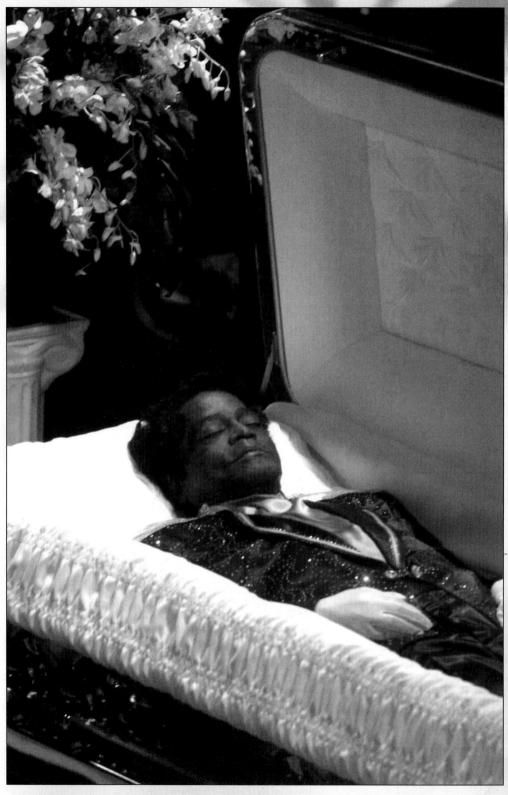

James Brown's final, poignant Apollo appearance on December 28, 2006. Crowds filed past the coffin to pay their final respects to a man who so often lit up the famed theatre. (LFI)

for a man in his late, late thirties. The one-chord bass drive of 'I'm A Greedy Man' was his final release in 1971 and 'Talkin' Loud & Sayin' Nothing', left from the Bootsy sessions of October, 1970, was a No. 1 R&B hit 16 months later in February, 1972. Then, a single on a par with 'Don't Be A Dropout' in its attempt to use his position to urge social change. 'King Heroin' was a poem written by Manny Rosen, who worked in the Stage Delicatessen on Seventh Avenue in midtown Manhattan. He lost a daughter to drug addiction and an overdose. Manny gave the song to Brown who set it to music with arranger Dave Matthews, an ex-symphony orchestra player from Cincinnati, who assumed the role played by Sammy Lowe during the Sixties. Matthews, of whom Bootsy spoke so warmly, was in fact much more in tune with Brown's music than Lowe. He went on the road with the singer, arranged the brass and all round had more "hands on" involvement. The New York session musicians were drawn from the new jazz–funk players such as guitarists Joe Beck and Hugh McCracken, drummer Billy Cobham, the keyboard player Richard Tee and horn players such as Joe Farrell, Dave Sanborn and Michael and Randy Brecker.

The bigger recording budgets Brown was able to command at Polydor meant that he could rise to the challenge of the mature soul works of Marvin Gaye, Stevie Wonder and Curtis Mayfield. With some notable exceptions, few of his King albums had been recorded as such, the vast majority were fairly hastily slapped-together. His first Polydor album, 'There It Is', although rarely mentioned in the same breath as 'What's Going On' or 'Innervisions', is as much of a statement about black life in the USA as those landmark Motown albums. Of course, Brown takes a considerably less melodic approach. But with 'King Heroin' and its anti-drug sequel, 'Public Enemy No. 1', 'Talkin' Loud & Sayin' Nothing', 'I Need Help', credited to his son Teddy, 'I'm A Greedy Man' and the title track there's enough social commentary for a small pamphlet.

Tracks on the double 'Get On The Good Foot' album were recorded between October, 1970 and September, 1972 but, despite their diversity, hang together as well as if they'd been cut at one session. Fred Wesley remembers the 'Good Foot' horn lines as purgatorial to play, especially at the tempo. The simple line was repetitive and hard to play, but Brown's energy gives vitality and life to the hyperdriven track. From the feet food of that title track and the album's other hit, 'I Got A Bag Of My Own', through remakes of hits like 'Cold Sweat', 'Ain't That A Groove', 'Lost Someone' and 'Please, Please, Please' to 'Recitation By Hank Ballard', a spoken tribute to the Godfather of Soul by one of his old King sparring partners (lately signed to James Brown Productions), the album is an affirmation of the funk according to James Brown. 'Recitation' is a track the like of which will doubtless never be heard again. Ballard welcomes the listener to The James Brown World, soberly advertises the songs and musicians to be heard therein and extols the leader's virtues. Ballard's mood turns sombre and his voice gets more world weary as he warns about the perils awaiting those keen to join their superficially glamorous and attractive life and "fight through the mean, vicious jungle of show business", a "hell that chews you up alive". By contrast, Brown's philosophising on 'The Whole World Needs Liberation' and 'Nothing Beats A Try But A Fail' is modesty incarnate.

Brown's raps at this time were far removed from the rhyming invective of the Eighties and Nineties. The straight, affecting recitation of 'King Heroin' was a long way from his own gospel-rooted screams of anguish or ecstasy in the Sixties and the anger and aggression expressed by rappers whose words were often laid over samples lifted from The Godfather's tracks. They're much more conversational, often laying out his thoughts in an unstructured, rambling fashion. The lyrics to his songs had rarely been written to convey much besides the joy of love, the pain of loss or the pursuit of a good time. His new lyrics did not give a full, coherent description of "blackness" but few other writers were getting as close to expressing the spirit of the experience as Brown. In fact, it was argued in the early Seventies that there was more expression of black experience in the punctuating "oo-weees!" and grunts of James Brown than in almost all other lyrics written by African-American composers. That is both condescending and inaccurate, but one can see what the "right-on" writers were getting at. It would be closer to the truth to say that Brown's tracks as a body of work paint the most accurate picture of contemporary black experience.

In tandem with his own recordings, he was producing and writing for his troupe, notably Lyn Collins on People and Bobby Byrd on Brownstone, a label started by Brown with Henry Stone and quickly assimilated into the Polydor empire. These were variations on current James Brown themes, such as Byrd's 'Hot Pants, I'm Coming, Coming, I'm Coming' and 'Keep On Doin' What You're Doin'' in 1971 and Collins' much-sampled 'Think (About It)' (1972) and 'Rock Me Again And Again And Again And Again And Again And Again' (1975). Known as The Female Preacher, Collins was from Abilene, Texas, though she'd been born in Lexington on June 12, 1948. Her father wasn't around much, she worked as a chasier in a grocery store at the age of 14, sang with local groups like Charles Pikes & The Scholars and in the church choir, which was not where she learned to smoke her trademark cheroots. She pestered Brown with tapes and letters and finally met him in Dallas in 1969 claiming never to have sung outside the Lone Star state until she joined his revue. She was in the show's tradition of big-voiced women singers, not quite as much of a powerhouse as Vicki Anderson, the woman she replaced, but assertive and declamatory enough.

The JBs, too, became a strong recording force, notably with 'Doing It To Death', a Fred Wesley feature that became a long-standing stage favourite after its 1973 release and the political riposte 'You Can Have Watergate Just Gimme Some Bucks And I'll Be Straight'. Maceo Parker had rejoined shortly before 'Doin' It To Death' was recorded. "I did a flute solo for a while and later I did an alto solo. That was during the time that he switched me from playing the tenor to the alto, he said I had too much power for the tenor which is again something that he saw about me that I didn't even realise myself, but I do realise now that he was right, once again he was right."

Brown's run of hits had tailed off in the last months of 1972. The adverse reaction to his prominent political affiliations to Nixon had shown no sign of abating and were now affecting his record sales and concert attendances. His Soul Bowl show in Baltimore had been picketed by supporters of "a politician of race" who was critical of Brown for meeting with Nixon. In November, the singer took the unusual step of buying a four-page advertorial in *Jet* magazine to set out his thoughts. Under the headline "Has James Brown Sold Black People Out Or Sold Them In?", he insisted that he'd been in the White House fighting for rights and jobs for his brothers and sisters and a public holiday on Martin Luther King's birthday, denied that money from any of his shows was going to Nixon's re-election fund but that he would continue to do benefits in aid of sickle-cell anaemia, anti-drug-abuse programmes and a Black Muslims' hospital-building project, the proceeds of a future Yankee Stadium date being ear-marked for that. He pointed out that James Brown Enterprises had 137 blacks on his payroll and that Charles Bobbit had risen from valet to president of the company. In conclusion he invited one and y'all to 'Get On The Good Foot' and support his initiatives.

It must have been a relief to get out of the country and visit Europe where his credentials as Soul Brother Number One were taken as read by the vast majority. He toured abroad regularly now, an act of immense international stature. In 1970 he'd made another visit to Africa playing Lagos, Ibadan, Benin and Kaduna in Nigeria and Lusaka and Kitwe in

Zambia and we've seen how he progressed between 1966 and 1971 in Europe. Not all of the critics had been carried along by Brown's revolutionary soul music. *Melody Maker* complained that his third Apollo live album, 'Revolution Of The Mind', and his live shows were riffing hell with nil music content. Now, in the early spring of 1973, he was back to promote the 'Good Foot' album. He appeared in London, at the Royal Albert Hall, and was banned from appearing there again after trouble in the audience. "We have nothing against the artist," the Hall's manager Frank Mundy said, "but it would seem that some concerts attract a certain type of audience ... Women's handbags were being snatched and stewards were threatened with violence by people who burst in. Our stewards are mostly middle-aged people who give their services for free and we just can't allow them to be subjected to this type of unruly behaviour." (The Royal Albert Hall had recently banned several acts. The Nice [and by extension Emerson Lake & Palmer], Chuck Berry, Frank Zappa and Funkadelic had all been banned for a variety of reasons ranging from obscenity to burning the Stars and Stripes.) When he played at the Rainbow Theatre in north London, one policeman was stabbed and two ushers wounded in struggles at the entrances.

But one of the biggest concerts was to be at the Musikhalle in Hamburg where Polydor had its headquarters just around the corner from the Intercontinental Hotel. Surrounded by tall Aryan men from the record company, his bushy Afro swaying to one side as though he'd been sleeping on it, Brown shuffled into the lobby like a prize fighter surrounded by trainers, managers and promoters, which was pretty much his relationship with Polydor. The centre-piece of the penthouse suite was a three-tier cake, the bottom layer a yard wide and decorated with a chocolate icing portrait of the singer. Perched on the top tier is another cake in the shape of a dismembered foot, also covered in chocolate. The legend in white icing reads 'Get On The Good Foot'.

Journalists from all over the world – Japan, many European countries, GIs from the US bases in what was West Germany – had gathered under the usual rules of engagement: address him as Mr. Brown, no questions about politics. "Musically," he said, "I've been kind of a loner. I use my own chords in my own way. I don't write according to any laws or restrictions ... I'm wondering, do I still play music?" Because the vast majority of people in the room did not have English as a first language, it took some while before the assembly realised he'd made a joke. Some never got it at all. Thus the pressure of the international star. He actually cracked quite a few jokes.

158

Children? He had six. "The youngest is three months old so you can see I'm still in good spirits."

But terrible tragedy was not far off. In June, 1973, all temporary disappointments were put into stark relief by the death of his son, Teddy, who still lived in Toccoa with Velma, Brown's first wife. Bob Patton vividly recalled the time. "Teddy drove up to New York with two friends. He had a band called Teddy Brown And The Fabulous Flickers [in his autobiography Brown says they were called The Torches] and they weren't that bad. He stayed away from the office until he knew his dad was gone. James loved him, but he found it hard to say that. Teddy was driving a little car and they went out to Harlem to visit some friends ... Teddy was just getting out of school to start private school." From there, they set off to visit another friend in Canada. The car was doing 80 mph when it hit a bridge abutment near Elizabethtown, New York, the driver having apparently fallen asleep at the wheel. Teddy was 19. He was buried in Toccoa; one of The Famous Flames, Sylvester Keels, supplied the music at the service. Brown had actually fulfilled a couple of contracted dates between Teddy's death and his funeral. It helped him get through the shock and pain. At the grave, Patton remembered, "James turned away and went back to the car when they lowered the casket. He didn't want to see that. I'll never forget the ceremony. There was a guy there named Senator Johnson, a black senator from Georgia, who was trying to talk James into doing a show for his campaign while they were walking out of the church, getting ready to bury James's son. I grabbed him but Bobbit pulled me back. And all of James's ex-wives and girlfriends were there. He had 'em in all different hotels for his son's funeral. I don't think he spent time with them. And dee-jays were there, all of 'em looking for handouts."

Teddy's death hit Brown hard. Although constant touring and recording meant that he was rarely home to enjoy his family life to the full, it's fair to say that he liked being a Dad. He must have. He had children – six that he owned up to – with three women, two of them his wives. His three sons were the product of his first marriage to Velma Warren, and he had two daughters with second wife Deidre (DeeDee). He had another daughter by Yvonne Fair and, although he always denied that he was the father, settled a paternity suit brought by the former secretary of his San Francisco fan club.

There was plenty of work to distract the singer's mind from grief. In late 1972, he had written, with Fred Wesley, the score to *Black Caesar*, a typical low-budget blaxploitation movie starring Fred Williamson. On the soundtrack album Brown adopted for the first time the title The

Godfather of Soul, a fittingly dynastic sobriquet for a bandleader whose former players showed loyalty in the face of a stern lawmaker and his occasionally despotic rule. (Interestingly, the *New York Times* suggested that this sobriquet subconsciously suggested fatigue and a distancing, a kind of fading grandeur.) Before Isaac Hayes (*Shaft*) and Curtis Mayfield (*Superfly*), movie soundtracks featuring African-American musicians had been limited largely to the use of jazz musicians as players – Sonny Rollins on *Alfie*, Jimmy Smith on *Walk On The Wild Side* and so on. But the defining contribution came from arrangers and orchestrators such as Oliver Nelson and Quincy Jones. (This, of course, excludes the many rock'n'roll films of the Fifties where the music was the *raison d'être* of the film, not incidental to it.)

Hayes and Mayfield used contemporary soul structures in the context of the movie score. Brown and Wesley widened the James Brown funk palette, for example by using jazzier strains of his instrumental albums (and the trombonist's own inclinations). It wasn't like doing film music Wesley said, it was doing music for James Brown for a film with Brown pulling one way and Larry Cohen, the writer-producer-director, pulling the other. "We've had a little trouble in that area," Brown told *Black Stars* magazine, "because people try to tell us how to be black and how to write black music. Later for that." The album sold 300,000 within three weeks of release; the movie grossed over $1m in the same period.

He signed to do another three soundtracks and wanted to act in the sequel to *Black Caesar*. "I know I can act," he told *Jet*. "All blacks can act. The only reason we survive today is because we've had to act a certain way for the white man." But in the end he wrote only one more soundtrack, *Slaughter's Big Rip-Off*, directed by Gordon Douglas, Jim Brown starring. (He wouldn't act until much later, when he took a cameo role in an episode of the TV show, *Miami Vice*, thrillingly titled Missing Hours.) In common with much of the white business world's exploitation of black culture, blaxploitation films were poorly made at low cost, given minimal promotion and the market was quickly flooded with them. Allowing for such a cynical attitude, it is scarcely any surprise that the boom lasted only a few years and African-Americans resumed their predominantly bit-part role in Hollywood until Spike Lee's *She's Gotta Have It* (1986) started a quieter, more resolute and sustained revolution.

While Brown was writing and recording those film scores, and dealing with the loss of his son, his presence on the singles charts waned. But at the end of 1973 he found the energy for one last great push. Barely six weeks after Teddy's funeral, Brown recorded the rhythm track to 'The Payback' in

Augusta, adding brass and backing vocals in New York the following month. It was the start of work on the soundtrack for Cohen's next movie, a sequel to *Black Caesar*. A disagreement with Cohen resulted in Brown leaving the project, with his tracks. He recorded feverishly over the next four months and the new songs – mostly written by combinations of Brown, Wesley, Charles Bobbit and John "Jabo" Starks – formed the basis of two double albums. The music was rounded by the return of yet more old colleagues, Maceo Parker, Jimmy Nolen, Charles Sherrell among them. "I rejoined the group after being away and again it was exciting, that James Brown mystique," Maceo said.

At the end of 1973, 'Stone To The Bone', the first single, also appeared as a relentless 10-minute album cut off 'The Payback' double album. The second 45, 'The Payback', has opening horn and guitar parts clearly written in a style fashionable for blaxploitation movies but evolves into a typical James Brown extended funk extemporisation with screams. It went to No. 1 on the R&B charts, No. 26 pop. Cohen's film was released as *Hell Up In Harlem*, (with an Edwin Starr score); Brown, exhibiting an unexpected touch of irony, called his next album simply 'Hell'. He thought it had a better concept, addressing global issues both from the perspective of leaders and the way in which the problem affected the "ordinary Joe". Although the title track breezes through contemporary issues, it is one of his most varied collections, mixing old songs (a lilting 'Please, Please, Please', 'Lost Someone', 'I Can't Stand It '76' – he was going to call the latter 'Stone To The Bone – Again' but decided to own up on its real genealogy), traditionals and standards done with reverence to the spirit if not the exact structure of the "accepted" versions ('When The Saints Go Marching In', 'Stormy Monday', a surprisingly affecting version of the ballad 'These Foolish Things', which had been a hit for Brown in 1963), strongly muscled dance tracks ('Hell', 'Coldblooded', 'Papa Don't Take No Mess' and 'My Thang', the last two both No. 1 R&B hits) and philosophical musings ('A Man Has To Go Back To The Cross Road Before He Finds Himself' and 'Don't Tell A Lie About Me And I Won't Tell The Truth On You'). The title track, with its vision of hell on earth, is a grim reminder of Brown's roots, the sort of problems day-to-day existence brought most African-Americans and of the singer's abiding reverence for the institutions of the United States of America and the difficulties of being President – "in the White House, it's hell".

Come the new album, come the new investiture. After a short reign as The Godfather of Soul, he is now James Brown – Minister of New,

New Super Heavy Funk. At the same time, the reunited members of The James Brown Orchestra who were helping to spread the Minister's gospel, had been given recording contracts of their own and were proving excellent apostles. The 1974 album 'Damn Right I Am Somebody' by Fred Wesley & The JBs marked the first time Brown had allowed anyone else's name to be affixed to his band since Al "Brisco" Clark (1964) and Alfred "Pee Wee" Ellis (1968). The tracks, recorded during 'The Payback' sessions, offer a familiar mixture of covers (Marvin Gaye's 'You Sure Love To Ball'), thorough dance workouts ('Same Beat', 'If You Don' Get It The First Time, Back Up & Try It Again, Party') and ghetto comment (the title track and 'I'm Payin' Taxes, What Am I Buyin''). It marked Wesley, Maceo and Jimmy Nolen as players with a far broader range than the casual listener might expect had they heard only the hit singles. Maceo's own album, 'US!!', features him almost exclusively on alto and the effect is to push his instrument further to the front of the group making it more of a lead voice than his tenor. The straight ahead JBs record had rearrangements of 'Soul Power' and 'Doing It To Death', three cover versions and a longer and slightly portentous piece, 'The Soul Of A Black Man'.

This latter piece was not an attempt to update W. E. B. Du Bois' 1903 tract 'The Souls Of Black Folk' to sound of funky music but one of several recorded in the early Seventies which Brown used as a platform for reminiscence about the hardness of his upbringing, the notion of "blackness" as expressed in music and his views on the present and future state of the nation. Ostensibly, Maceo's saxophone playing is 'The Soul of a Black Man' but the horn man's words – "I've learned so much from you, your teachings" – inviting the singer to rap some more give an entirely different impression. "Thank you, Mr. Parker. We start with respect," which he felt had been "lost along the way". He indulges in typical word play, such as the three meals a day he ate as a child: "Oatmeal, no meal and missed meal." He had "so many holes in my clothes that even a blind man could see them." Another monologue-based track he recorded around this time, in December, 1972, found him in a very similar frame of mind. 'Like It Is, Like It Was' was so titled on the *Black Caesar* soundtrack but in its original, unedited form was known as 'The Blues'. The fuller version is more revealing of his frame of mind. "I have been broke and hungry many times in my life," he began and there is a similar remembrance of the state of his clothes on the way to school, the bed, or lack of one, at home, the fact he was nine before he had proper underwear to wear. Then he began to talk about, and sing, the blues. He stopped. "I don't know how to sing the blues like I used to, but I can always sit back and think about it. He picked up the theme later on. He couldn't sing the blues because "I ain't got no environment no more ... We got to admit we have lost some of our heritage."

CHAPTER 13

"He was doing some smoking back then [in the mid–Seventies] of weed which had a little bit of the California weed that people who worked with the acts like Elton John and Joe Cocker had gotten to him," Bob Patton said. "It wasn't as strong as what he got into but I took two hits off it and sat up in his dressing room one night about two or three in the morning. That was the only time I smoked with him. There was a knock on the door, I went to the door and it was Danny Ray. Danny came in and I said, 'What are you doing here? James and I are here sitting talking.' He says, 'Mr. Patton, it's eight o'clock in the morning'. I said, 'No, it can't be, James and I ...' and I turned around and James'd been long gone. I'd been sitting there talking to nobody. So I figured I didn't want to smoke that shit anymore. James was smoking a whole one of those every night before he'd go to bed. If that was strong, I don't wanna know about no PCP. I didn't really knock him but I've told anybody that knows me that I wanna see him get help, I want to see him get back his feeling. At his age, he still could be a great entertainer. Just let him get his health back. He doesn't have his health while he's tied down with that drug. He doesn't have that drug, the drug has got him."

Problems of every imaginable type from every imaginable source combined to hasten the commercial decline of James Brown in the mid-Seventies. Yet even the most pessimistic prognosis of the changing tastes in music would not have foreseen the dramatic collapse of the influence and appeal of the hardest working man in show business. Naturally, the death of his son had hit him hard but work seemed to sustain him. His dissatisfaction with Polydor was at a stand-off while they enjoyed the successes of 1974.

In August, he took the opportunity of his success to call Polydor and ask for a $400,000 advance to pay off his income tax (the Internal Revenue Service first became interested in his finances in 1968). Problem was, the record company claimed he still owed them $470,000 plus $363,000 in recording costs for the first eight months of the year. Sales had clawed back $276,000 but his account was still $557,000 in the red. In the end, he received a loan of $500,000 but had to use his shares in the Dynatone, Golo and Tansoul publishing companies as security, along with future recording or producer's royalties and advances enshrined in his 1971 contract with Polydor and his writer's or publisher's royalties and other sums from the three publishers previously mentioned plus Jadar and CriTed and any producer's royalties.

Then, in January, 1975, his tax problems intensified when the State of New York Department of Taxation and Finance served a tax collector's levy on Polydor as garnishee in respect of unpaid tax claims against Brown and his wife Velma. This obliged Polydor to transfer all personal property and pay any money due to the singer under his recording contract to the Department of Tax and Finance until the amount of the levy, which was $85,411.53, was satisfied. In effect, before Polydor could get their hands on his royalties to pay off the loan he had from them, they had to hand over the money in the States taxes.

James Brown began to feel (a) everyone was out to get him, (b) he was losing control of his career, (c) most of his faithful lieutenants were deserting him.

"I actually worked with James until '77 but from '75 I went off solo and charged him for anything I did," Patton said. "I'd set up shows in Canada or wherever and charged him 10 per cent of it. Then he'd come up with a thing like, 'You only get 10 per cent if we do two shows'. Bobbit tried to look out for me. I actually made as much money until 1977 as I did before but I had to be paid for everything on one gig before I'd set up another." Patton left when Brown's demand for loyalty went too far. "My daughter was born in July, 1975. We were doing a big concert in New Orleans, an outdoor thing, and I came back to Nashville, which is where I was based at the time, and I called James in Augusta. I was at the hospital, my wife was having the baby. He says, 'Where are you?' I said, 'Well, I wanna tell you first that we're sold out and Mr. Bobbit and Mr. Holmes are in New Orleans and I'll be back there tomorrow night for the show.' He said again, 'Well, where are you?' I said, 'Well, I'm in Nashville.' He said, 'What are you doing in Nashville?' I said, 'I'm at the hospital. My wife is having a baby.' He got real quiet. He says, 'Mr. Patton, are you a doctor?' I said, 'James, you know I'm not a doctor.' He says, 'Well, you go to New Orleans – she don't need you, she needs a doctor. What are you gonna do for her? Your job's working for me.' And I hung up the phone."

Patton said that Brown got another of his managers to ring him back in Nashville and reiterate his importance to the organisation and smooth running of the concert before showtime. "So I went back down. But after that I started being less used. To this day I still love James and respect him. You have friends that you know are not going to be right to you but you're still …" He paused. "They're great entertainers and he's probably one of the greatest entertainers to me. I don't know if I would ever work for him again but I'm glad I did because the rest of this is easy. I did some work with Elvis, because of working with James, when he went out on the road in '69/70. I promoted some of his shows."

Charles Bobbit left Brown's organisation a year or two after Patton. "The record company wasn't doing anything for [Brown]. He wanted to do everything himself. He was starting to get paranoid and I think that's what finally led him to where he is now. You see, we had been the team behind James, not Polydor. And we'd all come over from the King era. At King, James was responsible for 75 to 90 per cent of the sales. He was King Records. And actually, at the black department of Polydor, he was 75 per cent of the sales but still they never respected him. 'You can't call us at four o'clock in the morning and then hang up on us'. And James used to do that to each different president that worked there. [Polydor] just didn't care about James Brown. They've done more in the last few years in re-releasing his records and CDs.

"He's always had that touch of paranoia and I'd say since 1974/75, when he started going downwards, I think that was the turnaround. He wasn't with King, he wasn't in control, he couldn't force them to do things. When he was first with Polydor, he'd call and say 'Well, I want to go into the studio, unless you give me $200,000, unless you fix my plane, unless you pay all my people …' and they'd do it. All of a sudden they're saying, 'Hold it, you owe us two million dollars, we can't give you anymore.' 'Well, I won't work.' 'OK, so you don't work.' "

After 1974, it is clear, too, that Brown became less decisive about the direction of his own music. African-American music had fragmented into sweet soul, hard funk and disco. In the last-named style, all rough edges were smoothed and polished out of existence, spontaneous emotional expression was being supplanted by the chanted chorus, the melody was simple and the lyrics were in a mundane love-and-good-times bag. The arrangements became predictable, the beats-per-minute count on a record became one of its selling points. Brown was far too raw for that market. He'd used overdubs and speeded a track up or slowed it down but he was at essence a bandleader and singer who cut tracks live in the studio with a band when they were hot. The new studio techniques, particularly that of recording tracks in layers – rhythm, then brass, string and finally vocals, were anathema to him.

Stylistically, he stuck with the hard funk but here the slew of self-contained bands who took 'Papa's Got A Brand New Bag' and its aftermath as a launch pad were mostly younger and their visual flash began to make Brown's show, for so long the foundation of his empire, look very dated. Sly Stone's talent had burnt out but George Clinton's Parliament and Funkadelic troupe led the funk forward followed by The Ohio Players, Kool & The Gang, Maurice White's Earth Wind & Fire, and Larry Blackmon's Cameo, among many others.

The 1974 album, 'Reality', featured the No. 4 R&B hit 'Funky President (People It's Bad)'. Recorded in New York with a band of local session musicians at a time when Gerald Ford was providing interim Presidential leadership after the downfall of Nixon, the track encouraged ordinary folks to take charge of their destiny, just as Brown was losing control of his own, control he'd fought to establish for two decades. But, after more than 20 years of 300 dates a year with recording sessions fitted in whenever and wherever, the hardest working soul brother number one finally started to show signs of strain, wear-and-tear and exhaustion. He was still the biggest-selling African-American performer of the 20th century but the respect he received from the American establishment was negligible. They had used him when their cities were about to burn in the late Sixties. Added to the demands of creating and performing, he'd been running his own businesses since the early Sixties and, a mixture of spiritual figurehead and political leader, had the responsibility of carrying the hopes, dreams and expectations of African-Americans. The Reverend Al Sharpton's upward political trajectory passed through Brown's orbit in a quasi-managerial capacity. Sharpton's family had moved to a house a few blocks from Brown's in Queens. His only memory of his father is that he took young Al to see James Brown at the Apollo. He had met James's son Teddy shortly before the fatal car crash and was introduced to the Godfather in 1973 before a concert at the Newark Symphony Hall. At the time, Brown was doing benefits for Reverend Jesse Jackson's PUSH and the SCLC. Soon after, he did two benefits for Sharpton's National Youth Movement at the Albee Theater in Brooklyn and took the young man around the country for a year, accompanying him to gigs, radio and TV shows. Sharpton tried to set up branches of the movement wherever they stopped. "When we honour Brown," the

Reverend said before a Madison Square Garden show in 1974, "we really honour ourselves because he has in the past 20 years outlived the effectiveness of many civil rights organisations in pointing the way for a generation of black young men and women." Heavy load.

The strain was most manifest in Brown's records, which no longer made trends but followed them. Almost everyone who was anyone was in the disco now and the trouble was off the streets. Like an ageing sportsman who'll suddenly give a glimpse of the glories of his youth, Brown could hit the spot with the occasional track. 'Get Up Offa That Thing (Release The Pressure)', a lively, if straightforward dance hit which got to No. 4 on the R&B charts in 1976 is a prime example. "Jimmy Nolen and I were down in Miami and we was just messing around in the dressing room and we came up with this rhythm track," Charles Sherrell said. "So we took it to James and said 'Hey, Mr. Brown, we got this real nice thing. We gonna let you hear it and just go ahead and cut. So he says, 'Great, great, great, great.' So we got the guys together and we laid it down. It was just a hot song." Well, not great to the power of five, perhaps, but a complete return to form in comparison with the previous year's confused and lamentable 'Everybody's Doin' The Hustle & Dead On The Double Bump'.

The old order was collapsing. Elvis Presley, the only white artist of similar stature from the same generation (Brown was roughly 20 months the elder), died in 1977. They had met but, Bob Patton recalled, "they weren't really friends. Elvis was a true fan of Jackie Wilson. Now the guys who worked for Elvis, his crew, Sonny West and those guys, they loved James. I'd always have to get them into the shows. And Elvis came to see him and shook hands with him but they weren't close."

Patton doesn't remember them singing gospel together, as the Godfather claimed in his autobiography, but Brown certainly attended Presley's funeral. "James wanted to get into Elvis's funeral. It was arranged to get a limousine to pick James up and take him direct to the house [Graceland] for the 'viewing' and everything. And James did that. In fact, when James was there, he was talking to Priscilla and a couple of people and he was standing next to the casket, leaning on it. Fred Davis [a former dee-jay from Texas who joined Brown's organisation] started to turn white. He says, 'Mr. Brown, Mr. Brown.' James looked over and says, 'Can't you see I'm talking to people'. So Fred whispers to him, 'Mr. Brown, you're leaning on Mr. Presley'. If James Brown ever turned close to white, that was it. It took him about a minute and then he recovered."

The latter part of his career has not been so resilient. In spite of all of his troubles in the United States, Brown's stage performances continued to pull in good-sized audiences abroad. The shows were increasingly stylised, the road bands played with a studied rather than rampant energy and the singer's own contribution was, quite naturally, less athletic and the authority in his voice was less sustained. The hardest working man in show business couldn't work so hard any more and found nothing to replace the sheer physical vigour that made his shows so compelling. Perhaps, if he had been able to maintain the last great road band of the mid-Seventies, he could have developed his show along more overtly musicianly lines but his erratic behaviour had finally convinced even the most loyal players that their futures lay elsewhere. Fred Wesley, his lips bleeding and teeth aching from blowing the trombone for 10 minutes solid on the 'Funky Good Time' brass riff would silently curse when Brown yelled "Hey, Fred! When I say blow ..." and give up a solo, either disinterested, exasperated or bug-eyed with exhaustion. As bandleader and musical director, Brown expected him to be on 24-hour call, seven days a week. When the money ceased to be worth it, and the fines, when he paid them, became infantile and the fact that he got no respect from his constituency – jazz musicians – began to irk and embarrass him, he walked. Fred had some fun with George Clinton as leader of The Horny Horns, blew jazz and latterly hitched up again with Maceo and "Pee Wee" Ellis.

Maceo Parker quit, again, in 1975 at the end of a tour which had begun the year before. During the African leg of the lengthy jaunt, after a concert in Zaire, a plane carrying James Brown and the band, B. B. King and musicians, The Detroit Spinners, The Crusaders and Lloyd Price only just cleared the runway because it was almost terminally over-loaded with Brown's personal effects. In one of his most outrageous and potentially lethal outbursts of unrestrained egotism, Brown insisted that other passengers had their luggage thrown off to make way for the Godfather's excess baggage and even then the plane scarcely got into the air. Parker left with few regrets but would return one more time. George Clinton, interviewed in 1995, said of the Brown's horn section to whom he gave safe harbour [Maceo Parker, Fred Wesley among them] said: "There's nobody in the world that is as dedicated to each other," making them sound like war veterans, "or to anybody that they played with for that matter. I guess after you've played with James Brown, and they all used to talk about it like they didn't like it but they talked about it so much that you knew that they had to like it. And now they can see it, because they had so much discipline, they can appreciate almost anything else and there ain't nothin' hard to them after going through that." They could also talk it. "Very rarely do people impress me by trying to put interpretation on music, especially funk because funk is anything that you want it to be as far as I'm concerned. But they can do it and sound so intellectual and be right on the money."

Brown toured Europe regularly – 1977, 1978, 1979 and 1981 – and recorded his final Polydor album in Tokyo in December, 1979. He went back two decades for his next label. His old friend Henry Stone had recorded Brown's '(Do The) Mashed Potatoes' in Miami under the pseudonym Nat Kendrick & The Swans and released it on his Dade label in 1959. He'd brokered the deal for Brad Shapiro to produce Brown. Now, he came to Brown's assistance again and released 'Rapp Payback (Where Iz Moses)' on his TK label, one of those sudden bursts of in-the-pocket funk that the Godfather of Soul could still cut. The 1980 JBs, particularly bassist David Weston and long-serving guitarist Jimmy Nolen, generated a locked-tight drive few previous orchestras or JBs would be ashamed of. But the single reached only No. 46 on the R&B charts – TK's national distribution or promotion wasn't the best but, more to the point, the tastes of Brown's African-American audience had changed once and for all. 'Soul Syndrome', the album built around the single, sounded out of step both with hard funk and the slicker dance music of 1980. But Brown's older grooves continued to be popular in the USA at the grass roots level. A new wave of acts both white and black, from Pere Ubu to James "Blood" Ulmer, were playing with JB funk. James White & The Blacks (or James Chance & The Contortions) attempted to build a career on reworkings of old hits like 'I Can't Stand Myself' and 'King Heroin'.

As if to emphasise the windblown lack of direction of his career, he appeared at the Grand Ole Opry, Nashville's bastion of red-neck country & western music. "I could throw up," one old-timer told *Country Music* magazine in May, 1979. Singer Jean Shepard refused to appear on the show. But the magazine went on to say that Brown eventually won over the audience. Two years after the event, Porter Waggoner, the performer who'd taken Brown to the Opry, told the same magazine that he did it to add another milestone to the Grand Ole Opry and get world-wide news coverage, "The King of Soul Music appears at the Grand Ole Opry!" But some in the C&W establishment questioned his loyalty. *Country Music* wondered whether the prejudice was racial rather than musical. "That could have been a factor," Waggoner admitted, adding that if his critics knew James Brown "they wouldn't have felt that way. [He] is one of the greatest men, one of the most professional men that I have ever met."

But just as the audience which had been his life blood for 25 years was deserting him utterly, he found a new generation of white fans. After his success with the *Black Caesar* and *Slaughter's Big Rip-Off* soundtracks there had been talk of a starring role in a movie. One visualised him as an African prince while another, *Come To The Table*, would give Brown the part of the world's No. 1 pool player named Youngblood – presumably a sort of Augusta Fats. Gil Moses was to direct and there were roles for Charles Bobbit and Lyn Collins. The film never materialised, although a movie titled *Youngblood* was shot starring Lawrence Hilton-Jacobs, Ren Woods and Bryan O'Dell. It bore little, if any, resemblance to the synopsis of Brown's aborted project. The group War wrote and performed its soundtrack.

The offer to take a cameo role as Reverend Cleophus James, a hot gospel minister of the Triple Rock Church Spiritual Choir, in John Landis's *The Blues Brothers* movie in 1980 proved a wiser decision. The appearances of Brown and Aretha Franklin as the owner of soul food restaurant, John Lee Hooker as a street musician, Ray Charles as a calamitous musical instrument store manager and Cab Calloway provided interludes of righteous and soulful verisimilitude which hover on the brink of patronising in the pedestrian plot designed as a vehicle for the comic antics of John Belushi and Dan Ackroyd. Not that Brown felt remotely patronised. "I was going through a bad period at the time, having trouble getting my records released" he told *Musician* magazine. "Truth is truth, and I was not in demand, not wanted."

"*The Blues Brothers* introduced me to an audience from a gospel concept," Brown said. "but it's still James Brown the way I did it. But I wouldn't do disco or a sexy dance or a regular James Brown dance. I would go from side to side, they call it sailing. But the movie introduced me to a total audience and everybody got a chance to see me from all nationalities."

Alas, they did not find any new James Brown material in the record stores to excite them. The cameo jump-started demand for his live shows in the United States but not in the black theatres – many had closed, hit badly by disco and the recession – but in the clubs like the Lone Star. And he again began to get more TV appearances. In 1976, Brown had conceived and started producing and directing his own TV show, *Future Shock*, which he filmed in Atlanta. The show was by blacks for blacks and gave African-Americans from all walks of life a platform. To keep control, he bought air time on TV stations and sold his own advertising time. His organisation claimed it was on in a dozen cities in the South and South-west. At the end of 1976 it was due to be sold to 42 African countries, it was claimed. One network offered the programme a three-month trial; Brown demanded a five-year contract. In 20 years time, he expected to control a large segment of what American TV viewers watched. In reality, *Future Shock* had no future. But after *The Blues Brothers*, Brown was still in demand as a guest on TV shows.

In February, 1982, he was in Los Angeles to record a show called *Solid Gold* when he met Adrianne Modell Rodriguez, the show's make-up and hair stylist and sometime actress on soaps such as *Days of Our Lives* and *The Young And The Restless*. They wed in late 1984. A marriage licence wasn't the only contract he put his name to that year. In March, 1982, Island Records signed Brown. "The deal is one of the most exciting in the company's history," they announced, "and it represents a fresh chapter in Brown's career." He was to start work that spring at the Compass Point Studios in funky Nassau with the hit team of drummer Sly Dunbar and bassist Robbie Shakespeare and the rest of the studio's house band – Mikey Chung (guitar), Wally Badarou (keyboards), Sticky Thompson (percussion). Brown, said Island, would produce the album and write the material and bring some of The JBs International band with him including Jimmy Nolen, Fred Wesley, St. Clair Pinckney and trumpeter Holly Ferris.

If not exactly a marriage made in heaven, this intriguing juxtaposition of the great soul singer and funk minister with the heavy, heavy reggae team could have been a fascinating combination of styles. Paul Wexler, son of Jerry, the producer of so many great Atlantic Records hits, had ushered the deal through as Island's US artist & repertoire (A&R) co-ordinator, and saw it slip through his fingers like water. "He was really excited about breaking the cycle of recording for yet another major label," Wexler told *Billboard* as sessions on the album, tentatively titled 'Country Funk', got under way. "He's looking forward to the prospect of a little personal attention from a smaller company. James doesn't have to be hot. This is an artist whose contribution speaks for itself." However, he would never again be in a situation where he could exert the sort of power he had at his previous small label, King, because the industry had changed. Brown reported between five and eight new songs in the bag, one called 'Bring It On', and was aiming for "a mass appeal record". He looked forward to working with the hot reggae team. "There's a feeling they get that I can identify with."

Alas, Brown's ego, never dormant for long, was in volatile mode. He arrived three hours late for a welcoming party thrown by label founder Chris Blackwell and local dignitaries, a social gaffe blamed on the tonsorial problems the humidity gave Henry Stallings as he tried to tame Brown's hair. All was soon forgotten as Brown, Wesley, composer Wally Badarou and The All Stars got down to work. The sessions developed, stickily enough, but came to a head when, Wexler alleged, Brown demanded publishing rights to a song written by Dunbar and Shakespeare as though he were back in the King Studios in Cincinnati with The James Brown Orchestra. Soon after, the unfortunate Stallings succumbed to bleeding ulcers. Brown was certain he had been poisoned by the studios' staff and fled Nassau with his entourage. Wexler later said he'd go through the turmoil again without a second thought. "All the bruises on his creative psyche and fears of exploitation that stem historically from very real abuses and rip-offs, [he] is indisputably a talent of monumental proportions. History has repeatedly shown that his finished product has always made any hassles *en route* seem awful paltry in retrospect."

John Belushi died of a drugs overdose while Brown was working with Belushi's former partner Dan Ackroyd on another film, *Dr Detroit* (it featured 'King Of Soul' and a new version of 'Get Up Offa That Thing') and the anti-drug homily the singer delivers in his autobiography about Belushi's death is particularly grim in view of the direction in which his personal life was heading. A third movie, 1985's *Rocky IV* (Sly Stallone nukes Dolph Lundgren in unbelievably crass sequel to the sequel of the sequel to *Rocky*), brought an even greater breakthrough as Dan Hartman and Charlie Midnight wrote a theme tune, 'Living In America', performed in the film in glorious Technicolor by Mr Brown.

After the 1980 set 'Soul Syndrome' on TK, Brown had featured later that year on *The Blues Brothers* soundtrack album, taped a live double album at Studio 54 in New York which would come out in 1981. His only new studio recordings had been 'Nonstop!' for Polydor in 1981 and 'Bring It On', based around one song from the aborted Island project, released on his own Augusta Sound label in 1983, neither of which caused much commercial excitement. But 'Living In America' illustrated what Brown needed to get to a new, younger pop market: new, younger pop writers and producers. Of course, the invaluable promotional exposure of a multi-million dollar budget Hollywood movie did not hurt the sales of 'Living In America'. Driven with lumbering rhino-power, the single thundered up the US pop charts to become only his second Top 5 pop hit, 20 years and two months after the last, 'I Got You (I Feel Good)'. Only five acts had had bigger spans between Top 5 hits – Frank Sinatra, Smokey Robinson, Stevie Wonder and Johnny Mathis among them. As 'Living In America' peaked, Brown was inducted into the Rock'n'Roll Hall of Fame, one of the first 10 members. Twenty-one years after winning his first Grammy for 'Papa's Got A Brand New Bag', 'Living In America' brought him his second, for Best Rhythm & Blues Vocal Performance, Male, at the 1986 awards. The competition this time was somewhat smoother – Al Jarreau, Luther Vandross, Oran "Juice" Jones and Billy Ocean. But did Brown like the record, the first on which there was almost absolutely no input from the Godfather of Soul apart from the vocals?

As Hartman said before his death in March, 1994, Stallone had wanted a Led Zeppelin sound with a James Brown vocal. Certainly, the writing and production team thought it a tall order producing a "semi-patriotic James Brown-type dance track" because his timing had greater sophistication and his voice was much tougher than was normally heard on pop hits of the Eighties. So they replaced patriotic overtones with Working Man realism. Hartman recorded and sang a basic track and sent it to Brown who requested horns to add to the fat rock rhythm section sound. The Uptown Horns, on tour with Robert Plant, were contracted. It was at Brown's suggestion, Hartman later claimed, that he and Midnight completed an entire album with Brown, 'Gravity'. According to Tony Cook, a James Brown road drummer for some 10 years from the mid-Sixties, the writers/producers studied the band on stage, record and video and recorded tracks in a very fair approximation of their style. In addition to 'Living In America', Hartman and Midnight consistently fitted out Brown with new rock-biased tracks – 'Goliath', 'Repeat The Beat (Faith)', 'Turn Me Loose, I'm Dr Feelgood', 'How Do You Stop' and the title track – that clicked with a white rock market as well as part of the younger African-American audience, the crowd he was really keen to reach again. (It showed what could be done if Brown would bite-the-bullet and work with the many younger writer/producers keen to work with him. Hartman was hot at the time, working on the soundtracks to various movies, mostly comedies – *Fletch, Krush Groove, Ruthless People, Down & Out In Beverly Hills* – but also the baseball light drama *Bull Durham*. He produced Tina Turner's 'Foreign Affair' album.)

Actually, the young audience had been listening to him all along albeit once removed. Entire new, younger music scenes were awash with singers and players steeped in the hard funk message of James Brown *circa* 1965–75. Dee-jays working with rappers, the first generation of hip-hop acts, the whomping House bands in Washington DC playing Go-Go, which was funk by another name, and countless British post-punk funk bands were some of the new apostles. His sound, his rhythms, were re-emerging recycled or lifted straight off the record as samples. It was deafeningly apparent everywhere. There was no emcee prefacing their acts with a litany of titles like 'Out of Sight', 'Papa's Got A Brand New Bag', 'I Got You', 'Cold Sweat', 'Lickin' Stick', 'Say It Loud', 'Mother Popcorn', 'Funky Drummer' but the songs were there, either in the notes, the beats, the spirit or the feel. It was estimated that between two and three thousand records in the second half of the Eighties used a James Brown sample. Royalties, if paid, would have been considerable. Eric B & Rakim, Public Enemy, Ice T, Run-DMC,

Beastie Boys, Fat Boys, Heavy D, Spoonie Gee, DJ Polo & Kool G Rapp, Sweet T & Jazzy Joyce, Scott La Rock, Fresh Gordon, producer Teddy Riley, Hammer. It's a big, big list. They couldn't find the musicians to play a lick, so let James Brown's band or voice come in and do the Popcorn! The artistic legitimacy of this kind of exploration of a music's roots is complex but it sure paid them dividends. Later, in 1991, Brown observed that "How can we make rap become what it needs when their music came out of the streets and not out of the church. They know one-note songs but they can't take it all the way. It's a sad thing but they're happy with it." Three years further down the line he called time on rappers using JB samples in songs with bad, as opposed to baaad, language when he objected to samples being used in Pharcyde's 'I'm That Type Of Nigga' and Salt 'n' Pepa's 'Sexy Noises Turn Me On'. "I don't think songs like that should be played on the air where your kids or sister or brother will have access to it."

The influence was global. When he played The Venue, a London rock club, in 1979, parts of Public Image, Pop Group and The Pretenders walked up to see and hear; dozens of others such as The Gang Of Four, Rip, Rig & Panic, Pigbag, A Certain Ratio sounded as though they'd only just been weaned off Soul Brother No. 1. Later, more commercially inclined acts like George Michael, Sinéad O'Connor and The Fine Young Cannibals put songs into orbit using sampled 'Funky Drummer' quotes as a launchpad.

Head hip-hop heavy Afrika Bambaataa felt no inhibition about giving Brown full credit for his influence and in 1984 collaborated with the Godfather on 'Unity', a six-part 12 inch single for the Tommy Boy label. Bambaataa was a Brown fan from the Sixties – he'd seen him outside the Yankee Stadium gig in New York in 1963 – and saw him again ten years later when Brown visited the mother of one of his dancers who lived in the East 174th neighbourhood. Another 10 years on, Brown went to see Bambaataa at a Zulu Nation date in Mount Vernon, New York and they talked again. One business meeting later and a deal was struck. 'Unity', a message of peace, unity, love and having fun against hard electro-funk beats, was swept aside by noise of on-rushing *Rocky IV*.

In July, 1984, in the first issue of a magazine called *Soul Survivor*, Brown said "If a record company would turn me loose today and say, 'Do what you want to do', I would have hit after hit. But the system don't want that, they don't want an artist to have that many hits, they only want an artist to have a hit every two or three years." And, indeed, after 'Living In America', Brown was virtually silent for three years.

The promise held out at the start of the Eighties by a reinvigorated live show – his band and singers, now known as The JBs International and The

Sugar Bees, had less to offer but by judicious pacing and a much shortened set he was able to give remarkably compelling performances – was dissipated on vinyl. The silence, on record, was broken in 1988 when Full Force, a good, tough six-piece band from Brooklyn who'd dedicated their 1986 album 'Full Force Get Busy 1 Time' to Brown (and to "The Original Sly and The Family Stone") produced the album 'I'm Real'. At a time when rappers were sampling his voice and blasts of the horn section for their own records, Full Force said, it was right and essential that the kids could hear the original in a format they could relate to. Contrary to the sampler's traditional defence, there was little reason to believe that just because a kid heard a two second "oooh-wee" or horn "daaa-dap" tape splice on a rap or hip-hop record he or she would read the small print and go out and find the record from which the sample came. Get real, said Full Force, this was not the same as hearing a complete cover version and then going out to find the original. So the group "mixed in a lot of his styles with a lot of [our] sounds and with a lot of street beats". As if to prove that, given the context, Brown could still sell, the title track went to No. 2 R&B.

In the meantime, Polydor had been consistently alerted to the fact that there was currency to be made out of the treasure trove in their possession known as The James Brown back catalogue. When prodded sufficiently they would reissue a single – in Britain a revival of Sixties Mod fashions in 1979 prompted the re-release of 'Papa's Got A Brand New Bag', joyously re-reviewed – and Cliff White set about telling the story from day one with the 'Roots Of A Revolution' double CD in 1984. Repackaging continued well into the Nineties by which time Brown had again been back in the headlines for the wrong reason.

CHAPTER 14

James Brown had been arrested many times in his life. As a teenager in the Forties for various car crimes, in the Sixties for alleged obscenity during a concert, in the Seventies for alleged "disorderly conduct" after a concert. He is American. He is black. Arrest and harassment came with that territory. The Civil Rights struggle, he said in the early Eighties, had counted for little. The jails were still full of black men. Were black men the only people committing crime? The jails were still full of poor people. Were poor people the only ones committing crime? James Brown was his own man, self-possessed to the point of arrogance – and as an innovator in music he had a lot to be arrogant about – wealthy and very high profile. None of this will have prepared him for 1988, the worst year of his life.

After his spell in jail as a teenager, the charges brought against him as an adult were invariably dropped. Apart from a few years at King when he was virtually the only act left on the roster, he seemed to be in permanent dispute with every record company he was signed to. He was investigated over allegations that dee-jay Frankie Crocker had received payola, Brown's former colleague Charles Bobbit testifying in 1976 that he had handed over $7,000 on Brown's behalf. The singer denied this, under oath, and the evidence was dismissed on a technicality. When the Internal Revenue Service got on his case big time, he alleged harassment and sued them. When the FCC were slow to grant him a licence for one of the radio stations he wanted to buy, he thought they were after him too. He alleged that the failure of his records in the early Seventies was due to collusion between the FCC and Philadelphia International Records, the label owned by Kenny

Gamble and Leon Huff which produced slickly orchestrated disco and social message hits for The O'Jays, Harold Melvin & The Blue Notes featuring Teddy Pendergrass and others. By the early Eighties, he feared he was under surveillance by the Federal Bureau of Investigation and the Central Information Agency. This was a man, you had every right to believe, dogged by trouble. He had given African-Americans a chance, for example when he appointed black managers to run his radio stations. They ended up bankrupt. His Lear jets had been repossessed. He had built an empire and lost it. He was tired, tired, tired. Except when he got on stage. The records were patchy going on moderate, so was his band, but like the baseball hitter itching for one more chance at the plate, he could still get on the good foot. But he couldn't be on stage all the time.

On May 6, 1988, way too high on PCP, or angel dust as it's known on the street, he had to cancel a show at the Lone Star Café in New York. Despite the increasingly peculiar, incoherent interviews, riddled with non-sequiturs and nonsensicals, and the rumours, emanating from the James Brown entourage, about an escalating drug intake in the Eighties, the image of the hardest working man in show business, the indestructible Godfather of Soul who rapped 'King Heroin' and 'Public Enemy No. 1' strung out on a vicious, extremely addictive drug like PCP was, literally, soul destroying. He had been on President Ronald Reagan's anti-drug task force for seven years while, as Bob Patton said, smoking extremely powerful marijuana, perhaps laced, for many years. Come show time he had got his act together. But not in 1988. In fact, that spring, Brown and his wife were scarcely ever out of the headlines for drugs, weapons or domestic violence offences. His wife alleged that he tried to kill her and the bruises from the beating were photographed for the edification of *National Enquirer* readers. Adrienne later said these were a publicity stunt – and the livid bruise on her arm does indeed look painted on – but she had been complaining to the local police since 1984 about Brown's treatment of her. Others in his entourage told *Rolling Stone* magazine that he had beaten his previous wife, Deidre, and other women close to him, including Tammi Terrell.

Then, on September 24, he lost it. As though the set-up for a bad joke, the catalyst was the toilet. He burst in on an insurance seminar, which was being held in a building next to his Augusta office, brandishing a pistol and a shotgun and complaining that his office's private bathroom had been used. Someone in the startled audience summoned the police and there started a chase across the State border into South Carolina, Brown's truck leading a small procession of police cars. It was not on national TV. Brown drove through a road block, allegedly attempting to run down two policemen.

The chase ended when police marksmen shot out the truck's tyres – even then he drove on the rims for six miles before running into a ditch. On arrest, it was alleged he sang 'Georgia' and did the 'Good Foot' dance. In court, Brown said he was more scared than he'd ever been in Vietnam. The details of the chase do not bear out Brown as a danger to anyone, except perhaps himself. His shotgun was found to be busted; his truck had 23 police bullet holes in it. His actions after bursting into the insurance seminar seem like those of a confused and frightened man first trying to get back to his home in South Carolina, then heading for the Terry in Augusta, where he'd been raised. Released on bail, he was arrested again in the Terry within 24 hours for driving under the influence of PCP.

Brown and his wife were defiant, later alleging various conspiracies and set-ups against Brown himself, against their marriage and an over-reaction on the part of the police, who shot up his truck and then pressed him to plead guilty to attempted murder. Ultimately, he said, he was offered 90 days if he pleaded guilty to everything, including the drugs, or six years. He said no deal and got sentences of six years from both Georgia and South Carolina, the sentences to run concurrently, time to be served at the State Park Correctional Center outside Columbia, South Carolina. He must have known what to expect from sentencing in Georgia. He'd experienced it 40 years previously. Whatever the evidence, the sentence for the particular offences smelled to a lot of African-Americans of prejudice and persecution. What would a white person of similar cultural stature receive in similar circumstances – jail or time in a rehabilitation centre with, perhaps, community service to follow? Problem was, Brown resolutely denied the drugs charges, the ones for which there was good evidence, and the locals well knew the history of domestic disturbances, shootings and drug related fracas which had been going on for several years. "He's one of our regular customers," a local sheriff had said in May, 1988, detailing seven arrests in 18 months.

Already, he had been charged three times in the previous 12 months for offences concerning either cars or PCP and guns. There had been two arrests in 1987 resulting in four charges concerning speeding, leaving the scene of an accident and avoiding arrest for which he was fined. In March, 1988, Adrienne had filed for divorce on the grounds of cruelty, the latest episode had been a beating with an iron pipe as she tried to leave their house at Beech Island, South Carolina. Adrienne later dropped the charges. In April she was arrested at Augusta airport for possession of PCP. In May, Brown accused her of setting fire to their hotel room in Bedford, New Hampshire. Shortly after, he was arrested for beating her. PCP was found on him. Each accused the other of planting PCP on the other. Quite brilliantly, she demanded all charges against her be dropped on the grounds of diplomatic immunity – she is married to the Ambassador of Soul. Drugs, cars, guns, beatings, arson. Even before the car chase denouement, which seemed to have sprung from a low-budget TV cop series, there were enough misdemeanours on the sheet to keep a court working for a week, plus overtime. But Brown, friend of the Presidents (when it suited them) since the Sixties, expected release at any moment, after a day, a week, a month. Surely one of his old, white "friends" in the big house would put in a word? Not a chance. Worse, the black organisations he'd helped, the stars he'd influenced, very few visited, and not many spoke up. Not about his guilt, but about the severity of the sentence. It hurt him badly.

While he had been in jail, at least two white rock and pop figures escaped jail sentences for alleged drugs and arson offences. What happened to him, he said, was proof positive that racial prejudice was alive and well in the southern States. "If I was white, I'd have got probation from the start ... it's just that I was the wrong colour." He resolutely denied involvement with drugs, saying that he'd been under medication for dental implant surgery, which treatment he'd certainly undergone. But more to the point, his spell in the Correction Center had convinced him that the country had regressed 25 years because bad education still kept doors closed to blacks, who made up 90 per cent of the prison population. The younger folks knew he'd been given a bum deal – he should have been in therapy, not custody.

A very few months after sentencing, a heavyweight "Free James Brown" campaign was under way, led by rappers Melle Mel, lately of Grandmaster Flash & The Furious Five, and Van Silk. Senator Jesse Jackson met Carroll Campbell and Strom Thurmond, respectively Governor and Senator of South Carolina, to plead for mercy on Brown's behalf. Reverend Al Sharpton, his long-time aide and spiritual adviser, Little Richard and Dick Clark, among others, worked for his early release. Brown spent his time working in the kitchens and with the gospel choir, writing songs and after a year he was put on a work release programme. TV presenter Arsenio Hall offered him a job as a "special music correspondent" because he didn't want the Godfather to be doing a menial job. He played a Christmas Show for GIs at nearby Fort Jackson when their leave was cancelled because of the Gulf War. Conditions might have been worse. State prison regulations allowed inmates to have no more than $50 in their possession while inside. A search revealed he had $48,000 in cashier checks and $600 cash and he was moved from a minimum security facility to a cell block. The IRS, still claiming an estimated $11m, filed a notice of levy on his lawyers.

James Brown was released on February 27, 1991, having served two-and-a-half of the six years sentence. He had to report to a parole officer until October, 1993. He set about successfully suing people like the producers of the film *The Commitments* who had used archive footage without his permission and shoe manufacturers who had used his image in a particularly tasteless advertisement about "two great things with sole under lock and key". Brown also announced that he was talking to several labels about a new recording deal which came as a surprise to Scotti Bros label who were owed five albums.

More immediately, he announced a Freedom Tour proclaiming that the time in jail had cleared his mind. "I've formulated a new sound – Universal Sound – which is still super heavy, heavy funk but is now more in line with what's happening in the Nineties." He kicked-off with *James Brown: Living In America*, a pay-per-view concert for Warner Bros Pay-TV promoted at the Wiltern Theater in Hollywood on June 10 by boxing promoter Butch Lewis. It was typical Hollywood wham-bam razzamatazz which opened in unexpectedly serious fashion by the Reverends Jesse Jackson and Al Sharpton offering a prayer. The African-American arts contingent turned out big-time to show support – Quincy Jones and Gladys Knight, Denzel Washington, Blair Underwood and Mario Van Peebles from the movie world, short sets from En Vogue, The Boys, Tone Loc, Al B, Sure, Bell Biv Devoe, C&C Music Factory, Kool Moe Dee and M.C. Hammer before Brown's performance climaxed by a jam session with guests Rick James, Bootsy Collins and Georgia rival and fellow survivor from way back, Little Richard.

If anything, interest in his life and work had increased while he was in jail. "I'm hotter now then I ever was in my life," he said with some exaggeration. A documentary-cum-tribute, *James Brown: The Man, The Music & The Message*, had been made for TV by On The Potomac Productions, a Washington DC company, and at PolyGram Cliff White, Harry Weinger and Alan Leeds had for 18 months been working on a four-CD box set covering the majority of Brown's hits from 1956's 'Please, Please, Please' to 1984's 'Unity', with some unedited, alternate takes and previously unreleased material among the 72 tracks. It was released by Polydor in May. 'Love Overdue', a "new" album on Scotti Bros Records which sounded a lot like tracks recorded before his incarceration, did not suggest that he was ready to break new ground in the recording studio.

In 1992 he went British, working with producer Trevor Beresford Romeo, better known as Jazzie B, the young Londoner behind Soul II Soul, and his partner Will Mowatt, on six tracks for 'Universal James'. Released on the Scotti Brothers label, the album had one song, 'Can't Get Any Harder', from the Clivilles/Cole production team and three by Brown including 'Everybody's Got A Thang' and 'Make It Funky 2000'. The third Brown track, 'Georgia-Lina' is still in his live show, as heard on a fourth 'Live At The Apollo', taped in 1995 because, on stage, the flame still flickered.

CHAPTER 15

It is the Fourth of July, 1991, and, irony of ironies, The James Brown Freedom Tour has reached London's Wembley Arena on American Independence Day. There is resonance, too, in his first London appearance since his release because it is a quarter of a century since his first-ever London date and 35 years since his first-ever hit.

The Arena, part of a sports and entertainment complex in north-west London, is the biggest, regular indoor concert venue in London set adjacent to Wembley Stadium, one of the world's most famous soccer grounds, home of the FA Cup Final and England's home international matches. The Arena's forecourt is a circling confusion of ticket touts and punters, hamburger stands, limousines and taxis, friends looking for other friends. Inside the Arena, the throng outside is matched by queues at the counters for a variety of over-priced food, ice-cream, weak beer and soft drinks as they come. James Brown merchandise over there, lay-deez 'n' gen'mun.

Tonight's audience is mainly white. These days, it always seems to be that way unless a young African-American act like Boyz II Men or R. Kelly flies in. The age range of the audience spans fifteen, maybe younger, who might have seen *Rocky IV* – to fifty-five, maybe older, who want to know if papa's found a brand new bag since his release. There is palpable excitement in their fetid air. It is an extraordinary show, as much because of the emotion of the night as its musical quality. But for European audiences, there is too much florid, gushing, Hollywood-style decoration through which the real James Brown is only glimpsed intermittently and faintly.

He is back to repeat the feat just five months later and now the Arena is more sparsely populated, though the age and racial mix is as before. But by now The Soul Generals, out of mothballs, are locking tight as a unit because history is in the driving seat in the shape of Brown's veteran road drummer Tony Cook. And tall, slim, soft-spoken saxophonist St. Clair Pinckney, the silver quiff in his hair getting wider by the year, who'd known the Hardest Working Man at school in Augusta, finds the puff for a chorus or two more. The Sugar Bees – Martha, Cynthia and Lisa – sing an unexpectedly bitter-sweet version of 'What The World Needs Now' before, in a blaze of resur-rectin' light, gud gawd, it's Jaaaay-mes Brown! He is dressed as a ringmaster, basically the Living In America robes, and six leggy dancing girls cavort. As the set blasts on, with little space between the songs, it becomes clear that perhaps James Brown is reaching a new audience. They're less accustomed to the fake endings and sudden continuations of songs. After 'Man's World' he looks out at the crowd and announces, with some satisfaction, that "I'm working hard every day and feelin' clean." He is fit and in good voice, a scream in 'It's Too Funky In Here' might have come from the Apollo, *circa* 1966, and the set is paced to give him long rests during solos. He does jus-tice to the oldies, 'Prisoner of Love', 'Try Me', 'Cold Sweat', 'Papa's Got A Brand New Bag', 'I Got You (I Feel Good)', 'Out of Sight' and the climac-tic 'Please, Please, Please'. But the music's visual decoration provided by repeated appearances of the six dancing girls, each time in a new costume, seems an ill-judged sop to some imagined Nineties audience. Somehow, James Brown took this on board and as the Hardest Working Man in Show Business moved into his sixties, the show got better.

Brixton, south London, 1995. The June Wednesday has been sunny. Heat on the street, city dust in the face, a dry, dry day. The shadows are lengthen-ing now, it is an in-between time. The commuters from the City and the West End have just got home, the night folks haven't come out yet. Three drivers waiting for fares, jive-talk Anglo-Caribbean style, outside a minicab office. Two doors away, a steady trickle of fans – dress code: shorts in vari-ous lengths, T-shirts – walk up to the Brixton Academy, an art-deco venue, acoustically and atmospherically the best hall of its size in London (approx-imate capacity 4,000). The Academy is the subject of a bid by Bishop Edir Macedo's Universal Church of The Kingdom of God (est. 1977), who wish to turn it into a place of worship. Tonight, however, it is the Church of the Universal James (est. 1933), and the hardest working Minister of the New, New Super Heavy Funk is back among his International flock in London for the fourth time in four years.

Inside, the Academy is comfortably full. A James Brown concert flickers on video screens in the bars, which are doing brisk business, but most of the crowd has already set up territorial rights on the hall's floor, which slopes steeply from the auditorium doors down to the stage. In keeping with the nature of Brixton, the audience is a more cosmopolitan mix of races than was attracted out to Wembley. By 9.30pm, the bars have all but emptied in expectation of "Showtime!". Local radio stations, which might be expected to play Brown's music and mention the show, have been boosting support singer Jhelisa who is Vicki Anderson's niece. She lately released a well-received album but live her sound lacks depth, despite dynamics and volume which shove the bass beats into the chest cavity with the thud of a Mike Tyson jab. It is a one-dimensional techno-sound. Never trust a band that has no drummer.

The Soul Generals, on the other hand, have two drummers plus a percussion player, four horns, two guitarists, a bass player and before the first tune's done they're hollerin' "can we give the drummer some?!". A military-looking band, in red jackets and black trousers. To the right of the Generals, six women singers, clothed in angelic white, form a formidable looking choir. After 20 minutes, showtime becomes "Star Time!". The man who brought you 'Payback!' – 'Try Me!' – 'Doin' It To Death!' – 'Please, Please, Please!' – 'Sex Machine!' – 'Living In A-mer-i-cah!' Ladies and gentlemen, the Godfather of Soul, Mister Jaaaymes Brown!!

'Cold Sweat', with the horn section hitting clean, is followed by a surprisingly spring-heeled 'Funky Good Time', which gets tremendous applause. There are now four guitar-playing Generals and for the new arrangement of 'Get. On The Good Foot', two dancers squeeze on. They do it the way he once did, not the same moves, but they carry the load. At 62, a man's man's man's joints aren't what they were. When once he would have been doin' the Mashed Potato, he now conducts the horns or the choir, who in the scheme of James Brown things have replaced The Famous Flames, in a doo-wop introduction to 'Try Me'. And as this happens it becomes clearer that at last, in the four years since his release from jail, on stage at least, he has discovered how to present himself to several new generations. In terms of stature, he should be venerated alongside the last of the blues greats like B. B. King and John Lee Hooker. Certainly his music has proved as advertising-agency friendly as theirs. But the egotism which he insists necessarily sustained him as an artist through the Fifties, Sixties and early Seventies, had by the mid-Eighties left him open to as much approbation as any maverick African-American act of a younger generation, like Prince. There may be no new songs or great new records but he has accepted that the role of The Godfather of Soul is an honourable one and not to be undertaken lightly.

Of course, misjudgements recur, such as the waif, draped in gossamer, making quasi-balletic swoops and passes to a dramatic 'It's A Man's, Man's, Man's World'. These Terpsichorean interludes, rock critics tell us, are part of Brown's attempt to appeal to a Las Vegas audience. Obviously, they know nothing – why should they? – of his vast history and of the Revue style shows he headlined at the Apollo in the Sixties, with his first dance troupe The Brownies, with Elsie "TV Mama" Mae, a risqué marriage of blues shouter and comedienne, or the many other dancers who've frugged with ferocity in the service of Mr. Please, Please himself. The occasional dancer is not a sudden, aberrant manifestation of a desperate artist aiming for the sober retreat of the white cabaret lounge. The nubile is a part of the traditional presentation of African-American music and, in one form or another, has been part of James Brown's act since the mid-Sixties. Certainly in the early Seventies he had an extremely vigorous go-go dancer doing severe damage to her sacroiliac but so compelling was his show that her gyrations next to the drum riser kept the stixman warm but were largely ignored by the audience.

"POWER! Is what we need," James Brown sings at the top of his voice. "Soul Power! Soul Power! Soul Power!" He stands centre stage, essaying a few steps as though from memory while the band thunders on. He takes no chances and does no dances. Right now his moves in 'I Got You (I Feel Good)' may be more reminiscent of callisthenics and karate kicks at a class for the imminently aged, but as the Soul Generals storm into 'Sex Machine' there is a sudden and unmistakable sense that here is the root of funk, and the feeling grows that this is not some sterile lesson in a genre's history but a living, breathing, thrilling music that has a whole lot of life left in it yet.

CHAPTER 16

Intermittent turbulence and generous acclaim, simmering controversy and tumultuous tributes, these were Brown's constant companions during the next 11 years. He was firmly in that period of life when citation, trophies, plaques and laurels for achievements and contributions in his chosen field were a fairly commonplace occurrence. As mentioned earlier, as long ago as January 23, 1986, he had been one of 10 inaugural inductees into the Rock and Roll Hall of Fame in New York (it was eventualy sited in Cleveland, Ohio), and six years later, on February 25, 1992, had been awarded a Grammy for Lifetime Achievement. The following year he received a Lifetime Achievement Award at the Rhythm & Blues Foundation Pioneer Awards, and in January 1997 he was inducted onto the Hollywood Walk Of Fame and immediately afterwards moved on to perform at Billboard Live, a music venue on Sunset Boulevard associated with the American music business publication. In June 2000 he was inducted into the New York Songwriters Hall Of Fame and in December 2003 received a Kennedy Center Honors award and a Black Entertainment Television (BET) Lifetime Achievement Award. He was even granted a pardon from South Carolina for crimes he committed in that state.

By this time, too, signposts pointed to many and various geographical locations named after the Godfather of Soul. It was no surprise that many of these were in Augusta, Georgia – James Brown Boulevard was a portion of 9th Street between Broad Street and Twigg Street (a statue of the man himself stood nearby on Broad Street), and the city's civic centre was renamed the James Brown Arena in 2006. Less expectedly, the good folks of

Steamboat Springs, Colorado, voted in 1993 to rename a bridge over the Yampa River as The James Brown Soul Center of the Universe Bridge. Taking it to the Bridge, he performed there on at least two occasions, in May 1993 and July 2002.

Brown's keenness to embrace and be embraced by successive US Presidents, no matter what their party, allegiances or performance, continued. At the end of June 2001, he made his umpteenth trip to the White House, this time to meet George W. Bush during a photo opportunity to mark Black Music Month at which gospel singers Shirley Caesar and Bobby Jones, jazz vibist/drummer veteran Lionel Hampton, and singers Nancy Wilson and Lena Horne were honoured.

All of this was part of Brown's gradual rehabilitation as one of the most profound influences on 20th, and now 21st Century popular music. He was no longer able to reinvent, regenerate and revive on record, but his all-pervasive influence on hip hop, soul, R&B, rock and, indeed, jazz was self-evident, loud, clear and funky on the airwaves for all to hear.

In the debit column was a recurring theme of a less palatable stripe playing itself out at Brown's family home on Beech Island, South Carolina, just across the Savannah River from Augusta, the area hymned in his ballad 'Georgia-Lina'. In December, 1994, Brown had turned himself in to the Aiken County authorities in South Carolina having been accused of pushing his wife, Adrienne, during a row, but the charges were dismissed in March 1995 when she refused to testify against her husband. This had been a repetitious plot line in the saga of the Browns' 10-year marriage. In May that year Adrienne was being treated for a prescription drug overdose at the Aiken General Medical Centers, and by the end of October Brown was charged, yet again, with domestic violence after Adrienne alleged he had assaulted her. She was taken to the same medical facility in South Carolina. Brown was arrested and later released by the Aiken County Magistrate on a $940 bond. But the tempestuous marriage had almost run its course. On January 6, 1996, Adrienne died in Los Angeles at the age of 45, two days after cosmetic surgery. The LA coroner's office ruled that PCP intake and atherosclerotic heart disease were the immediate causes of death, with her heart disease, lung infection and obesity all contributing to a susceptibility to the mixture of prescription painkillers and PCP in her body. After a memorial service in Los Angeles, her body was flown back to Augusta, Georgia, for burial at Walker Memorial Gardens.

Later that year, Brown met the woman who became his next partner, and a backing singer and featured vocalist in his act, Tomi Rae Hynie. Thirty-six years his junior, Hynie had been in a hard rock band, Hardly Dangerous, who were for a time signed on a development contract to Madonna's Maverick label. A former waitress at the Rainbow in Los Angeles, she was not unfamiliar with the rock'n'roll lifestyle. By 1996, Hynie was enacting the role of Janis Joplin in the Dead Legends Live segment of Legends In Concert show, a Las Vegas-style entertainment of long standing, and now auditioned for Brown's show, singing Joplin's 'Mercedes-Benz'. In February 1997, Hynie married Javed Ahmed, a Pakistani, in Houston, Texas, later claiming that the marriage was never consummated, and that the wedding was purely a business arrangement so that she could get some much-needed cash. The marriage was later annulled, but not before Hynie married James Brown in December 2001 in a private ceremony at his Beech Island home. The couple's son, James Joseph Brown II, was born on June 11, 2001. In common with his previous marriages, there would be periods of separation and charges against him of domestic abuse.

For fans of his music, however, 1996 had marked 40 years since Brown's first hit 'Please Please Please' and a two-CD 'JB40 40th Anniversary Collection' celebrated the fact. A 40-track compilation produced by Harry Weinger, linernote essay by Cliff White, music by Brown, essentially the hardest-working team behind the 'Star Time' box set, the CD is the best and most complete introduction to the world of James Brown anyone will ever need. When sated by the 'JB40 40th Anniversary Collection', or when overcome by curiosity to know more, you just move on up to 'Star Time'. There would be a steady supply of CD compilations in the next few years and any of them bearing the stamp of Weinger as compiler, producer or annotator are worthwhile, but particularly 'Foundation Of Funk A Brand New Bag: 1964–1969' from 1996, with Alan Leeds, and two years later a second Weinger/Leeds double-CD compilation, 'Dead On The Heavy Funk: 1975–83'. Of more arcane interest was a 2002 'Remembering The Roots Of Soul' CD featuring James Brown and Eddie Floyd, 'Soul Brothers', apparently, but only in the sense that their early recordings had been licensed for release in the UK by the Ember label, which was set up in the 1960s by Jeffrey Kruger. The dozen James Brown tracks on 'Soul Brothers' were, in fact, those which comprised his fourth King album in the USA, 1962's 'The Amazing James Brown', which had been retitled 'Tell Me What You're Gonna Do' for UK release on Ember, with 'The Bells', 'I Don't Mind', 'Lost Someone' and the title track as its standouts.

By the late 1990s, Brown himself wasn't the only focus of repackaging interest as the ongoing proliferation of samples on rap and hip hop tracks had turned his entire archive into an industry in its own right. Thus 1998's

'James Brown's Original Funky Divas', a two-CD collection of sought-after tracks by Vicki Anderson, Lyn Collins, Marva Whitney, Yvonne Fair, Tammy Montgomery (Tammi Terrell) and others, and 'James Brown Funky People's Greatest Breakbeats', a 2006 bag full of much-sampled music by The J.B.'s, Fred Wesley, Lyn Collins, Maceo, Bobby Byrd and other followers. The booklet to the latter CD, and to the James Brown collection 'Greatest Breakbeats', gave some indication of the astounding number of times his tracks had been sampled.

After the death of his third wife – there were no children from the marriage – Brown showed few signs of slowing down or taking stock. Another arrest, in 1998, after a car chase, led to a 90-day sentence to a drug rehabilitation course, so at last perhaps the immediate cause of Brown's behaviour had been identified, admitted and addressed. Certainly that year held a host of positive developments to encourage a brighter view of his future, most notably a new album titled with confident emphasis 'I'm Back' and released on Eagle Records. Predominantly co-written by Brown and producer Derrick "New Funk" Monk, the 14 tracks included three mixes of 'Funk On Ah Roll' – Brown's original and two Club mixes by Steven Wills and Cat Gray. The track, a pounding funk stomp, was Brown's last new recording to reach the British Top 40, which it did in the early part of 1999.

The hardest working man had waited years before finding the deal that led to 'I'm Back', but the follow-up was respectably prompt. Again mostly produced by and co-written with Derrick Monk, 2002's 'The Next Step' (CNR/Fome) welcomed back old collaborators Bobby Byrd and Charles Bobbit on the lyrics to 'Send Her Back To Me', 'Why Did This Happen To Me' and, a lingering echo of his socially concerned efforts such as 1966's 'Don't Be A Dropout' campaign, 'Killing Is Out, School Is In'. That said, it was undeniable that among the soul aficionados who had once hung on every James Brown downbeat, there was as much excitement over the several new recordings by former Brown band members and singers as created by either 'I'm Back' or 'The Next Step'. Acknowledging this drift, in June 2003 Universal re-released the 1986 compilation 'In The Jungle Groove', and 1988's 'Motherlode', both of which were laden with heavily sampled tracks by successive generations of hip hop and rap acts, such as 'Funky Drummer', 'It's A New Day', 'Talkin' Loud And Sayin' Nothing', 'Soul Power' and 'Hot Pants'.

And all the while, Brown was touring with his Soul Generals who by now were an extremely well-drilled, tight and smartly functioning band, and if they lacked the inspiration and innovations of previous James Brown Orchestras and J.B.'s line-ups, well, that was no longer the function of the

James Brown show. Giving the people what they wanted, funk from the Godfather's mouth, was the name of the game and he continued to stagger and impress new audiences. There were periods when, to older fans, the act had become too predictable, and the pauses when Brown vacated centre-stage to recover his breath while dancing girls executed quasi balletic moves were perhaps too numerous, but his energy and charisma left a strong impression on neophytes. In July 2003, Brown did just that at the Royal Albert Hall in London. Although the show was by now very familiar to me, it was clear that the power of the band, Brown's ability to conjure believable emotion from very well-worn lyrics and the sheer conviction of his every move was a compellingly persuasive argument that convinced any new JB watchers that he was a genuine one-off.

But that month there was further domestic upheaval as Brown took out a full-page advertisement in the entertainment magazine *Variety* to announce that his marriage to Hynie had broken up. Hynie later gave her version – an argument on an aeroplane flight had started the train of events, but that Brown told her not to worry about it, it was all good publicity. What it actually achieved was to continue the acceleration of a perception that James Brown's life was a fascinating sideshow.

A show of a more appealing nature appeared in October that year. *Soul Survivor* was a Channel 4 co-produced 90-minute documentary on Brown's life and times featuring extensive contributions from the man. At the launch screening at the Barbican in London, director Jeremy Marre told a story about the start of filming which illustrated Brown's mischievous and not always understood sense of humour. The evening before the commencement of filming, Marre and Brown had dinner together and discussed what was to happen on the following day. On that next morning, Brown arrived in the room, dappled with snowflakes and accompanied by his usual, sizeable entourage.

"Who's the director of this film?" Brown brusquely inquired. "Well, I am," replied Brown's somewhat puzzled dinner companion from the previous evening.

Brown stared hard. "What do you know about me?" "I've read your autobiography, and books about you, and listened to the records, looked at footage," Marre patiently explained.

"You read some books and listened to some records," Brown glowered. "Who are you to make a film of my life, to suppose that you know me? You don't know me, you can't know me, 'cos I don't know you. I am a black man, what do you know about my experience? What do you know about my life? What?!"

There was a deafening silence, recounted Marre, as the director gazed at the ground and wondered how to formulate a response. When he looked up again, Brown was grinning broadly. "Where are the cameras, man, why ain't they rollin'? You just missed your first shot!"

In July 2004 came my next, and final, meeting with James Brown. He was in London to receive a Lifetime Achievement Award from *MOJO* magazine, and as the old soul servant on that publication I was to chaperone the Godfather of Soul. He had indeed by then become a cherished and revered elder statesman of contemporary music, despite the continuing drip of bad press courtesy of his private life. Not that he was averse to publicity. On the contrary, he seemed increasingly willing to share with more writers a glimpse, if only from a perspective of over 60 years distance, into the unimaginably hard life that ushered him through childhood and his teenage years, surviving to become the eternally driven, sometimes suspicious, often confrontational and argumentative, consistently egocentric and bravura genius of African American music.

The *MOJO* Award ceremony was to be during the day at The Banqueting Hall, Whitehall, a building most commonly used for State ceremonies and functions. The focus of the main hall was a throne on which the monarch, and only she, we were warned, was permitted to perch. Our duties as chaperones were to get the rock dignitaries into the building, past the photographers, and, at the appropriate time, up the stairs to the hall for the presentation ceremony. Most people came with business or social partner. James came with almost a table full. In addition to Mr Brown there were his managers, SuperFrank and the long-serving Charles Bobbit, among them and a British bodyguard of considerable size. Rather than join the bibulous scrum in the reception area, James wanted to get to his seat right away in the empty hall, and immediately after his Lifetime Achievement presentation wanted to escape to his limousine and rest at his hotel before continuing with the rest of that day's diary. The usual, and unusual, stipulations had been laid down – address him as Mr. Brown, entourage to be treated likewise, no alcohol on the table, because of the rules of his latest parole – and plans for the hasty getaway implemented. Although the hall was only on the first floor, two short flights of stairs up, Mr Brown's scarred and battered knees meant a slow climb. Despite it being *MOJO*'s first ever Awards, the ceremony went smoothly, and as James was presented with his particular piece of statuary, the roar and applause, the loudest and most heartfelt of the afternoon from an audience that included Jimmy Page of Led Zeppelin, Ray Davies of The Kinks, The Who's Roger Daltrey, Roger McGuinn of The Byrds, Love's Arthur Lee, Sting, The

Shadows, the Red Hot Chili Peppers, The Clash's Mick Jones, Noel Gallagher of Oasis, Morrissey, Marianne Faithfull, Lemmy of Motörhead, the Manic Street Preachers, Television, Beth Orton, The Libertines before Pete Doherty became a one-man reality TV show, and many more, left a deep impression.

Of many clear memories of that afternoon is of Black Eyed Peas' Will.i.am hovering at Brown's table and expressing a very strong desire to work with the Godfather. Apparently the young producer made a good impression because Brown later called him and showed up at the studio to sprinkle some funk dust on the proceedings.

★   ★   ★

There had been no outward indication that he was unwell, but by December 15 of 2004 he had survived a successful operation for prostate cancer at the Midtown Urology Surgical Center in Atlanta. Although he had for years been suffering from diabetes and from knee joint ailments brought on the the punishment meted out to them during that athletic and exhausting stage act over many years, he remarkably contrived to keep up a rigorous schedule of touring.

January 2005 brought with it more legal disputation when Jacque Hollander claimed in a federal lawsuit filed in Chicago that Brown had raped her at gunpoint in 1988 which subsequently caused her to suffer from Graves' disease, an autoimmune complaint that affects the thyroid gland. She sought $106 million in damages. In 1988, Hollander said, she was working as a publicist for Brown when that attack occurred. "This is what you call a shakedown in its most stupid form," one of his legal team rejoined. "It's too little, too late and baseless." The statute of limitations on rape had long run out but it was alleged that Hollander's thyroid disease was diagnosed in 2000, and three years after that her doctor said it was caused by the alleged assault. A federal judge threw the case out of court and although Hollander's lawyers said they would appeal, Brown's attorney said the lawsuit "would be frivolous in any court. A stupid case is a stupid case." Hollander continues to press her case against the Brown estate.

As the years passed, more of Brown's former bandmates and singers died. In February 1999, after suffering from emphysema for some years, St. Clair Pinckney, tenor saxophonist and flautist in the Brown horn section for many years, left the stage. Instantly recognisable because of his hair's distinctive streak of grey, and a rich and robust tenor sound, Pinckney was a solid, calm and dependable character, the kind of cement that held a band together through knowing the leader's ways and how best to survive them.

After his time with Brown, he made two solo albums, 1988's 'Private Stock' and 'Do You Like It?' in 1992. Fred Wesley called him "the unannounced liaison between the members of the band, the bandleader and Mr. Brown". In addition to a large contingent of Orchestra members, J.B.'s and Soul Generals, Pinckney's employer attended the funeral at the Bethlehem Baptist Church in Atlanta, Georgia, and spoke warmly of the musician and the man. His last recording was laid down in October 1998 for the Jabo Starks and Clyde Stubblefield album 'Born To Groove'.

A year later, Alphonso "Country" Kellum, Brown's guitarist from 1964 to 1970, died. Kellum played second guitar, with the late Jimmy Nolen, on signature Brown tracks such as 'Papa's Got A Brand New Bag' and 'Say It Loud, I'm Black And I'm Proud' and with Nolen evolved the chicken scratch style of rhythm guitar that was an integral part of Brown's sound. In 1970 Kellum joined the mutiny that saw the formation of Maceo And All The King's Men, but unlike Maceo, Nolen, Fred Wesley and others, he never rejoined the Brown bandwagon. Although not as innovative a guitarist as Nolen, who in a previous life as Johnny Otis's guitarist had adapted the Bo Diddley rhythm for 'Willie And The Hand Jive', Kellum was nonetheless a key member of a terrific outfit.

And on March 13, 2005, Lyn Collins, 'The Female Preacher', died after a choking fit brought on a seizure. Only a month previously she had been fit and extremely vibrant during a live performance at London's Jazz Cafe with her friend and fellow Brown Revue graduate Martha High. She was 56. Born in Dime Box, Texas, on June 12, 1948, and raised in Abilene, by the age of 14 Collins had married a man who promoted James Brown's shows locally. Brown heard her sing – she had also sent tapes to King Records in Cincinnati – and when Vicki Anderson quit the revue Collins joined and for the first time in her life got to sing outside Texas. She stayed with Brown between 1971-76. Possessed of a strong, demonstrative voice and commanding stage presence, Collins was an effective vocal partner in Brown's show and recorded some powerful funk tracks with him, best known of which was 1972's 'Think (About It)', a US Top 10 R&B hit. (The song had a long afterlife when, in the 1980s, her vocal was sampled by Rob Base and DJ E-Z Rock's 'It Takes Two', a single that reached Number 24 in the UK charts in the spring of 1988 and 49 on re-entering in the spring of the following year.) In the end, over 70 artists sampled 'Think (About It)', including Eric B & Rakim, EPMD, Afrika Bambaataa, Kool Moe Dee (several times), Janet Jackson, Public Enemy, DJ Jazzy Jeff & Fresh Prince, PM Dawn, Boyz II Men, New Edition and De La Soul. Just as soulfully assertive a Collins performance came on 'Mama Feelgood', her contribution to the

1973 *Black Caesar* soundtrack, while she gave Bill Withers' 'Ain't No Sunshine' and Isaac Hayes' 'Do Your Thing' convicing interpretations. Like all of Brown's musicians and singers, Collins contributed to the writing of the material but received scant acknowledgement and little in the way of royalties for their work. Recording on Brown's People label, she made effective singles like 'Just Won't Do Right' and, a duet with Brown, 'What My Baby Needs Now'. Another James Brown soundtrack, 'Slaughter's Big Rip Off', found her in sexy form on the lubricious 'How Long Can You Keep It Up', but following a second album for People, 1975's too apologetically titled 'Check Me Out If You Don't Know Me By Now', she retired from touring in 1976 after her final single of the period, 'Mr Big Stuff', failed to chart. "I would have preferred," she said, long after her time with the Revue, "to sing more and scream less." But she continued to sing sessions and for a time worked in Los Angeles at the Record Plant studios. The revival of interest in her work that started in the 1980s lured her back out of retirement and by the end of her life she'd become a strong attraction, particularly in Europe, all over again.

Actually, many of Brown's former musicians were keeping busy, but in 2006 none were as sought after as the man himself. A frequent transatlantic flier, on July 4 he performed at a special concert at the Tower of London and returned in October to perform at the BBC Electric Proms at a recently reopened Roundhouse in Chalk Farm, north London. A month later, on November 14, Brown was back in London for an appearance at the Alexandra Palace, an even older, grander north London venue, where he was inducted into the newly founded UK Music Hall of Fame.

As December 2006 and the Christmas holidays approached, James Brown's schedule focused on the seasonal occasions in Georgia, such as the Thanksgiving event at which he customarily donated 800 turkeys to the needier local residents, and the toy giveaway on December 22 for the children of the area. But it rained heavily on the day of the toy giveaway and Brown, whose health had been giving cause for concern for some weeks, got chilled. Over Christmas, the singer was due for dental procedure on the work-in-progress on his teeth. As Charles Bobbit later told *MOJO* magazine's editor Phil Alexander, he was so concerned about his employer that he arranged for a doctor to be on hand at the surgery of his dentist, Terry Reynolds, in Atlanta on the Saturday, to check up on Brown before the work went ahead. Brown "looked very drawn and he was coughing like mad," Bobbit remembered. After an examination, the physician immediately suggested Brown be taken to hospital, suspecting his patient was suffering from bronchitis or pneumonia.

Rushed to Emory Crawford Long Hospital, Brown was diagnosed with congestive heart failure and pneumonia. He spent the Sunday, unwell, but resting, and talking from time to time, but as Bobbit told Phil Alexander, at 1.20am on the morning of Monday, Christmas Day morning, Brown said, "I'm going to leave here tonight," sat down on the bed, laid back, sighed three times, and, despite frantic attempts to revive him, was gone.

The shock in that hospital room was echoed and amplified around the world in the homes of those who had been touched by Brown's music because the life force defined by his great works, his biggest hits, seemed so indestructible and elemental and his death seemed so parochial and commonplace. "One of the main things that I miss, is that he used to call every night between 11p.m. and 1a.m. and we used to talk for one hour," a deeply saddened Bobbit said. "My body is used to that call coming and I'm still waiting for that call that will never come any more."

★　★　★

The chaos of attempts to revive him would be mirrored, too, in the months after his death as his adult children, Tomi Rae Hynie, their legal representatives and interested parties sought to fairly and properly divide his wealth. Having seen the many and various legal wars over the estates of deceased music stars of equal stature – his close friend Elvis Presley, for example, or that other black music pioneer, Jimi Hendrix – James Brown must have known that settlement of his estate after his death was never likely to be a smooth, amicable, litigation free affair. So it transpired. But first came the funeral.

James Brown's death did not inhibit his ability to draw a crowd. Far from it. His body was taken from Augusta to New York, to the Apollo Theater in Harlem, scene of so many of his greatest live shows, starting from support slots beneath billtopper Little Willie John in the mid-fifties, and where he had recorded classic, soul defining live albums in 1962, 1968 and 1971. And there, in a gold coffin, he was laid in state as the queues stretched along 125th Street. The Reverend Al Sharpton, Brown's younger friend and long-time confidante since 1973, had accompanied the star's body on the long journey through the night from Georgia, until it was transferred from van to a carriage drawn by two plumed white horses for the final procession through the Harlem streets. A crowd of several hundred followed chanting, "Say it loud – I'm black and I'm proud", and the mood was pumped up by celebratory blasts of Brown's music from the stores and shops around the theatre, and from the portable stereos carried by fans as they waited in line, some dancing and singing, for a chance to file past Brown's body, dressed in a blue stage suit, white gloves and silver boots and laid out in the empty auditorium. This was a genuine street celebration of a life, a carnival almost, but once inside the theatre the mood was more sombre as the line filed past Brown's coffin, while his music pumped through the hall.

The tributes poured in from close friends, like Reverend Sharpton and the Reverend Jesse Jackson, and stars such as Little Richard, the fellow Georgia star who Brown imitated back in the long ago as he first tried to make an impact, and Mick Jagger, who tried to imitate and adapt Brown's moves after watching the star on *The T.A.M.I. Show* back in the 1960s, to Michael Jackson, whose dancing was clearly based on Brown's moves, and Chuck D, former linchpin of Public Enemy whose rap and hip hop was largely founded on Brown's funk riffs and rhythms.

But even before the tributes were digested, the wrangling began. On Boxing Day, the day after Brown's death, Tomi Rae Hynie arrived at the Beech Hill mansion home she had shared with him and their now five-year-old son, to find the iron gates firmly padlocked and entry barred. One of Brown's lawyers, Buddy Dallas, asserted that Hynie's marital status was still unclear at that time, although she claimed a judge told her that her 1997 marriage, to Javed Ahmed, had been annulled, but not before she wed Brown in 2001. They had had periods of separation, notably in 2003, and after his arrest on January 28, 2004 for domestic abuse he filed for annulment of their marriage the following month, claiming Hynie's previous marriage was still valid. But by April the couple were reconciled. Until, that is, September 2005 when Hynie moved to Los Angeles and filed for divorce with drugs, beatings and verbal abuse cited in the papers. Outside the mansion that December 2006, Hynie said she had nowhere else to go. Dallas insisted she had another home nearby. Moreover, Hynie had not been living at the Beech Island residence for some weeks before the singer's death because she had been recuperating in California after recent concert dates. "I was taking antidepressants," she said. "So he sent me to the beach. He paid $24,000 for me to go. He was a difficult man to live with, but he was a great man. I was the only one who could handle James."

Meanwhile, Brown's coffin was moved from New York back South to Augusta, Georgia where it was to be displayed at the James Brown Arena for the funeral, on December 30, which was televised live. Former band members such as Bootsy Collins and Fred Wesley, star fans such as Michael Jackson, and the Reverends Jackson and Sharpton attended and even Tomi Rae Hynie sang 'Hold On, I'm Coming', the Sam And Dave hit she'd often sang with the Soul Generals in Brown's revue. Amid the grief there seemed to be a constant jockeying for position. But still the accolades kept coming.

At the funeral, he recived a posthumous doctorate from Paine University in recognition and honour of his many contributions to the predominantly black college in Augusta.

From the Arena, Brown's sealed coffin was taken to the Beech Island mansion where it was kept in a specially chilled room while the family, lawyers and interested parties wrangled over where the body should be interred and how the will should be interpreted. Hynie's representatives were insistent that she would receive 50 per cent of Brown's estate and the trust, and that her son, James Brown Junior II, would receive a one-seventh share of the other 50 per cent, along with Brown's six other children from his first two marriages. The family were equally insistent: when Hynie married Brown in 2001 she was still bound by a previous marriage. Although this was later annulled, the couple never officially remarried and she had remained, in fact, a companion and girlfriend but not a spouse.

Brown's will had been drawn up and signed on August 1, 2000, Brown's probate attorney Storm Thurmond, Jr told the *Augusta Chronicle*. Thus it predated both his invalid 2001 marriage to Hynie and the birth of their son. Consequently, when it was read in Aiken, South Carolina, there was no mention of them in it. The document called for his personal effects (clothes, jewellery, cars and so forth) to be divided equally between his six adult children, Terry, Larry, Venisha, Yamma, Deanna and Daryl. Hynie's lawyers contended that American laws did not allow the exclusion of a spouse if they marry after the will is drawn up. Hynie's lawyer, Robert Rosen, claimed that in South Carolina his client was entitled to a third of the estate no matter what the will stipulated. However, when questioned by the *Augusta Chronicle*, local lawyer James Huff told the newspaper that if a will names some children but excludes others, the excluded children have no claim on the parent's assets, no matter when they were born.

Nothing daunted, approximately a week after James Brown's death, Tomi Rae Hynie, "sad" and "angry", had been interviewed live on the Larry King Show on CNN, in which her allegations of exclusion and harsh treatment by Brown's representatives were rebuffed by one of his legal team, Debra Opri. Concurrent with the reading of the will, Brown's body, still in the gold coffin, was moved out of the mansion to a secret and secure location. (Agreement on a permanent resting place was not reached until late February, nearly two months after his death, the burial site to remain "confidential".)

A further complication came from the trust, set up by Brown in 2000, which was said to hold most of his holdings, such as his Beech Island home, and business assets, notably the invaluable music rights. A project to turn the Beech Island mansion into something along the lines of a Graceland attraction, the former Elvis Presley home in Memphis, was suggested. But by the end of January matters had not improved and Brown's six adult children were demanding the removal of the estate's trustees, alleging that said estate had been mismanaged and that a portion of Brown's assets were in danger of being lost, dissipated or stolen. The trustees included Buddy Dallas, who had been an attorney and friend of Brown's for nearly a quarter of a century. Hynie was finally allowed into the Beech Island mansion to collect her clothes, furniture and James Brown Jr's toys but only when accompanied by the estate's trustees and three of Brown's adult children.

Distinct from the immediate family there was a much larger Brown 'family', the business, band and entourage, who had relied on the singer for their daily bread and here everyone was keen to erect a "Business As [Almost] Usual" sign. Brown had been in the process of recording a new album, 'World Funk Against The Grain', and was booked to record two new tracks in Montreal in the first week of January. One new track, 'Gutbucket', had appeared on a CD, 'James Brown's Funky Summer', given away with *MOJO* magazine in August 2006. His current band, The Soul Generals, would almost certainly continue to tour because it was verging on the criminal to let all of that training and sweat go to waste, and the promoters of shows of his former bandmembers were quick to bill them as James Brown Tributes.

The Hollywood machine swung into action and just two days after Brown's death Paramount Pictures announced that Spike Lee would direct a biopic of the Godfather of Soul's life based on his autobiography, Brown having signed the contracts for the project before he died. With expectations that the film would be even more popular than Taylor Hackford's biopic *Ray*, in which Jamie Foxx won an Oscar nomination for his portrayal of Ray Charles, Brown's preferred choice for the lead was said to be Cuba Gooding Jr. Another film in production, *Life On The Road With Mr and Mrs Brown*, a documentary featuring new footage of his more recent stage shows, archive material, and interviews, was further along the line. The film's co-writers and directors, Camille Solari and Sheila Lussier, had previous credits that included titles such as The Bliss and Hookers Inc., over which it is best to draw a veil.

If the not unexpected unseemly wrangling over Brown's estate presented a mostly disharmonious image, the obituaries and more balanced tributes were fulsome indeed, notably one in *Rolling Stone* by Gerri Hirshey, author of an excellent book on soul music, *Nowhere To Run*, and a friend of Brown's for about 25 years, and another in *MOJO* magazine, by Michael Hurtt. On the internet, too, there were touching reminiscences from ex-employees, such as former tour manager Alan Leeds. As a young white man working for a black man based in the South in the 1970s, when militant black empowerment and residual institutional white racism put him between a rock and a very hard place, Leeds' memories of his years with Brown provided an illuminating memoir.

None of the major tributes or celebrations shied away from or attempted to hide much less justify his history of dometic abuse, but most made some attempt to set it in the social context of his upbringing, his background and his whole complex and contradictory life. Unlike, it has to be said, a few white middle-class British columnists whose comments on Brown's life focused solely on domestic abuse, as if this crime was the only occurence of note in his 73 years, choosing to ignore the child he had been, one effectively given up for dead at birth, abandoned by his mother at the age of four, living in poverty, afforded absolute barest minimum of education, poorly fed and clothed, dumped at a brothel, beaten, and forced to scuffle for a living as a shoeshine boy and petty criminal until as a teenager in jail, music became his salvation. The sheer effort of will and determination to survive and prosper, to get out from under, to earn and then demand respect, *Mr.* Brown, all this set his character. And, miracle of miracles, he lived to the age of 73 to become one of the foremost icons of African American culture. The debate "Can we separate great art from the flawed human being who creates it?" is, sadly, too long to enter into here, but even a proportion of artists from the most pampered backgrounds – the European literary, fine art and classical music fields, say – have their litany of flawed human beings down the ages whose contribution to their field of art has not been diminished by history.

Those who worked with him, and had experienced his stringent and not always fair or logical regimes, and indeed received many fines from him, were quick to acknowledge his prominence in their lives and development as musicians and artists. Lois Wilson, a British soul expert and *MOJO* contributor, interviewed many of them in the days after James Brown's death and all were keen to set on record their debts to their former employer, no matter that many of them had, in the intervening years, been understandably emphatic in their anger at many aspects of his business practices.

One of the most outspoken in this respect had been legendary trombonist Fred Wesley, whose autobiography, *Hit Me, Fred*, nevertheless took its title from Brown's shout-out for a Wesley 'bone riff. Fred had been a jazz buff, into Miles Davis, Curtis Fuller, JJ Johnson, but when Henry Freeman turned down an opportunity to join Brown's orchestra, "Pee Wee" Ellis and Waymond Reed coaxed Wesley into joining. As a musician, Brown taught Fred to venture outside music theory, and let music flow from creativity. But the lessons he received about music publishing were just as valuable. Wesley co-wrote 'Soul Power', and Brown offered him cash up front or 25 per cent of the publishing. Fresh from California and headed for New York, Fred needed money for a warm coat so that's what he chose. But Brown gave him the money *and* the publishing and told him to take the publishing every time. Publishing earns forever; money is just temporary.

Like Wesley, "Pee Wee" Ellis was another horn player with a powerful attachment to the jazz world, but accepted Waymond Reed's invitation in the mid-Sixties to join the Brown travelling show. He went to the Howard Theater in Washington DC, and watched from the wings. "The first show I saw, my mouth just fell to the floor, it was so incredible, so exciting. Up to his death, his show was still one of a kind." He eventually became arranger and MD. Outside of music, Ellis said, Brown stood up to "the race problem" and was a positive influence, gave money to organisations, to churches, to soup kitchens. "He was the head of a big, big machine, to have that platform was special. James Brown was a big man."

Richard "Kush" Griffith became MD towards the end of 1969 and was given the task of creating arrangements for cover versions in the set, and coming up with a fresh arrangement for 'Please, Please, Please'. But lessons on stage presence, pacing oneself and, mostly, pleasing the crowd. was everything. "The real payoff was the applause, the money was only wages." But he was unimpressed when, in the wake of 'Say It Loud – I'm Black And I'm Proud', the then 19-year-old Griffith was instructed to cut off his big mushroom afro so that Brown would be the 'blackest' and 'proudest'.

Griffith was hurt, offended. Most of the rest of the band were five years older and "from an era when you were a good, upstanding negro. I was the first one that was black, I was black when I came to James Brown. But he had that intimidating authority as a part of his make up... He got Pee Wee [Ellis] to be the messenger, he didn't even tell me himself."

But still, as Kush's fellow trumpeter, Joe Davis, told Lois Wilson, at every job he's had since the James Brown Orchestra, the people who hire him, or those in the band with him, the one issue they all want to ask him about is being a James Brown musician. This is almost certainly true of every musician ever to have passed through the JB ranks and with some that probably always will rankle. Many, however, are able to take a balanced view and see that whatever the drawbacks there were during their time with the ensemble, the benefits, most obviously the doors subsequently opened by the JB connection, have given them a life's work of the most enjoyable kind imaginable – playing music.

Almost every musician has a tale about Brown's notorious system of fines. What Brown invariably got right, was rhythm and feel, and in that sense the drummer was arguably the key component of the band, and the most vulnerable if things went wrong. Among his most famous stixmen, Jabo Starks and Clyde Stubblefield both joined in 1965. Brown had been trying to lure Starks from Bobby "Blue" Bland's band since 1963, and his initiation ceremony was the same as for any musician: watch the show from the wings, get an idea of what's going on. But with four drummers already on stage, Starks was unsure where he'd fit in. It was much the same for Stubblefield, who Brown spotted in a Macon club and two weeks later invited him to a date in Augusta. "I went to the auditorium, it was jam packed. There were five sets of drums. He said, 'Pick a set', I did and then with that the band and audience cranked up. He gave me $100 for my performance, I got my ride back to Macon and two weeks later they wanted me to join a show in North Carolina. I did. We always looked forward to playing live. It was a great show."

Of course, the anchor of the band's functioning, the rhythm section was not immune to the odd fine or four. "That was one of the worst things," Stubblefield told *MOJO* in January 2007. "I would make $200 a week, hotel would cost $15 a night, we had to get our clothes cleaned, had to eat and pay our own hotel bill out of our salary plus we got fined and I had a family to take care of back home. I'd be playing and I'd see a hand go up, 5, 10, 15, 20, that's a $20 fine and I didn't know what I was doing wrong. You never knew when he was going to fine you. You didn't know what was going down, but he had the idea you weren't doing it right."

Jabo Starks, though, explained to Lois Wilson that he had leverage. "I told him I don't pay fines... I said, 'When you fine me you are not taking money from me really, you are taking money from my family and I refuse to let you do that to my family. So therefore you tell me what you want me to do and how you want me to do it and there's no need for you to take a fine from me.' We had a good relationship."

Of course, the most difficult times with the James Brown Orchestra were undoubtedly experienced by the women in the entourage. Equal opportunity and the women's liberation movement were concepts foreign to most areas of business from the late 1950s, when Brown's travelling show first included women. Many of the women singers in his act have since died

(Lyn Collins, Yvonne Fair, Tammi Terrell among them) but Vicki Anderson, was even-handed in her assessment of Brown.

Anderson was a gospel vocalist with a Church Of God In Christ (COGIC) Singers choir whose manager said they could record a gospel album if they did one rhythm and blues track for him. Anderson sang 'Nobody Cares', a track her manager took to Brown when Anna King left his show. Hired on the spot, Anderson was taken to Miami to meet the band and found Brown, her future husband, Bobby Byrd, and the musicians working up a new song, 'I Love You'. After a brief run through the song was cut in one take. A challenge, Anderson told Wilson, but "If you can sing gospel you can sing anything, it didn't bother me." Anderson stayed with Brown for many years, off and on, because you could only stay with him for a finite period. "When it got too rough for me, I'd leave and go home."

In general they were on good terms, "all except me not getting paid my money and my husband not getting paid his money". More than fines, disputes over publishing royalties have angered former colleagues. For example, the only fine Anderson can recall ever getting was enforced because she had the temerity to attend the funeral of her sister-in-law and thus missed a show. Brown levied a $75 fine, Anderson refused to pay and the impasse was only overcome, she said, when Charles Bobbit stepped up to the plate and paid the fine for her. But Brown could be generous. He sent her money when her mother died, and he paid for her hospital care when she fell ill. "He did do good things, but when he wanted to and how he wanted to."

Brown undoubtedly had a special regard for Vicki Anderson, wife of the man who befriended him all those years ago when he was in Toccoa jail. When other singers left the show, he would ask her to come back until he found another singer. "He did love Bobby and me, but James was James and you had to love him to understand him. There were times when he'd give a few thousand dollars here and a few thousand dollars there, but it really didn't mean anything to us because he wouldn't have had to do stuff like that if we had got our money that was due us anyway from our work. But my life was changed because of him. If I didn't know the Almighty, I'd be bitter, but Bobby and I aren't bitter."

★ ★ ★

James Brown had no intention of dying. He was booked to tour through 2007 starting on New Year's Eve 2006 with appearances at the Count Basie Theatre in New Jersey and at B.B. King's club in New York with other shows pencilled in running up until August. In addition to the new recording mentioned earlier, his very first singles were being reissued in a series of two-CD releases, another mammoth undertaking by Harry Weinger and Alan Leeds, and reportedly he had heard the first volume ('The Singles Volume One: The Federal Years 1956-60') and fell into a spell of happy reminiscence. The second volume, covering his switch from Syd Nathan's label Federal to the proprietor's main imprint King, would not have disappointed him.

Fred Wesley once said that Brown's fear of a return to poverty was the demon that drove him. The desire that kept pushing him on at an age when many men would have long-since opted for the comforts of pipe, slippers and grandchildren was not easily stilled, but surely a lack of money would never again be a problem. After all, he'd regained control of his music publishing and negotiated a $30 million bond on Wall Street against his future royalties, a deal similar to one struck earlier by English rock star David Bowie, and one Brown was in the process of renegotiating. The insecurities and paranoia that fuelled his need to control the lives of those around him and who worked for him, and that once made him forbid the use of computers at the offices of his company, James Brown Enterprises, ought to have been abating as the awards piled up, surely at last convincing him that, for his musical achievements at least, he was truly cherished. Because his music is where Michael Jackson learned to dance, where Prince learned to project and to organise a band, where Sly Stone and George Clinton heard something that they could pick up and run with, where every funk band of the Seventies found a way to groove on and where many, many jazz musicians found a way to broaden their music and their market. And it's where rappers and hip-hoppers and samplers of the Eighties and Nineties found a wealth of raw material on which to base their careers.

But die he did. As his daughter Venisha poignantly told the world, "Y'all lost the Godfather of Soul, but I lost my father. I know the whole world loved him just as much as we loved him, so we're not mourning by ourselves."

And so the Hardest Working Man In Show Business was finally wrapped in his cape and left the stage after the final encore to find his resting place in a tomb on his daughter Deanna's farm in South Carolina. Whether it will be James Brown's permanent resting place – surrounded by a wooden fence, the burial place certainly had a temporary look about it – remains to be seen because the legal wrangling over his estate drags on. Indeed, at writing a bill of $70,000 for his funeral costs and care of his body for three months remained unpaid.

His passing left an immense cultural void as significant as those left by his fellow 20th century African American icons, Louis Armstrong, Duke Ellington, Miles Davis, Ray Charles, the architects of jazz, R&B and soul, the music styles of the previous century which form the United States' great cultural legacy to the world.

Selective Discography

A comprehensive list of all of James Brown's known, original vinyl 45 and LP releases up to 1985, and his productions of his bands and revue singers, was included in his 1986 autobiography *The Godfather Of Soul*. Brown's own releases were then updated to 1989 in the booklet enclosed with the CD box set 'Star Time' (see below) and variations on the theme have been reprised in publications such as *Record Collector* (UK) and *Goldmine* (USA). Sometime in the not too distant future US researcher Alan Leeds will publish his complete session discography of all of James Brown's recordings and productions, a book in itself. Here, instead, is a splash of recommended CDs, as far as known all still in catalogue at August 1995 unless otherwise noted.

An arbitrary, 18-track compilation of James Brown's past recordings was first reissued in the 'new' CD format by PolyGram's US Polydor division in 1985. (It was titled 'The CD Of JB' – these were early days.) Ten years on we are faced with a bewildering multiplicity of James Brown CDs from many territories around the world. BEWARE!! The vast majority of apparently bargain examples are constantly recycled, differently packaged live recordings, sometimes a 1980 New York City concert, most times a 1983 Augusta, Ga, performance – these frequently presented as 'Best Of' or 'Greatest Hits' or similar. Nothing wrong with getting each of them once at a cheap price (although they cannot be enthusiastically recommended) but if you're not careful you'll end up buying the same live recordings several times over. Read the small print.

A good rule of thumb is to remember that PolyGram Records Inc owns the record rights and master tapes to all of James Brown's recordings from 1956 up to 1980, except perhaps for a few of his independent Sixties productions and a couple of overseas Seventies concerts that have surfaced recently. So if the James Brown CD you are contemplating buying is not on Polydor, or clearly licensed from PolyGram Special Products, the odds are it will either be a post-1980 recording or a bootleg.

And so to your digitally enhanced, home entertainment unit. First, the big one for big pockets …

STAR TIME
Polydor 849 108–2

A 4-CD, 72-track, Grammy-winning 'long box' set with an informed, well illustrated, 64-page booklet. Principally remastered from original session tapes (as are all US Polydor originated reissues), this chronological odyssey gives copious account of the reasons James Brown is a living legend, including all of his major hits, other influential recordings and three previously unissued revelations. It is deliberately light on Brown's early, unsuccessful recordings and, as only one critic carped, perhaps doesn't do The Godfather's Seventies years full justice. These gaps are adequately filled elsewhere.

For those of slimmer pocket, 35 of Brown's key recordings (generally edited versions of the longer tracks) have been distilled onto two volumes of **THE VERY BEST OF JAMES BROWN**, subtitled **SEX MACHINE** Polydor 845 828–2 and **FUNKY PRESIDENT** Polydor 519 854–2.

Early days and influences …

ROOTS OF A REVOLUTION
Polydor 817 304–2

MESSING WITH THE BLUES
Polydor 847 258–2

Two double CDs with plenty to read in the pocket. 'Roots' gives a chronological account of Mr. Dynamite's R&B years, 1956–64. 'Blues' presents his re-interpretations of songs by other R&B stars who inspired or impressed him over the years, also an extraordinary monologue. Both have previously unissued alternate takes, studio chat, etc; both, originally issued in jewel boxes, are being re-presented in slipcase format.

Let's take it to the stage …

LIVE AT THE APOLLO
Polydor 843 479–2
Recorded at the Apollo Theater, NYC, 24 October 1962.

LIVE AT THE APOLLO #2
Polydor 823 001–2 Same venue, 25 June 1967.

LOVE, POWER, PEACE
Polydor 314 513 389–2
Recorded at The Olympia, Paris, France, 8 March 1971.

REVOLUTION OF THE MIND/LIVE AT THE APOLLO #3
Polydor 314 517 983–2
Back at the Apollo, NYC, 24–26 July 1971.
Some acts deliver live albums as contractual cop-outs, not so here. These four are ESSENTIAL to the understanding of the evolution of James Brown's music, his dynamic force as a live entertainer, and the brilliance of his changing ensembles of musicians during his heyday.
Later live recordings include **HOT ON THE ONE** Polydor 847 856–2, recorded late 1979 in Tokyo, Japan, the aforementioned concerts in Studio 54, NYC, 1980, and Chastain Park, Augusta, Ga, 1983, also **SOUL SESSION** with assorted guests, Scotti Brothers 8340852, 1987 and numerous Seventies, Eighties and Nineties performances on video. At the time of going to press it has been announced that his latest album with be **LIVE AT THE APOLLO #4**, recorded late 1995. All of some interest, of course, to the hardcore James Brown fan – but the four recommended above are something else again: milestones in the history of African-American music.

Jump start those funky retro 'rare grooves' …

IN THE JUNGLE GROOVE
Polydor 829 624–2

MOTHERLODE
Polydor 837 126–2
Issued in 1986 and '88, respectively, these two compilations were deliberately aimed at the new generation then rediscovering James Brown's late Sixties early Seventies pulse and sampling That Thang for their own aspirations. 'Motherlode' (a random delve into, mainly, previously unissued recordings) has subsequently been deleted but is still around and will be revised in future reissues. 'Jungle Groove', featuring full-length versions of eight funk anthems and the first example of a major record corp providing would-be samplers with a 'Bonus Beat Reprise' (a looped segment of

'Funky Drummer'), remains in catalogue precisely because it achieved what it set out to do: remind the new wave technocrats where the old school was founded, and by whom.

Step by step from 'Sex Machine' to the edge of the precipice …

SEX MACHINE
Polydor 314 517 984–2
CD of King double LP K1115, 1970, half live, half overdubbed.

HOT PANTS
Polydor 314 517 985–2
As Polydor LP PD4054, 1971, plus unedited, long 'Escape-Ism'.

THERE IT IS
Polydor 314 517 986–2
As Polydor LP PD5028, 1972, with fresh edits.

GET ON THE GOOD FOOT
Polydor 31452 3982–2
As Polydor double LP PD3004, 1972.

BLACK CAESAR Soundtrack
Polydor 314 517 135–2
As Polydor LP PD6014, 1973.

SLAUGHTER'S BIG RIP OFF Soundtrack
Polydor 314 517 136–2
As Polydor LP PD6015, 1973.

THE PAYBACK
Polydor 314 517 137–2
As Polydor double LP PD3007, 1974.

HELL
Polydor 31452 3983–2
As Polydor double LP PD9001, 1974.

REALITY
Polydor 31452 3981–2
As Polydor LP PD6039, 1975.
Filling in the shortfall of 'Star Time', these are Brown's most important individual Seventies albums.

NB. At least 10 of Brown's earlier King albums have been reissued 'as was' on CD by Japanese Polydor, who have also released – and sublicensed to Japanese P-Vine – several CDs of his People label productions. These tend to be expensive in Western markets and duplicate many tracks with our recommendations. Wealthy completists won't worry about that.

A big hand for the boys in the band …

SOUL PRIDE: THE INSTRUMENTALS 1960–69
Polydor 314 517845–2
THE JBs: FUNKY GOOD TIME/THE ANTHOLOGY (1970–76)
Polydor 31452 7094–2
Never underestimate the unsung heroes. Two double CDs with authoritative annotation tracing Brown's bands through the high times, from his first, regular, tight little R&B combo which gradually evolved into a blistering jazz/funk 'orchestra' ('Soul Pride'), on through the most inventive and influencial years of the magnificent JBs ('Funky Good Time'). The latter a must for all funketeers; the former a pocket history of how it all came together in the first place.

And for the boys and girls in the troupe …

JAMES BROWN'S FUNKY PEOPLE #1
Polydor 829 417–2
JAMES BROWN'S FUNKY PEOPLE #2
Polydor 835 857–2
26 (13 apiece) of the hottest tracks by The JBs/Maceo & The Macks (some duplication with 'Funky Good Time') and singers Vicki Anderson, Hank Ballard, Bobby Byrd, Lyn Collins and Marva Whitney. Brown's urgent instructions are stamped all over these powerhouse productions.

BOBBY BYRD GOT SOUL (THE BEST OF BOBBY BYRD)
Polydor 31452 7987–2
22 tracks chronicling Byrd's own important contribution to the evolving heatwave, 1963–72.

Soul sauce for your yuletide pudding ...

JAMES BROWN'S FUNKY CHRISTMAS

Polydor 31452 7988–2

Never let it be said that Phil Spector's 'A Christmas Gift For You' is the only remarkable alternative to Bing Crosby or The Harry Simeone Chorale at that 'special time of year'. 17 tracks drawn from several of Brown's festive seasons may not have you believing that Santa Claus Goes Straight To The Ghetto but every one is a cracker.

And ever onwards ...

SOUL SYNDROME PLUS

UK EMI CDP 7977022

14 tracks comprising Brown's 1980 TK album, with both mixes of the hit, 'Rapp Payback', plus bonus single sides by Bobby Byrd and The JBs.

GREATEST HITS OF THE FOURTH DECADE

Scotti Brothers 75259

From 'Living In America' to 1991.

LIVE AT THE APOLLO

Scotti Brothers 723927580–2

A fourth album recorded at the scene of James's triumph. Includes one bonus new studio recording.